Stoic Virtues

Continuum Studies in Ancient Philosophy
Series Editor: James Fieser, University of Tennessee at Martin, USA

Continuum Studies in Ancient Philosophy is a major monograph series from Continuum. The series features first-class scholarly research monographs across the field of Ancient Philosophy. Each work makes a major contribution to the field of philosophical research.

Aristotle and Rational Discovery, Russell Winslow
Aristotle's Metaphysics, Jeremy Kirby
Aristotle's Theory of Knowledge, Thomas Kiefer
The Enduring Significance of Parmenides, Raymond Tallis
Happiness and Greek Ethical Thought, M. Andrew Holowchak
The Ideas of Socrates, Matthew S Linck
Parmenides and To Eon, Lisa Atwood Wilkinson
Plato, Metaphysics and the Forms, Francis A. Grabowski III
Plato's Stepping Stones, Michael Cormack
Pleasure in Aristotle's Ethics, Michael Weinman
Pythagoras and the Doctrine of Transmigration, James Luchte
The Socratic Method, Rebecca Bensen Cain
Stoic Ethics, William O. Stephens

Stoic Virtues

Chrysippus and the Religious Character of Stoic Ethics

Christoph Jedan

continuum

Continuum International Publishing Group

The Tower Building   80 Maiden Lane
11 York Road   Suite 704
London SE1 7NX   New York NY 10038

www.continuumbooks.com

British Library Cataloguing-in-Publication Data
A catalogue record for this book is available from the British Library.

ISBN: PB: 978-1-4411-9794-8

Library of Congress Cataloging-in-Publication Data
Jedan, Christoph.
Stoic virtues : Chrysippus and the theological foundations of stoic ethics/Christoph Jedan.
   p. cm.
Includes bibliographical references and index.
ISBN-13: 978-1-4411-9794-8

1. Stoics. 2. Virtue. 3. Virtues. 4. Chrysippus, ca. 280-207 B.C. I. Title.

B528.J43 2009
171'.2–dc22   2009016385

Typeset by Newgen Imaging Systems Pvt Ltd, Chennai, India
Printed and bound in Great Britain by the MPG Books Group

To Rina

Contents

Part Four: Practices of Virtue

Acknowledgements

I began working on the project that eventually resulted in this book at the University of Münster in 1999. During the years that it has taken me to finish the manuscript I have accumulated debts of gratitude to many more individuals and institutions than I can mention here.

However, I am indebted to the Ministry of Education, North Rhine-Westphalia, for funding my research project entitled 'Ethik der Lebensgestaltung: Die Entfaltung der griechischen Tugendlehre und ihre Bedeutung für die Gegenwart' from 1999 to 2001. Soon afterwards, I concentrated my research on the religious aspect of Stoic virtue ethics. My interest was triggered in the first place by Maximilian Forschner's stimulating publications on Stoic ethics. I am particularly grateful to Hermann Weidemann, my supervisor in Münster, for his tireless support of the project and for his detailed discussions of my work. My thanks also to Burkhard Hafemann and Thomas Leinkauf, two other colleagues in Münster, and to Klaus Engelhard, for their response to my early attempts on the Stoics.

I spent the academic year 1999–2000 as a visiting scholar at the Faculty of Classics in Cambridge. I am grateful to David Sedley for inviting me and for discussing on several occasions, then and later, drafts of my work. My thanks also to Malcolm Schofield and Geoffrey Lloyd, who, although not directly involved in the project, helped make my stay in Cambridge and at Darwin College a fruitful one.

Since 2003, I have worked at the Faculty of Theology and Religious Studies in Groningen. I am grateful to my colleagues at the faculty in particular to Jan Bremmer and Patrick Vandermeersch, for their support.

An earlier draft of the book was submitted and accepted as a 'Habilitationsschrift' at the Humboldt University Berlin in 2005–6. I am indebted to Christof Rapp for making possible the 'Habilitation' of an external candidate and for his comments on the text. My thanks for comments and suggestions also to Dominik Perler, and to Hermann Weidemann and David Sedley who, together with Christof Rapp, acted as referees.

My preparation of the text for publication was greatly aided by a sabbatical leave financed by the Netherlands Organization for Scientific Research (NWO) in 2007–8.

My thanks to the staff at Continuum for seeing the book through the press and to Michael Rice for his invaluable help with correcting the proofs.

Let me end with my family. I am grateful to my parents for their support over the years. Most of all I want to thank Rina, my wife, for sharing the burdens of a protracted work on virtues I do not possess. The book is dedicated to her.

Abbreviations

For abbreviations of the titles of ancient philosophical works, see the Index of Cited Passages.

ANRW	*Aufstieg und Niedergang der römischen Welt*
EK	Fragments of Posidonius, ed. and trans. Edelstein and Kidd
FDS	*Fragmente zur Dialektik der Stoiker: Neue Sammlung der Texte mit deutscher Übersetzung und Kommentaren*, ed. Hülser
IG²	*Hellenistic Philosophy: Introductory Readings*, ed. Inwood and Gerson. Second edition
KP	*Der kleine Pauly*
LAW	*Lexikon der alten Welt*
LS	*The Hellenistic Philosophers*, ed. Long and Sedley
OCD	*Oxford Classical Dictionary.* Third edition
OSAP	*Oxford Studies in Ancient Philosophy*
PBACAP	*Proceedings of the Boston Area Colloquium in Ancient Philosophy*
SVF	*Stoicorum veterum fragmenta*, ed. von Arnim

Introduction

Like its ancient rivals, Stoic ethics centred on the concept of virtue. From Chrysippus of Soli onwards, a systematic discussion of virtue was part of Stoic ethics. Yet, in spite of its centrality to Stoic ethics, the concept of virtue has not yet received a sustained, book-length examination.[1] The topic of virtue fares less well than other aspects of Stoic ethics: the passions and 'appropriation' (*oikeiōsis*), for instance, have been scrutinized in a number of detailed studies.[2]

The lack of research into the Stoic concept of virtue is perhaps due to the complacent view that Stoic ethics is, after all, a form of virtue ethics, and that 'we all know what virtue ethics is about'. That, however, is doubtful. The *de facto* predominance of Aristotle's ethics[3] threatens to narrow our view of what ancient virtue ethics could have been about and, consequently, to distort a fair appreciation of Stoic virtue ethics. This should not be taken to mean that the Stoics must have formulated practical concerns that were markedly different from the concerns of Aristotle (or, for that matter, other ancient authors) and thus must have endorsed recommendations on courses of action which set them apart from other philosophical schools. On the contrary, I suggest that we should be sceptical about such inflated claims regarding the novelty and uniqueness of Stoic practice.[4] What I argue here is that Stoic virtue ethics is, as an intellectual enterprise, quite different from the virtue ethics formulated by Aristotle.

The use of the word 'Stoic' instead of reference to specific individual Stoic philosophers has probably made the reader suspect what in fact is the case: this book discusses the school's unified central doctrines—as it were, the theoretical core of Stoic ethics. Historically, this doctrinal core has been identified with Chrysippus' attempt to systematize and enhance Stoic philosophy. Without neglecting the developmental aspects of Stoic ethics wherever they are relevant to the argument, this book focuses on Chrysippus' contribution. I am aware that this focus is deeply questionable to some scholars. Is not the history of Stoic philosophy, they might ask, a succession of theories which are so markedly different that it is, perhaps, better to speak of the rise and fall of several, quite different Stoicisms? Nevertheless, while doctrinal developments and discontinuities are reflected in our sources, we should not be tempted to overstress them. Hellenistic philosophers were members of schools. Even if it is difficult for us to grasp the plethora of factors involved in the membership of an ancient philosophical school,[5] it is hard to imagine that membership went without considering oneself part of an ongoing tradition. Chrysippus is a good example: he chose (some time after 260 BC) to join the Stoic school, which had been founded more than a generation before (*c.*300 BC). The evidence points to Chrysippus' considering himself the systematizer and defender of a pre-existing doctrinal core to which he was clearly committed.[6] Even though he rejected some doctrines that he thought indefensible and emphasized some doctrines more than his predecessors had done, he did so in a spirit of continuous engagement with the doctrinal basis of his school. Indeed, without the prevalence of such a spirit, the continuity of the Stoic school (as well as that of the other ancient philosophical schools) cannot be explained. I support this view by showing, for instance, how Chrysippus' virtue table stemmed from a critical engagement with Zeno's thought and remained an important point of reference for Panaetius, at a later and apparently very different stage of Stoic thought.

There must have been a core of common beliefs and a common outlook that defined what it was to be a Stoic, even if stances on practical ethical questions were radically contended. That core, I suggest, was formed pivotally by the religious orientation of Stoic ethics. I am convinced that religion is the single most important perspective from which we can understand the specific shape and coherence of Stoic virtue ethics. The observation that the philosophy of the Stoics and *a fortiori* their ethics were religious through and through is not exactly novel. In his book on Stoic theology, Daniel Babut has called this observation a banality.[7] Banal though it may be, it has not yet been shown in sufficient detail what role religion played in Stoic ethics.[8] In recent literature, we even find tendencies to disregard or downplay the role of religion, particularly in the context of the neo-Aristotelian interpretations of Stoic ethics.[9] Apart from the currency of a specific reading of Aristotelian ethics mentioned above, such interpretations can perhaps be attributed to a certain embarrassment of hindsight. We should be warned, however, by Plutarch's report that Chrysippus prefaced every one of his ethical treatises with theological doctrines and wrote that it is 'impossible to find a different principle of justice and a different beginning than the one from Zeus and from universal nature'.[10]

And so this book takes Stoic religion seriously, and it attempts to show how the religious tenor of Stoic philosophy provides the key for an adequate understanding of Stoic ethics, not only across time but also structurally, by helping us to understand a number of counterintuitive and seemingly incoherent Stoic statements. I argue that such apparently paradoxical claims as, for instance, the sufficiency of virtue for happiness and the non-graduality of virtue can only make sense if we see them in the light of the religious character of Stoic ethics.

This book deals with the historical form of Stoic ethics rather than the applicability of Stoic doctrines to today's discussions. It resists the temptation to reformulate Stoic philosophy in the language of the present age. This historical approach to our sources undoubtedly comes at the cost of making the Stoic position more alien in terms of today's philosophical discussion, but it undoubtedly has the advantage of enabling us to understand what we grasp at no time better than when talking to cultural strangers: the historical situation of our own assumptions and perspectives.

The historical approach implies also that the book is wary of forcing undue unity on Stoic teachings. It argues that for all their efforts, the Stoics were left with some unresolved tensions in their outlook. Where other scholars have attempted to explain away such tensions by attributing the evidence to different historical stages, this book does not resort to such (more often than not dubious) stratagems. Instead of treating such tensions as potential sources of embarrassment that one should dispose of as quickly as possible, it highlights them as being of particular philosophical interest.

The argument proceeds in four parts. Part One offers an introductory overview of the religious world-view of the Stoics. It is pitched at non-specialists. Since the texts and debates rehearsed in this part are well known to specialists, they are invited to turn to Part Two directly.

Where Part One attempts to set accents of its own in a scholarly field already well studied, it is by stressing the tensions in the Stoic system, which remain, I argue, unresolved in spite of the Stoics' quest for a unified theory. The Stoics balanced three intellectual tendencies which pulled (at least potentially) in quite different directions. First, there was an adherence to traditional polytheistic religion which the Stoics attempted to defend. Second, the Stoics stood in the broader current of ancient philosophical theology with its tendency towards spiritualizing ethical interpretations of religion. In short, philosophical theologies tended to be critical of (some aspects of) traditional polytheistic religion. Third, the Stoics brought their natural philosophical theories into the bargain, which were shaped by the assumption that only bodies 'are'. If followed unmitigated, this philosophical tendency would certainly have suggested a reduction of the deity to a physical factor at work in the arrangement of the world and could thus have been disastrous for the imagery of a deity somehow transcending the world.

Of course, the Stoics laboured to forge a unity out of these three tendencies, limiting the impact of each one. I have already suggested that a degree of tension remained. This is perhaps best evidenced by the astonishing spectrum of theological rhetoric available to the Stoics, ranging from staunchly corporealist and pantheistic conceptions to the imagery of a personal God.[11] It allowed the Stoics to combine their rigorously corporealist natural philosophy with a sincere support for the traditional polytheistic religion of their time and to greatly enhance the wider acceptability of Stoic philosophy.

Chapter 1 analyses the corporealist physics of the Stoics and its shaping role for other parts of Stoic philosophy. Chapter 2 presents Stoic theology while focusing on the range of theological rhetoric available to the Stoics. Chapter 3 deals with the Stoic doctrine of human responsibility against the background of determination by fate. It manifests the interpretive changes that result from a historical perspective which does not attempt to purge the appearance of tensions at any cost.[12] In previous scholarship, it has been more widely accepted that during the first phase of the Stoic school two different pictures of fate were evoked: first, a fairly traditional picture of a 'personal fate', the predetermination of certain key events in human life. Second, a picture of fate as 'all-embracing'; that is, the exceptionless determination of every detail of the world process. While scholars have attempted to 'distribute' the endorsement of these two pictures of fate over the early phase of the Stoa,[13] I suggest that Chrysippus (unwittingly) employed both characterizations of fate. The fact that both pictures or concepts of fate were evoked, often intertwined, in ancient Greek literature makes it likely that Chrysippus failed to see the difference between them. It is far easier for us to appreciate the difference, profiting from the cultural distance between the ancients and ourselves. The assumption that two different pictures of fate were employed by Chrysippus can explain the range of rhetoric he employed, coupling the endorsement of an exceptionless determination of every detail of life to a rhetoric stressing individual human responsibility.

Part Two examines the Stoic characterizations of virtue and the virtues. Chapter 4 analyses the meaning of two Stoic definitions of virtue: (a) virtue is a 'perfect state' and (b) it is a 'consistent character' in the whole of one's life. Both definitions are closely related to the Stoic description of the virtues as forms of knowledge (*epistēmai*). The import of the claim that virtues are forms of knowledge is examined in Chapter 5. Chapter 6 focuses on Chrysippus' theory of how there can be several different, yet inseparable virtues. Chapter 7 discusses the Chrysippean catalogue of virtues we find in Arius Didymus and Pseudo-Andronicus of Rhodes. It argues that this virtue table was (and was probably intended to be) an *open* one, allowing additions and further refinement, rather than being 'complete' and 'closed'.

Part Three deals with Stoic theories of how human beings can become virtuous. The Stoics held that virtue is an extremely rare possession. Chapter 8 analyses how the Stoics argued that virtue is attainable in principle. The Stoics had to explain why nature, benevolently administered by God, does not carry human beings more frequently towards virtue. The Stoics needed an account of interfering factors for which the deity cannot be blamed.

Chapters 9 and 10 analyse the religious language in which the description of the acquisition and possession of virtue is couched. Chapter 9 attempts to show, in more detail than has hitherto been shown, the import of the description of the theological training indispensable for the acquisition of virtue as an 'initiation'. The terminology of ancient mystery cults employed in this description sheds light on how the Stoics perceived their theological training. Among other factors, the attempt of ancient mystery cults to achieve closeness to the divine is an important hint for the interpretation of Stoic virtue ethics. Chapter 10 continues the enquiry by analysing the theological rhetoric evoking such closeness to the divine. It focuses in particular on a passage in the *Tusculan Disputations*, where Cicero describes the acquisition and possession of virtue in terms of taking or sharing the divine standpoint. I suggest that Cicero's description, in spite of his being a rather late witness, with an argumentative and literary agenda of his own, in fact contains a valuable suggestion for the interpretation of early Stoic virtue ethics and one that can help us understand a number of otherwise inexplicable structural features of Stoic ethics.

Part Four studies the *practices* of Stoic ethics. The plural is chosen deliberately. In our sources we find evidence of a far-reaching flexibility and context sensitivity of Stoic practical prescriptions. We find, moreover, that different courses of action are prescribed by leading Stoics. Against the background of a contentiousness in Stoic practice it is pivotal to reconstruct how Stoic practical reasoning must have worked. Chapter 11 examines the evidence of the Stoic concepts of a natural law and action-guiding rules prescribing what is appropriate (the *kathēkon*). Against recent attempts to give the concept of rules a neo-Aristotelian, procedural role, I defend the older natural law interpretation of Stoic ethics and attempt to show how that interpretation can account for the sensitivity to context of Stoic prescriptions correctly highlighted in 'procedural' interpretations. Chapter 12 discusses the evidence for the versatility and contentiousness of Stoic practical prescriptions and suggests that the interpretation of Stoic ethics as a fundamentally theological system can help us to understand why the contentiousness of Stoic practice did not undermine the unity of the teaching of the Stoic school.

Throughout the book I quote translations of the principal Greek and Latin texts that my interpretation draws on. In the past decades, the English-speaking academic world has produced numerous excellent translations and I have been happy to use work that has been so admirably done. I have not pointed out minor alterations, such as capitalization. In the few instances, however, where I prefer another reading or a different translation of Stoic terminology, I have made this clear. I have given preference throughout to the translations of Long and Sedley's *The Hellenistic Philosophers*. In addition to the fact that these translations are excellent in their own right, Long and Sedley's work is an extremely useful standard of reference in a field of research where many editions are so scarce as to impede immediate consultation. For the same reason, I have added references to texts in von Arnim's collection *Stoicorum Veterum Fragmenta* wherever I thought this might be helpful.

Part One

A Religious World-View

Chapter 1

Stoic Corporealism

It has often been remarked that the Stoic world-view was religious through and through.[1] In order to integrate religion into their philosophical outlook, the Stoics had to strike a balance between three intellectual tendencies pulling in quite different directions. First, the early Stoics stood in the larger context of traditional polytheistic Greek religion which they attempted to integrate in their philosophical system. From the time of Zeno, the Phoenician founder of the Stoic school, a favourable attitude towards conventional polytheistic religion was part of the Stoic world-view.[2]

Second, the Stoics stood in the broader context of ancient philosophical theology.[3] While attempting a rapprochement between philosophical theory and traditional religion, philosophical theologies could at the same time be critical of aspects of popular faith and press for an ethical (re-)interpretation of cultic practices.[4] One need not doubt that such (re-)interpretations were conducted in a spirit of positive engagement with traditional religion. Given the fact that traditional religion was determined by the ideal of ritual correctness rather than by specific doctrines or a creed, by 'orthopraxy' rather than by orthodoxy, the ancient philosophers could well believe they were remaining within the scope of traditional religion.[5] Seeing that traditional religion was under attack[6] or indefensible in parts, they chose to defend it actively by providing a rational, argumentative basis for it, even if this meant that aspects of traditional religion had to be rejected as untenable.[7]

Finally, there was a third tendency that the Stoics themselves brought into the discussion: their own philosophical predilections, most notably perhaps a tendency towards a 'materialistic' ontology which was arguably not the easiest starting point to combine with a traditional theological outlook.

It hardly needs to be emphasized that the integration of such different tendencies is a difficult task and one that can, perhaps, never be accomplished seamlessly. In any case, philosophical theologies of all ages and descriptions inadvertently display a tension between deep-felt reverence for

a traditional deity—or, for that matter, for several deities—and the philosophical reconstruction explaining the nature of that deity and the role
that the deity plays in the universe. Among the ancient Greek philosophical theologies, those of Plato and Aristotle are striking examples of this
ubiquitous problem, and the Stoics are no exception to the rule.

The Stoics attempted to retain conventional religion while re-interpreting
it in the framework of a rigorous natural philosophy resulted in a highly
original blend of ideas. They tried to overcome potential tensions, not only
by selectively adopting motifs of traditional theology but also by adapting
their world-view to fit their theological intuitions. With this two-sided process, the Stoics achieved a high degree of unity. Yet, some tensions between
conventional theology and the philosophical reconstruction remained. It is
perhaps these remaining tensions and their argumentative consequences
that give the Stoic system its characteristic shape. The Stoics conceived a
pantheistic theology which they interpreted in terms of their physics as a
divine principle permeating and organizing matter. Yet at the same time,
the Stoics continued to employ the theological language stemming from
traditional polytheistic religion. The God of the Stoics had humanly recognizable qualities and virtues, which made a cosmos under control of such a
divine element a place tailored for the needs of human beings providentially looked after by God. This cosmos was a more agreeable place than
could be expected on the basis of physical analysis in terms of matter
permeated and enlivened by a fiery element.

In this chapter, I shall begin with an analysis of Stoic physics and its
implications for other Stoic doctrines, in particular for theology, which was
also seen as the 'crowning' part of physics. I shall discuss Stoic theology in
more detail in Chapter 2, with a particular emphasis on the tension between
the traditional religion that the Stoics wanted to integrate and the constraints imposed by their other philosophical assumptions, physical as well
as theological. I shall continue this argument in Chapter 3 by showing that
the Stoic doctrine of fate offers clear evidence of such residual tensions.

I have mentioned that the Stoics had a tendency towards materialism.
However, the Stoics conceived a materialism of a special kind, a materialism
which squared with their theology. Their 'materialism' does not picture
material processes as purely mechanical, like billiard balls colliding and
being thereby pushed onto another trajectory.[8] For the Stoics, the material
reality is formed and controlled by a divine principle. Body is 'alive and
intelligent all the way down'.[9] For present-day readers, who understand the
label 'materialism' against the background of early modern mechanical,
reductive materialism, it is therefore better to avoid the misleading word
'materialism' altogether and use the term 'corporealism' instead.[10]

The Stoics claimed that only bodies 'are'. Their insistence on this point is well attested.[11] For them, body is 'that which is extended in three dimensions with resistance' (τὸ τριχῇ διαστατὸν μετὰ ἀντιτυπίας), a definition also used by the Epicureans.[12] With it, a second Stoic definition of 'body' is adumbrated. According to the Stoics, only bodies can act (ποιεῖν) or be acted upon (πάσχειν).[13] It is probable that the second definition was a reaction to Plato's discussion of materialism in the *Sophist*.[14] There, Plato has the 'visitor' suggest that 'corporeality' (and, consequently, 'visibility' and 'tangibility') are not satisfactory definitions of 'being', since the soul and the virtues obviously are incorporeal entities (247A–B). Instead, he suggests that the ability to act or to be acted upon is characteristic of being (247D–E). In consequence, the Stoics claimed that everything that 'is' (including the soul and the virtues) is body, or a property of it.[15] The Stoics turned the tables on Plato's 'visitor': the corporeality of the virtues cannot be denied if they are to have causal efficacy in the world. However, if virtues, one of Plato's prime examples for incorporeal entities, are corporeal after all, it is difficult to avoid the conclusion that everything else is corporeal too.

Nevertheless, the Stoics acknowledged four 'incorporeals': place, void, time and the 'sayable' (λεκτόν). These incorporeals have a secondary ontological status, as is reflected in Stoic terminology. Incorporeals do not 'exist' (εἶναι), they 'subsist' (ὑφίστασθαι). All this is tantamount to stressing the special status of bodies in the Stoic world. Bodies are fundamental; everything else is related to them.[16]

The corporeal world is constituted by two principles (ἀρχαί): an active principle (τὸ ποιοῦν) and a passive principle (τὸ πάσχον). Diogenes Laertius reports (D.L. 7.134, trans. LS 44B and Hicks):

They [the Stoics] think that there are two principles of the universe, that which acts (τὸ ποιοῦν) and that which is acted upon (τὸ πάσχον). That which is acted upon is unqualified substance, i.e. matter; that which acts is the reason in it, i.e. god. For this, since it is everlasting, constructs (δημιουργεῖν) every single thing throughout all matter. This doctrine is laid down by Zeno of Citium in his treatise *On Existence*, Cleanthes in his work *On Atoms*, Chrysippus in the first book of his *Physics* towards the end, Archedemus in his treatise *On Elements*, and Posidonius in the second book of his *Physical Exposition*. They say there is a difference between principles and elements: the former are ungenerated and indestructible, whereas the elements pass away at the conflagration. The principles are also bodies ['incorporeal' (ἀσωμάτους), in the parallel text of the Suda] and without form, but the elements are endowed with form.

We learn from this text that the Stoics characterized the passive principle as 'unqualified substance' (ἄποιος οὐσία) and also as 'matter' (ὕλη). The active principle is called the 'reason' (λόγος) in matter, and also God (θεός). The active principle permeates matter and forms the corporeal world down to individual entities (ἕκαστα). The divine principle has the role of a creator (δημιουργεῖν).[17]

The next noteworthy characteristic of Diogenes' account is a long list of Stoic adherents to the concept of twin principles. The names range from Zeno to Posidonius. Diogenes indicates by the list that, at least on the level reached so far, the conception of the two principles is a theory held without exception by members of the Stoic school.[18]

The text also mentions the differentiation between principles and elements (στοιχεῖα). Whereas the twin principles—the primary constituents of the corporeal world—are eternal, elements have a merely secondary status. Constituted by the twin principles, they undergo processes of generation and destruction in the cyclical history of the cosmos.[19] This is crucial for the place of man in the world. Since the corporeal world at the level of the elements is in a constant flux, the only way to retain a sense of stability and permanence is to identify oneself with, and try to take the perspective of, the eternal, rational, world-controlling divine principle.[20]

The corporeality of the Stoic twin principles (as stated in the text of D.L. 7.134) has been debated. A parallel text in the Suda reads 'incorporeals' (ἀσωμάτους) instead of 'bodies' (σώματα), and some scholars have followed the Suda's reading.[21] There are, however, strong reasons to maintain the corporeality of the principles according to orthodox Stoic physics. First, the corporeality of the twin principles is far better attested by ancient reports.[22] Second, as mentioned above, the capacities to act and to be acted upon define bodies. It would be bizarre to conceptualize God as the formative principle of the world and yet deny this principle the power to act.[23] Third, the seemingly problematic conception of an interdependence between two bodily principles is understandable against the background of the theory that two bodies can occupy the same place, which forms the backbone of the concept of 'total blending' (see below).[24]

Part of Stoic cosmology, and particularly the roles of God and of the elements, is outlined by Diogenes in a passage following almost immediately after the one quoted above (D.L. 7.135–7, trans. Hicks):

God is one and the same with Reason, Fate, and Zeus; he is also called by many other names. In the beginning he was by himself; he transformed the whole of substance through air into water, and just as in animal generation the seed has a moist vehicle, so in cosmic moisture God, who is the seminal reason of the universe, remains behind in the moisture as such an agent, adapting matter to himself with a view to the next stage of creation. Thereupon he created first of all the four elements, fire, water, air, earth. They are discussed by Zeno in his treatise *On the Whole*, by Chrysippus in the first book of his *Physics*, and by Archedemus in a work *On Elements*. An element is defined as that from which particular things first come to be at their birth and into which they are finally resolved. The four elements together constitute unqualified substance or matter. Fire is the hot element, water the moist, air the cold, earth the dry. (. . .) Fire has the uppermost place; it is also called aether, and in it the sphere of the fixed stars is first created; then comes the sphere of the planets, next to that the air, then the water, and lowest of all the earth, which is at the centre of all things.

The text provides valuable information for our present enterprise. God is explicitly named as the creator of the four elements: fire, water, air and earth. Again, the identity of God and cosmic reason (λόγος) is emphasized. The Stoics offered etymologies of the names of traditional divinities that should make them compatible with the assumption of a single divine principle.[25] At 7.147, Diogenes Laertius enumerates some typical etymological explanations (trans. Hicks, modified):

He [God] is, however, the creator of the universe and, as it were, the father of all, both in general and in that particular part of him which is all-pervading, and which is called many names according to its various powers. They give the name Dia (Δία) because all things are due to (διά) him; Zeus (Ζῆνα) in so far as he is the cause of life (ζῆν) or pervades all life; the name Athena is given because the ruling part of the divinity extends to the aether; the name Hera marks its extension to the air; he is called Hephaestus since it spreads to the creative fire; Poseidon, since it stretches to the sea; Demeter, since it reaches to the earth. Similarly men have given the deity his other titles, fastening, as best they can, on some one or other of his peculiar attributes.

Apparently, the Stoics saw the cults of different divinities as endeavours to name and honour different aspects of the single divine principle. Seen in this light, the use of the names 'Fate' and 'Zeus' in Diogenes Laertius 7.135 is highly evocative. The names imply that the active principle is, as it were, a sovereign governor of the world process through time. The idea that

God providentially administers this process is indicated by the remark that
he undertakes a certain step in the creation of the world 'with a view to
the next state' (πρὸς τὴν τῶν ἑξῆς γένεσιν).[26] One of the concepts that the
Stoics famously used to illustrate the process of the providential creation of
the world was the concept of 'spermatic reason', or the 'seminal principle'
(σπερματικὸς λόγος). At Diogenes Laertius 7.136, God is identified with the
seminal principle of the world. A text of Aetius gives us additional material
on the cosmogonic role of God (*Placita* 1.7.33 = *SVF* 2.1027 part, trans.
Hunt 1976: 38):

> The Stoics declare that God is endowed with mind, a craftsmanlike fire
> going on its way to the generation of the cosmos, embracing in itself all
> the *spermatikoi logoi* in accordance with which the particulars come into
> being according to fate, and as *pneuma* pervading the whole cosmos being
> called by various titles according to the variations of the matter which it
> has pervaded.

Taken together, the two reports show how the Stoics described cosmogony
as a quasi-biological process of generation. The seminal principle determines the structure of the world, employing specific building plans of
particular entities which are also called 'seminal principles' (in the plural).
The world process is cyclical. A recurrent conflagration consumes the entities in the cosmos, until only fire (the divine principle) remains by itself.[27]
In the recurrent processes of world generation, the seminal principles can
account for the identical nature of the entities in different world cycles.[28]

Aetius' doxography employs the title of 'craftsmanlike fire' (πῦρ τεχνικόν)
to characterize the Stoic God. With this concept, the Stoics apparently
tried to incorporate Heraclitean ideas on the governing principle of the
cosmos. They enriched it by differentiating between two kinds of fire, the
generative heat of living things associated with the sun and the destructive
heat of ordinary fire.[29]

When Zeno spoke of God as craftsmanlike fire, he meant by that, of
course, the generative, productive kind of fire in opposition to the destructive, uncreative ordinary fire (πῦρ ἄτεχνον). The generative and productive
kind of fire is found in plants, animals and the stars.[30] Zeno's successors
Cleanthes and Chrysippus further developed his theory that a certain
form of heat governs the cosmos. Most probably it was Chrysippus who
introduced the theory which later became the standard Stoic view.[31] According to this theory, the governing force of the divine principle is transmitted
by 'breath' (πνεῦμα). Zeno had already defined the soul as 'warm *pneuma*'

(πνεῦμα ἔνθερμον), but there is no trace that he extrapolated from the working of *pneuma* in an animal's soul to the cosmic level.[32]

According to Chrysippus, *pneuma* permeates the whole cosmos and is the universal vehicle of divine reason.[33] On the level of physics, *pneuma* can be analysed as a mixture of air and fire.[34] In physical analysis, the role of *pneuma* as the universal controlling entity is based on its peculiar double movement, often called 'pneumatic motion' (κίνησις πνευματική). The *pneuma* moves simultaneously 'out of itself' (ἐξ αὑτοῦ) and 'into itself' (εἰς αὑτό),[35] or, as another source has it, 'outwards' (εἰς τὸ ἔξω) and 'inwards' (εἰς τὸ ἔσω).[36] The state resulting from this double movement is called 'tension' (τόνος) and, accordingly, the double movement is also called 'tensional movement' (κίνησις τονική).[37] The tension is responsible for the unity and the qualities of a thing. More precisely, the inward movement causes the being and unity of the object, whereas the outward movement produces the dimensions and qualities.[38] The tensional state of *pneuma* is called 'tenor' or 'holding' (ἕξις). *Hexis* is a generic term here. The constitution of different types of entities is the result of different degrees of the pneumatic tensional state present in an object. Chrysippus distinguishes four different levels of pneumatic tension.[39] On the lowest level, *pneuma* functions as 'tenor' (ἕξις, here in a specific sense), maintaining the unity and qualities of inorganic objects. On the second level, *pneuma* is 'nature' (φύσις), in the sense of the nutritive capacity of plants. The third level of pneumatic formation is 'soul' (ψυχή) in animals, whereas the fourth level of pneumatic instantiation is rational capacity ('intellect', νοῦς).

The universal application of the theory of the pneumatic tensional state expresses the governing role of the divine principle on the physical level. The tensional state is the cause not only of every quality of objects *within* the cosmos (and therefore also for every psychic quality); it also causes the coherence of the cosmos itself.[40] Therefore, the doctrine of fate—that is, the belief that there is complete control of the divine principle over the world, so that there is a complete causal connectedness between successive world states under the guidance of the provident divine principle (see Chapter 3)—is expressed in terms of the theory of *pneuma*. Chrysippus holds that fate is a 'power of *pneuma*' (δύναμις πνευματική).[41]

Chrysippus' theory of *pneuma* had to be supplemented by related doctrines. Since *pneuma* is a body, Chrysippus had to offer a theory how permeation of the corporeal world by another bodily entity could be possible. His solution was a theory of mixture that can explain how two bodies can occupy the same place.[42] According to Alexander of Aphrodisias, Chrysippus made the following distinction[43]: There is, first, a type of mixture in which different objects are merely in physical contact, yet without changing their individual qualities, just like beans and grains of wheat mixed together. Chrysippus called this kind of mixture 'juxtaposition' (παράθεσις). The second mode of mixture, 'through-and-through fusion' (σύγχυσις), is characterized by the destruction of the ingredients and the generation of a new compound body out of them. The compound has its own, new qualities. This is what happens in the production of certain medical drugs. However, only a third kind of mixture is, according to Chrysippus, 'blending in the true sense of the word' (ἥντινα τῶν μίξεων κρᾶσιν ἰδίως εἶναι λέγει). It occurs when

> certain substances and their qualities are mutually coextended through and through, with the original substances and their qualities being preserved in such a mixture (. . .) for the capacity to be separated again from one another is a peculiarity of blended substances, and this only occurs if they preserve their own natures in the mixture.[44]

According to Chrysippus, an example of blending in the true sense of the word.[45] is the dissolution of wine in water.[45] He held that these two substances are unified through and through—in an extreme case, even a drop of wine in the ocean[46]—but that they can still be separated, for instance by means of an oiled sponge.[47] The concept of blending provides the model for the permeation of *pneuma* in matter. Alexander reports (*De mixtione* 217.32–218.1, trans. Todd, modified):

> They employ as clear evidence that this is the case the fact that the soul, which has its own substantiality, just like the body that receives it, pervades the whole of the body while preserving its own substantiality in the mixture with it (for there is nothing in the body possessing the soul that does not partake of the soul); and the same holds for the nature of plants, as also the tenor in bodies held together by their tenor.

The theory of blending enabled Chrysippus to support his corporealism. He could maintain that all the characteristics of corporeal entities are caused by an entity that is itself corporeal, the *pneuma*. For instance, Chrysippus held that qualities like virtue, vice and knowledge are 'bodies' (σώματα), because they are states of the material *pneuma*.[48] Yet, with his theory of blending he was not committed to a reductionist type of materialism (see above). The corporeal *pneuma* is represented as a conscious rational agent creating and constituting the world as well as determining its course. Because of *pneuma*, the cosmos is a unified living being. The theory of *pneuma* spells out in terms of physics the role of God in the world. God, the ruling rational principle, is represented as controlling and providentially governing the cosmos.

The corporealism of the Stoics has marked consequences for their view of the soul. As we saw above, Chrysippus conceived of the soul as *pneuma* extending through the whole animate body. More precisely, he defined the soul as 'the *pneuma* innate in us, continuous, and penetrating the entire body, as long as the breath of life is in the body'.[49] In order to establish the corporeality of the soul, Chrysippus offers an argument which rests on the assumption that death is the separation (χωρισμός) of soul from the body:

> Death is the separation of soul from body. Nothing incorporeal is separated from the corporeal, for nothing incorporeal comes into contact with [or 'is joined to'] the corporeal. The soul is joined to and is separated from the body. Therefore the soul is corporeal.[50]

However, for Chrysippus this did not entail an immortality of the soul. On the contrary, the soul is not eternal, since it can only last, at the very best, until the next periodic conflagration of the cosmos (ἐκπύρωσις), when the divine element has consumed the other elements and remains alone until a new world cycle begins.[51] As to whether *all* souls last until conflagration, opinions differed. Whereas Cleanthes claimed that all souls last until conflagration, Chrysippus held more restrictively that only the soul of the sage does so.[52] In any case, conflagration was the endpoint of the soul's post-mortem existence. The Stoic doctrine of conflagration underlines the radical finitude of human existence in an ever-changing world. The only stable factor is the divine principle. To retain a sense of stability and permanence, the best strategy seems to identify with, and to imitate the permanence of, the divine principle as much as possible. And this was in effect what the Stoics suggested.[53] While the strategy of imitating the divine principle gives structure to Stoic ethics,[54] it is already present in the physical part of the Stoic system. Stoic psychology, for instance, stresses the natural link between man and the divine rational principle by claiming that the soul is essentially rational. The 'parts' or 'functions' of the soul are aspects of a unitary rational commanding faculty (ἡγεμονικόν) located in the region of the heart.[55] Physically, these functions are interpreted as a diffusion of *pneuma* into different parts of the body.[56]

Chrysippus believed that, in spite of being constituted by an essentially rational principle, the soul could display a deficiency of rationality in its working.[57] Normally human beings are in a state of deficient rationality, since the fully rational, God-like sage is only a rare exception. Deficient rationality is the cause of the 'passions' (πάθη), interpreted by Chrysippus as '(mistaken) beliefs' (δόξαι) which stimulate, by their immediateness, the wrong form of behaviour.[58] Plutarch's report in *De virtute morali* 441C–D offers us a glimpse of how Chrysippus conceived of the generation of the passions. Plutarch writes (trans. LS 61B):

> [T]he same part of the soul (which they call thought and commanding-faculty) becomes virtue and vice as it wholly turns around and changes in passions and alterations of tenor or character, and contains nothing irrational within itself. It is called irrational whenever an excessive impulse (τῷ πλεονάζοντι τῆς ὁρμῆς) which has become strong and dominant carries it off towards something wrong and contrary to the dictates of reason.

According to Plutarch, Chrysippus argued that, when reason lacks the stability identified with the possession of moral knowledge, the unitary rational soul 'wholly turns around' and forms the passions. Therefore, the production of the passions is the result of reason's failure to assent constantly to the right impressions in the right way.[59]

The Stoics' conception of a unitary soul made it difficult for them to account for phenomena like mental conflict (a mind divided between rational conviction and emotional attachment) and acting against better knowledge (ἀκρασία). For Socrates, who like the Stoics had emphasized the status of virtue as a form of knowledge, these phenomena were mere appearances. If a person has virtue, Socrates was convinced, virtue as stable knowledge has to prevail; where it does not, the claim to knowledge is mistaken.[60] Plato, with his concept of a tripartite soul developed in the fourth book of the *Republic*, could far better account for such phenomena: they are essentially a conflict between independent parts of the soul.[61] But Plato's answer, too, was not without difficulties. In order to make mental conflict and *akrasia* appear possible, the parts of the soul have to be independent. If, however, their independence is too strongly marked,[62] the communication between parts of the soul as well as the control exerted by the rational part become problematic.

Stoic psychology attempted to preserve the unity of the soul, but the Stoics had to explain how the appearance of mental conflict can arise. A Stoic suggestion seems to have been that the appearance of mental conflict is caused by an imperceptibly rapid succession of opposed mental states of the unitary rational soul.[63]

The Stoic model is not so wildly implausible as one might think. Not only is it irrefutable by experience,[64] it could even be considered the best representation of folk psychology: when we feel torn between different possible courses of action, do we not attempt to find out how it would *feel* to have taken the alternative decisions, do we not probingly *take* the alternative standpoints? Do not our ordinary experiences of weakness of will show that we *convince* ourselves that we may indulge a bit (say, by eating sweets) without any harm? In allowing for an imperceptibly fast oscillation between such standpoints, the Stoics could therefore have claimed that they merely extrapolated from common experience. Thus, they paid heed to the concerns underlying Plato's tripartite moral psychology without having to pay the price for it: they did not have to weaken the role of reason in virtuous action.

The rapid sequence of opposed mental states, which appear nevertheless to be simultaneous, is a sign of deficient rationality. If, however, an agent has true knowledge of what is right, that knowledge will prompt the right action without such conflict. But how could the Stoics explain the case of the *akratic* person, who claims to have acted against better knowledge? In the extant material we do not find an explicit treatment of this question, so we have to rely to some extent on guesswork.

Probably, the Stoics would not have accepted the claim that true knowledge is involved in alleged cases of *akrasia*. I suggest that the Stoics would have referred to their conception of virtue as knowledge. Virtue as *knowledge* in the full sense of the word is knowledge of a systematic body of information *plus* the unshakeable firmness of this knowledge. Concerning the content of knowledge, the Stoics distinguish two levels. It consists of (1) more detailed rules (παραινέσεις) and (2) ultimate principles (δόγματα) in which these rules are grounded. Without possession of the latter, the former lack the inherent stability which characterizes knowledge proper. As I shall suggest in Parts Three and Four, the ultimate principles are theological, and knowing them goes hand in hand with taking a new perspective on the world and one's place in it.[65]

I suggest that the Stoics would have denied that the *akrasia*-cases should be analysed as instances of acting against better *knowledge*. One can—up to a certain point—be *aware* of a moral obligation (a precept), but this awareness need not include the ultimate principles which ground the awareness of precepts in such a way that they become firm knowledge. Had the agent been aware of the ultimate principles and thus *known* his obligation, he would have unfailingly done what the precept commands.

Mental conflict and *akrasia* are cases of psychic instability. Against such instability the Stoics set the value of the continuous and stable shaping of life by reason. For Chrysippus, as we shall see later, the extreme form of such a rational form of life is living by the unitary true body of beliefs, whose possession is tantamount to taking the divine perspective on the cosmos: the standpoint of virtue.[66]

For the Stoics the virtues are ultimately analysable in physical terms. This is a corollary of Stoic corporealism, since only bodies can act (or be acted upon) and since virtue has an observable influence on the agent.[67] The Stoics conceptualize the corporeal nature of the virtues by characterizing virtue as 'a body disposed in a certain way'.[68] The body in question is the inborn *pneuma*, the soul or the 'controlling part' (ἡγεμονικόν).[69]

In their attempt to conceptualize the corporeal nature of the virtues, the Stoics went to extraordinary lengths. Every virtue is to be called a 'living creature' (ζῷον). Since the soul 'lives and has awareness', it must be considered a living being.[70] The virtues are 'in their being' (κατὰ τὴν οὐσίαν)—that is, in their material constitution—nothing else than the inborn *pneuma* which constitutes the soul. This made the Stoics vulnerable to arguments on the basis of iterated attributions, or so-called 'third man arguments'. The Stoics could not escape the inference that the characteristics which the whole living being has through the virtues could be attributed to the virtues themselves. Thus, virtue itself should have, for instance, *hormē* and virtue. Both a report in Stobaeus (2.64.18–65.6) as well as Seneca *Letters* 113 show that the Stoics did not find fault with this consequence.[71]

The Stoic claim that every virtue is a living being exposed itself to attack from competing philosophical schools: if every virtue is a living being, should it then not be the case that a multitude of living beings resides in the controlling part of the soul? Seneca *Letters* 117 records the Stoic defence against such attacks. Although every virtue can be described as a living being, the virtues are not *separate* living beings. If they were separate living beings, they would have to admit of a separate existence (*separati debent esse*).[72] However, this was not conceded by the Stoics. They could offer two arguments to support their stance: First, the virtues are instantiated *in* a living being; they are merely qualifications of a single physical component (the *pneuma* making up the controlling organ) of that being.[73] Second—on the basis of a complex theory to be discussed later—the virtues were, in spite of all the difference between them, ultimately inseparable.[74]

The physical doctrines related in this chapter are of great theological import: essentially they show that God is the only active principle in the world and thus maintains a complete control over the course of the world. In the next two chapters we shall see in how far the Stoics were able to square their conception of God with their attempt to integrate key elements of traditional polytheistic religion.

Chapter 2

Stoic Theology

In *De natura deorum* 2.3, Cicero's Stoic spokesman Balbus claims that Stoic theology was generally divided into four parts. The first part proved the existence of the gods, and the second dealt with their attributes; the third part treated the divine administration of the world, while the fourth discussed divine providential care for mankind. It is not clear what status can be attributed to this division of theology into four parts. Perhaps the *formal* division originated in Stoic teaching practice contemporary with Cicero, as has been suggested by Clara Auvray-Assayas.[1] This suggestion is attractive. Particularly where the refutation of objections raised by other schools was concerned, a clear-cut division of theology into four parts, each answering specific objections, must have been highly desirable. The fact that the older Stoics had dealt with the very same topics (albeit differently systematized), made it possible for later Stoics to cast their predecessors' theories into the four-part scheme. This would explain why Cicero's Stoic spokesman Balbus can draw so easily and extensively on the doctrines of Zeno, Cleanthes and Chrysippus.

However, the four-part division was too schematic to fit the arguments actually propounded by the early Stoics. This becomes particularly evident in the case of the Stoic arguments for the existence of God. In fact, the arguments rely on assumptions concerning divine attributes, the divine administration of the world, and providence for mankind.[2] Rather than being an independent part of theology, these arguments must be considered a focal point of Stoic theology where fundamental theological doctrines of the Stoics come together.

To give an impression of this focal role of the Stoic arguments for the existence of God, I reproduce here the outline of the ten arguments which Myrto Dragona-Monachou (1976) has ascribed (with varying certainty) to Chrysippus.[3]

1. 'If there is something that man cannot produce, that which produces it is superior to man. But the heavenly bodies and all the regular phenomena of the sky cannot be produced by man. Therefore the being which created them is superior to man. But that which is superior to man is God. (Therefore the gods exist).'[4]

2. 'If the gods do not exist, nothing in the universe can be superior to man, the only being endowed with reason, which is the most excellent property. But for any human being to believe that nothing is superior to himself is a sign of insane arrogance. There is then something superior to man. Therefore the gods exist.'[5]

3. 'If you see a beautiful house, you require a master, not a mouse, for whose sake it has been built. But the world is more beautiful and better-ordered than any house. Therefore it has not been created as the abode of man only, but for something superior to man. (But only god is superior to man. Therefore the world is made for the sake of the gods. Therefore the gods exist.)'[6]

4. 'It has been shown that the world is created for the sake of the gods. The higher position of a thing implies greater value and superiority. Man, as located in the densest and lowest region of the universe, that is, on the earth, is also lower than God—and therefore the world is made to be the abode of beings superior to man, therefore the gods exist.'[7]

5. 'Man gets all the elements of his constitution from the world . . . since nothing exists among all things superior to the world . . . nor can anything superior be conceived [. . .]; reason, wisdom etc. must primarily be possessed by this superior being from which man derives his own; thus the world is rational and thus God, and therefore the gods exist.'[8]

6. The sympathetic agreement, interconnection and affinity of things prove that the world is maintained in unison by a single divine and all-pervading spirit.[9]

7. Chrysippus claims 'that everything except the world was created for the sake of something else: the earth and its products for the animals, those for man, and man, as a fragment of the absolutely perfect being, i.e. the world, in order to contemplate and imitate the world. The world, as the absolute best, is also endowed with the best properties, such as intelligence and reason, since perfect things always possess better properties than imperfect ones do; therefore the world, as a perfect unity, possesses virtue as its most essential characteristic . . . therefore the world is wise and consequently is God'.[10]

8. 'Altars and other religious practices cannot be justified without the postulate of the existence of the gods.'[11]

9. 'If the gods do not exist, piety, the science of rendering service to the gods, is non-existent . . . But piety exists . . . Therefore the gods exist.'[12]

10. 'If the gods do not exist, divination does not exist either [being the science which observes the signs given by the gods], nor do inspiration and astrology, logic and prediction by dreams; But it is absurd to abolish so many things believed in by all men [that is, divination exists . . .]. Therefore the gods exist.'[13]

With these arguments, the Stoics intend to offer definite proofs for the existence of God. Take as an example the text of the ninth argument (Sextus Empiricus *Adversus Mathematicos* 9.123, trans. Bury):

> If gods do not exist, piety is not existent. For piety is 'the science of service to the gods,' and there cannot be any service of things non-existent, nor, consequently, will any science thereof exist; and just as there cannot be any science of service to Hippocentaurs, they being non-existent, so there will not be any science of service to the gods if they are non-existent. So that, if gods do not exist, piety is non-existent. But piety exists; so we must declare that gods exist.[14]

Probably this argument stems from Zeno, the founder of the Stoa, and was reformulated later either by Chrysippus or by someone employing his style.[15] However, I shall leave the question of ultimate authorship aside since it does not have any bearing on our present argument. For the moment I also leave aside the logical form of this as well as of other arguments.[16]

For our present purposes, it is more interesting to look at the argumentative resources that the Stoics drew upon. Ultimately, the ninth argument rests on the institutional fact of piety in society. The argument presupposes that some people *are* pious and that this is a truth-attaining cognitive state. This entails other propositions, for instance the proposition that the object of piety, the gods, exist. The motif is employed more frequently in Stoic theology. Other examples of it are the eighth argument on Dragona-Monachou's list, that 'altars and other religious practices cannot be justified without the postulate of the existence of the gods', and the tenth argument with its reference to traditional religious practices like divination. What these arguments have in common is that the Stoics *relied* on the truth of traditional religious practices. They took the broad religious consensus of their society for granted.[17] It is no surprise that these arguments support traditional, polytheistic religion. In fact, eight of the ten arguments (1–5, 8–10) infer the existence of *gods* (in the plural), whereas two arguments (6–7) argue for the existence of one divine principle permeating the world (6) or iden- tify the world with God (7). Yet the Stoics apparently saw no sharp divide, and certainly no incompatibility, between the two types of argument. This view is supported by the observation that the evidential bases of the two types of argument are not neatly separated: arguments for the existence of several gods (in the plural) draw not only on the institutions of polytheistic religion; they can also draw on physical speculation one would rather associate with arguments for a single divinity. Argument (4), which is based on physical speculation about different cosmic regions, is a case in point.

To all appearances, the Stoics must have been convinced that their arguments in support of the existence of a single deity and their arguments in favour of the existence of several deities were compatible and that they served the same argumentative goal.[18] A clear sign of this can be found in argument (5). Its intermediate conclusion is the Stoic pantheistic convic- tion that the world is God (see below), but the argument continues with support for a polytheistic stance. The issue is therefore not *if* the Stoics considered the polytheistic and mono- or pantheistic strands of their theology compatible, but how they combined the strands, and how much coherence they achieved.

It is well attested that the Stoics called their divine principle Zeus. They admitted other divinities in the Greek pantheon as aspects or manifesta- tions of the single divine principle and identified them as entities in—or rather, elements of—the world.[19] The Stoics attempted what can be described as 'allegorical interpretations'[20] of classical sources of traditional religious mythology, like Hesiod and Homer, and offered in this context etymologies of divine names.[21] By providing such interpretations, the Stoics could not only draw support for their own cosmological doctrines from venerated authors;[22] they could also relate themselves in a positive way (and thereby offer additional support) to traditional religion. Naturally, such support did not come without costs. The Stoics, who wanted to 'rediscover the original rationality of traditional mythology',[23] could not grant all the deities of the Greek pantheon the status of imperishable gods and god- desses. Only God, Zeus, is eternal. The 'lesser' gods are perishable, since only Zeus will remain in the cyclically occurring conflagration.[24] Regarding these lesser divinities as perishable, however, clashed with generally held convictions on the gods.[25]

While the constraints imposed by Stoic doctrines thus led to the abroga- tion of some aspects of traditional polytheism, the potential clashes were not infallibly resolved at the cost of traditional religion. On the contrary, the Stoics adopted so much of the rhetoric of polytheism as to incur tensions in their own philosophical system, even if that was certainly not the way the Stoics would have described their efforts. The clearest sign of such tensions can be found in what Keimpe Algra has termed the 'rather fluid conception' of the Stoic God.[26] According to Algra, the Stoic conception of God displays a 'monistic', a 'dualistic', and a 'more strictly theistic' perspective. The monistic perspective is employed where the world is identified as God, whereas the dualistic perspective comes into play where God is identified as a divine principle permeating matter (to different degrees). In the third, more strictly theistic perspective the Stoics can describe God more along human standards of intending and acting, related to persons. The Stoics speak of God as a craftsman of the cosmos, as a father.[27]

We can best think of these three perspectives as a rhetorical spectrum of descriptions of God which, to the Stoics' mind, were not mutually exclusive. Since the divine principle is the fundamental constituent of the world that cannot be distinguished from the world (other than conceptually), the Stoics would have felt justified in regarding the world as God (see below). By distinguishing conceptually between the divine principle and the matter it permeates, the Stoics were able to mark off a divine sphere from a subdivine sphere. In turn, the distinction must have made a rapprochement between the pantheistic and theistic ways of talking about God seem possible and even inevitable.

Characteristic of Stoic theology is the way it combines language from the different regions of the rhetorical spectrum. The Stoics argued that the world is divine because the divine principle permeates matter, and they described the pantheistic deity as having qualities that are recognizable and (at least in part) understandable from a human perspective. God represents, for instance, the virtue of wisdom. In this way, the Stoics could adopt part—but, of course, only part—of the theistic language of traditional polytheistic religion. In line with earlier philosophical theologies (e.g. Plato's), God is identified with positive, humanly recognizable qualities (virtues), while grosser representations of the Greek pantheon are shunned.

A good example of the tensions due to the employment of a veritable spectrum of theological language is the seventh Chrysippean argument. Since it is at the same time the most elaborate of Chrysippus' arguments and shows very clearly the importance of theology for Stoic ethics, I shall discuss it here in more detail.

The argument is reported in Cicero *De natura deorum* 2.37–9. This passage is preceded by a lengthy theological argument stretching from 2.20 to 2.36, where Cicero presents the basic strategies of Stoic theological reasoning. He begins with the contention that Zeno formulated his arguments in a contracted and dense way to invite criticism, in particular by the sceptical Academics (*ND* 2.20). Cicero later quotes some of Zeno's gems (*ND* 2.21–2), after disclosing his own intention to elaborate the implicit assumptions of Zeno's reasoning, obviously in order to render it immune to sceptical criticism.[28] Cicero does this by using arguments held within as well as outside the Stoic school. In the sequel to the passage (*ND* 2.23–36) he therefore adduces arguments advocated by Cleanthes and Plato (who was presumably quoted by the Stoics as an authority on the matter).

Ultimately, also, the passage *De natura deorum* 2.37–9 forms part of Cicero's enterprise to elaborate Zeno's argument and to present thereby standard Stoic theology. It is therefore quite unlikely that Cicero intended to reproduce in *ND* 2.37–9 an argument that originated with Chrysippus and was not to some extent a recapitulation of material already extant in Zeno. Indeed, this is precisely the impression Cicero wants to convey when he starts his account of Chrysippus with the phrase: 'Therefore Chrysippus did well . . .'[29] He presents Chrysippus as defending and elaborating on a core Stoic theology.

Here is Long and Sedley's translation of the passage (*ND* 2.37–9, trans. LS 54H):

For nor is there anything else besides the world which has nothing missing, and which is equipped from every point of view, perfect, and complete in all its measures and parts. As Chrysippus cleverly put it, just as the shield-cover was made for the sake of the shield and the sheath for the sake of the sword, so too with the exception of the world everything else was made for the sake of other things: for example, the crops and fruits which the earth brings forth were made for the sake of animals, and the animals which it brings forth were made for the sake of men (the horse for transport, the ox for ploughing, the dog for hunting and guard-ing). Man himself has come to be in order to contemplate and imitate the world, being by no means perfect, but a tiny constituent of that which is perfect. But the world, since it embraces everything and there is noth-ing which is not included in it, is perfect from every point of view. How then can it lack that which is best? But nothing is better than intellect and reason. Therefore the world cannot lack these. Therefore Chrysippus did well to prove by appeal to analogies that all things are better in perfect and mature specimens—for instance, in horse than in foal, in dog than in pup, in man than in child. Likewise, he argued, that which is the best thing in the whole world should be found in something which is perfect and complete. But nothing is more perfect than the world, and nothing better than virtue. Therefore virtue is intrinsic to the world. Indeed, man's nature is not perfect, yet virtue is achieved in man. Then how much more easily in the world! Therefore there is virtue in the world. Therefore the world is wise, and hence is god.

De natura deorum 2.37 begins with the statement that the world is perfect and complete.[30] This is a consequence of the vision propounded repeatedly before, that the world is a whole which comprises all other entities and is therefore the best of all that exists.[31] According to Cicero, Chrysippus expressed this Stoic vision well.[32] Chrysippus characterized the whole-part relationship between the world and the things it comprises by describing how entities are embedded in the world by means of teleological functions. The world itself does not have a function that links it to something exterior to it, since nothing (except void) is exterior to the world. With this, Chrysippus made use of the idea of a *scala naturae* extant in nature. Cicero had already presented the outlines of the theory in *De natura deorum* 2.33–4. The *scala naturae* ranges from (1) plants, (2) non-rational animals and (3) man as an entity that is (partly) rational to (4) entities that are naturally good and wise, i.e. completely rational. Already at *ND* 2.34 Cicero presents the theological use to which the *scala naturae* theory was put. What belongs to the fourth level of the scale must be identified as the divine and as the world itself. In the argument recapitulated in *ND* 2.37–9, Chrysippus begins by highlighting the teleological structure of nature with the examples of the shield-cover and shield and the sheath and sword. Everything comprised by the world is created in teleological patterns, standing to something else in the same relationship as the shield-cover to the shield and the sheath to the sword. For example, crops and fruits (entities from level (1) on the *scala naturae*) were made for the sake of animals (level (2)). Non-rational animals (level (2)) were made for the sake of man (level (3)). Man (level (3)) has the peculiar function to 'contemplate and imitate the world' (level (4)). The world itself does not have a teleological function, since it 'embraces everything' (*ND* 2.38). Chrysippus holds that the completeness of the world guarantees its perfection.[33] He argues that the perfection of the world entails that the world has the best properties, namely intellect and reason. Cicero has already mentioned a possible argument for this claim in *ND* 2.32. The status of perfection would be incompatible with only a part of the world (instead of the world as a whole) having the property of intelligence, for then the part would be better than the whole. In the text of *ND* 2.37–9 Cicero presents another argument by Chrysippus to this effect. Here, Chrysippus argues from experience that the perfect and mature state in nature is better; thus the horse is superior to the foal, and the mature dog is superior to the puppy. Similarly, the whole world is perfect and must therefore have the best properties.[34] Since virtue is the best property, it must be a property of the world.

The next lines (*ND* 2.39) form an additional argument for the thesis that the world has virtue, presumably anticipating the following objection: virtue would be the best property if it existed; however, it does not exist. Chrysippus holds that if man can acquire virtue, then it is far easier that the world should develop virtue. The argument is contracted and perhaps not rendered precisely by Cicero. Part of the argument relies on a thought reported earlier, at *ND* 2.35: the world as a whole, more than any part of it, must be able to attain perfection because, unlike entities within the world, the realization of the world's perfection cannot be impeded by external obstacles. At *ND* 2.36, Cicero presents the Stoic conviction that if the world had to develop virtue it would presumably never attain it.[35] In line with this, Chrysippus claims according to Cicero's *ND* 2.39 that the world would not attain virtue at some time, but that the world (always was and) *is* virtuous; this is evident from the summary characterization of the world as 'wise'.[36]

The last step of Chrysippus' argument as reproduced in *ND* 2.39 is the identification of the world with God. This step is extremely significant. When the Stoics asked their adherents to 'follow nature' they did not invite them to follow the limited perfection of an excellent human being (like the Aristotelian σπουδαῖος ἀνήρ); rather, they are invited to understand the rationale of the divine administration of the world, visible in the whole world process, and thereby to imitate the divine principle. The identification of the world and of God in this argument shows that Stoic ethics is a fundamentally theological theory.

However, we return to our purpose of analysing the tensions revealed in the theological language employed by the Stoics. Throughout the argument and its context we find a spectrum of assumptions about (and descriptions of) both the world and God that do not easily cohere. In the course of the argument, for instance, we witness a transition from a 'formal' concept of the world as the sum of all that exists to a 'substantive' concept of the world as an animate divine being possessing intellect and rationality. Closely related is the observation that in our passage the world as a whole is deified, whereas much of the argument preceding *ND* 2.37–9 makes use of the concept of 'breath' or 'vital power' (πνεῦμα, *vis vitalis*), i.e. a divine principle *within* the world. In short, we find here tensions between the monistic, dualistic and theistic regions of the theological rhetorical spectrum employed by Chrysippus. True, it would have been possible for Chrysippus to offer some arguments to make the tensions seem less marked. For instance, he could have argued that the divine principle is the fundamental constituent of the world in such a way that it renders the world a unified animate being and that the divine principle cannot be separated from the world. Yet, for what such arguments are worth, the fact remains that the spectrum of characterizations of God forms a source of tension. On the other hand, the very range of characterizations of God available to the Stoics was not only a problem but also an opportunity. The fact that Stoic theology was able to absorb central motifs of traditional religion to such an extent must have increased its appeal to a broader public.

For the Stoics, the integration of traditional religion was a core issue. This is confirmed by reconstructions of Stoic theological arguments which put the epistemological conception of so-called 'preconceptions' at centre stage.[37] The theory of preconceptions (προλήψεις) was introduced into philosophy by Epicurus.

The motivation behind the Epicurean theory of preconceptions must have been to find a starting point of inquiry that is beyond doubt.[38] It is highly significant that the Stoics—presumably led by Chrysippus—took over the Epicurean theory of preconception.[39] Applied to theology, the theory of preconceptions allowed the Stoics to hold that the traditional religious practices express a core of truth.[40] In turn, this allowed the Stoics to feel justified in highlighting certain aspects of traditional religion and integrating them into their theology.

The above may sound as if the Stoics had deliberately *chosen* a strategy to preserve elements of traditional religion and thereby to actively support traditional cults. This, however, would give too 'activist' an interpretation of the Stoics' stance towards traditional religion. Even if the Stoics were (in part) self-conscious re-interpreters and thereby intentional supporters of traditional religion, they must also, and perhaps primarily, have been guided by an implicit trust in the adequacy of the religious-institutional basis of ancient society. In the above list of the ten Chrysippean arguments, arguments (8) to (10) contain an explicit appeal to the religious institutional bases of ancient societies. Argument (10), for instance, contains an appeal to the truth of religious practices like divination.

For Chrysippus, divination is the 'power to see, understand and explain the signs that are given to human beings by the gods'.[41] Chrysippus, as well as other Stoics, argued for divination by invoking preconceptions of God as beneficent and caring for mankind and by pointing out how much foreknowledge of future events is in the interest of human beings.[42]

Yet, while adherents of traditional divination practices would have wished for a theory explaining the direct involvement of the gods with the minutiae of human affairs, it seems that the Stoic defence of divination did not go as far as that. Rather than seeing in divination the proof of a direct interference of the gods in human affairs, the Stoics explained signs as the result of the *general* layout of the world according to which 'certain things should be preceded by certain signs'.[43]

Chapter 3

Two Pictures of Fate

Chapters 1 and 2 have shown how the Stoics attempted to integrate key aspects of a traditional polytheistic theological outlook into the framework of their philosophy. It has become apparent that their concept of a divine pneumatic element could not match completely the traditional theological convictions they wanted to preserve. The residual tensions were evidenced by contrasting descriptions of the divine. On the positive side, the integration of quite different theological strands enabled the Stoics to draw upon a whole range of theological rhetoric, which must have enhanced the popular appeal of Stoic philosophy.

This chapter continues the analysis of the Stoics' religious world-view by interpreting their doctrine of fate. Stoic physics showed how the divine element exerts complete control over the course of the world and is ultimately the only true agent. The pneumatic force produces an ineluctable connection between causes and effects, a view that sits uneasily with human responsibility. However, Stoic theology harboured also the polytheistic strand that would give a far more limited role to the divinities. I shall argue that those tensions in Stoic theology translated into parallel tensions in the Stoic doctrine of fate. It has already been suggested by Long and Sedley that the early Stoics evoked two different pictures of fate.[1] I shall reiterate and elaborate their suggestion here. By interpreting the two pictures of fate as the rhetorical expression of underlying tensions between different theological strands in Stoic thought, I attempt to offer a broader framework that can support a differentiation between the two pictures of fate and explain its pivotal importance for our understanding of early Stoic doctrine.

In Long and Sedley's reading, the two pictures of fate differ as follows: The first picture is in line with the traditional Greek picture of fate. It is a picture of 'personal fate'[2] according to which 'certain landmarks in individual lives and in human history' are preordained: 'a victory, a hero's return home, an illness, someone's murdering his father, the date of one's own death. These things will happen whether or not we try to avert them. Far from threatening our independence, they provide precisely the proper context for autonomous moral choice.[3] This picture represents fate as something external to the agent, something providential, yet sometimes potentially opposed to his own wishes, something which sets limits as to the results he can achieve by his actions without, however, fully determining the way towards that result. I suggest that in making fate something external to the agent, the picture of personal fate is in line with the traditional (poly-)theistic theological outlook according to which Zeus (or a plurality of traditional deities) are forces external to the agent and with a limited range of influence. The picture of personal fate is exemplified by the following verses of Cleanthes (Epictetus *Ench.* 53, trans. LS 62B):

> Lead me, Zeus and Destiny, wherever you have ordained for me. For I shall follow unflinching. But if I become bad and am unwilling, I shall follow none the less.

In these verses becoming bad, not wanting to follow the divine preordainment, is depicted as a realistic possibility. The verses make no reference to fate itself making the agent willing or unwilling. It seems that the decision is ultimately up to the agent; it is not determined by fate. Nonetheless, the resolution of the human agent will be immaterial to the final outcome, which is preordained: even if the agent is unwilling, the outcome will be the same.

The second picture of fate described by Long and Sedley is characteristically different from the first. Bobzien (1998) has coined the name 'all-embracing fate' for it. Fate is seen as the ordering and complete determination of the succession of world states.[4] Gellius *Noct. Att.* 6.2.3 writes (trans. LS 55K):

> In *On Providence* book 4, Chrysippus says that fate is a certain natural everlasting ordering of the whole: one set of things follows on and succeeds another, and the interconnexion is inviolable.

The all-embracing character of fate thus understood, and the necessity of the succession of world states, are stressed in a number of reports. See, for instance, Stobaeus 1.79.1–12 (trans. LS 55M):

> Chrysippus calls the substance of fate a power of breath, carrying out the orderly government of the all. That is in *On the World* book 2. But in

On Seasons book 2, in *On Fate*, and here and there in other works, he expresses a variety of views: 'Fate is the rationale of the world', or 'the rationale of providence's acts of government in the world', or 'the rationale in accordance with which past events have happened, present events are happening, and future events will happen'. And as substitute for 'rationale' he uses 'truth', 'explanation', 'nature', 'necessity', and further terms, taking these to apply to the same substance from different points of view.

The same point is made, without using the attributes of fate, by Alexander of Aphrodisias (*De fato* 191.32–192.8, trans. LS 55N):

They [the Stoics] say that since the world is a unity which includes all existing things in itself and is governed by a living, rational, intelligent nature, the government of existing things which it possesses is an everlasting one proceeding in a sequence and ordering. The things which happen first become causes to those which happen after them. In this way all things are bound together, and neither does anything happen in the world such that something else does not unconditionally follow from it and become causally attached to it, nor can any of the later events be severed from the preceding events so as not to follow from one of them as if bound fast to it; but from everything that happens something else follows, with a necessary causal dependence on it, and everything that happens has something prior to it with which it causally coheres.

We will see later that this picture of fate, for all its dependence on Stoic physics, can also be understood as developing a different strand of earlier Greek theological speculation. For now, let us turn to the considerable interest that this picture of fate has raised in today's discussions on determinism and moral responsibility, and which has led, as it seems to me, to the picture of personal fate being crowded out of scholars' perception. Indeed, the characterization of all-embracing fate seems to address issues very much in line with modern, Laplacean formulations of determinism as a necessary succession of world states.[5] Compare the following quotation from van Inwagen (1993: 185):

Determinism is the thesis that it is true at every moment that the way things then are determines a unique future, that only one of the alternative futures that may exist relative to a given moment is a physically possible continuation of the state of things at that moment.

Of course, the Stoic doctrine of fate is not simply reducible to such a modern, mechanistic theory of determinism. For the Stoics, determinism is implied by their doctrine of fate. In Chapter 1, we have seen how the pneumatic tensional state causes the qualities of all things in the cosmos, even the coherence of the cosmos itself. This is the physical aspect of the Stoic doctrine of fate: the divine principle exerts a complete providential control over the world. The idea that a divine principle benevolently controls the succession of the world states in such a way that it is the ultimate agent of the world process must have influenced the Stoic attitude towards determinism. A deterministic world controlled by a benevolent god is certainly less threatening than a world that is not so controlled, i.e. a world that is deterministic and non-teleological. Thus, determinism would have appeared a less pressing problem to the Stoics than it is for modern philosophers who deal with a mechanistic, non-teleological variant of determinism.

Among scholars, it is undisputed that both pictures of fate were advanced in the early phase of Stoicism. However, more specific attributions and possible developments of the views held in early Stoicism are a matter of dispute. Long and Sedley have argued 'that Zeno and Cleanthes may have entertained no more than a fairly traditional Greek picture of [personal] fate'[6] and have suggested that it was only Chrysippus who tightened the screw further and proposed as well as defended what comes down to a concept of all-embracing fate.[7] However, as Long and Sedley point out, the traditional picture of personal fate was still evoked by Chrysippus.[8] Susanne Bobzien has disputed Long and Sedley's analysis. She argues—to my mind rightly—that, since it is attested that Zeno called fate the 'necessity of all things', it is likely that he defended a fully deterministic view of fate alongside the picture or concept of personal fate.[9] However, Bobzien denies—to my mind mistakenly—that Chrysippus himself maintained a picture of personal fate.[10] She does so by discarding what in my view constitutes clear evidence to the contrary. She dismisses *inter alia* the famous simile that compares the situation of human agents with a dog tied to a cart as un-Chrysippean in spite of the clear reference to Chrysippus.[11] Since the issue is pivotal for our understanding of Stoic attitudes towards fate and determination, I shall examine the evidence for Chrysippus' picture of personal fate in some detail.

In a passage of Cicero's *De fato*, we can catch a glimpse of Chrysippus' picture of personal fate (*De fato* 30, trans. LS 55S):

Some events in the world are simple, he [Chrysippus] says, others are complex. 'Socrates will die on such and such a day' is simple; his day of dying is fixed, regardless of what he may do or not do. But if fate is of the form 'Oedipus will be born to Laius', it will not be possible to add 'regardless of whether or not Laius has intercourse with a woman'. For the event is complex and 'cofated'. He uses this term because what is fated is *both* that Laius will have intercourse with his wife *and* that by her he will beget Oedipus.

The above passage is part of Cicero's account of Chrysippus' defence against the 'Lazy Argument' (*argos logos*). The Lazy Argument objects to (a naïve) fatalism on the ground that if an event *e* is fated, *e* will come about whatever the agent does, so that purposeful action is useless. Chrysippus responded to the argument by pointing out that many events are predetermined in a 'complex' way, such that purposeful human action is a necessary antecedent to the fated event *e* and, indeed, that such action is itself fated. This, however, is not the crucial point for our present concerns. It is pivotal that Chrysippus, even while proposing his theory of 'cofated' events, nevertheless asserted that some events are 'simple'. As an example he mentioned 'Socrates will die on such and such a day'. Obviously, Chrysippus acknowledged a picture of personal fate according to which the date of Socrates' death is predetermined, regardless of what Socrates decides or does.

It is tempting to interpret Chrysippus' example of a simple fated event as a reading of Plato's *Crito* 44A–B, as David Sedley has suggested.[12] Cicero had had his Stoic spokesman refer to *Crito* 44 A–B in the work immediately preceding *De fato*, the *De divinatione*. At *De divinatione* 1.52, the events related in *Crito* 44 A–B are presented as example of a veridical prophetic dream.

The context in the *Crito* is as follows: Crito visits Socrates in prison, planning to propose a scheme to enable Socrates to flee Athens. When Crito impresses on Socrates the necessity to flee swiftly, because the ship whose return is to mark Socrates' execution will arrive the next day, Socrates relates the dream he has just had (Plato *Crito* 44A–B, trans. Grube):

'I thought that a beautiful and comely woman dressed in white approached me. She called me and said: "Socrates, may you arrive at fertile Phthia on the third day."'

Socrates takes this dream with its quotation from Homer's *Iliad* to signify that he will die one day later. To a Stoic, Sedley argues,

it will have seemed that Socrates' decision to stay and die was to a large extent guided by the revelation that he was bound in any case to die on that day—a divine indication that it was morally preferable for him to do so willingly.[13]

From this emerges the picture of branching and reuniting causal chains that have certain events as necessary nodes, such as Socrates' dying on the third day. Different hypothetical paths all reach the same nodes. Socrates could flee, but would be struck by a lightening, drown at sea, or die of food poisoning, all on the third day. Clearly, this is not a mechanistic, Laplacean determinism, but one in which the Stoic deity plays an indispensable causal role in bringing about the necessary nodes.

Bobzien has objected to Sedley's interpretation that the Socrates example cannot play a role in refuting the Lazy Argument. It would be completely impossible for an agent, short of having prophetic dreams, to tell a simple fated event from a cofated event, since both types of event seem identical.[14] The objection, however, misses the point. In arguing for a difference between simple fated and cofated events, Chrysippus does not commit himself to offering rules to decide whether an event is simple or cofated. It is perfectly plausible that Chrysippus would have acknowledged at the same time (a) that prophetic dreams and divine signs are the only possibilities to recognize simple fated events and (b) that the interpretation of such signs and dreams ordinarily exceeds human powers. Only in this way can we understand the importance placed by Chrysippus on being guided by reasonable life rules in the absence of any clear knowledge of what is the divinely preordained outcome.[15]

There is, then, no reason not to take the following report at face value. Hippolytus writes (*Refutatio omnium haeresium* 1.21, trans. LS 62A):

> They too [Zeno and Chrysippus] affirmed that everything is fated, with the following model. When a dog is tied to a cart, if it wants to follow it is pulled and follows, making its spontaneous act coincide with necessity, but if it does not want to follow it will be compelled in any case. So it is with men too: even if they do not want to, they will be compelled in any case to follow what is destined.[16]

The simile expresses the same view of personal fate that we found in Cicero's *De fato* 30. Fate is something external to the agent. It determines (at least some[17]) outcomes in such a way that these outcomes come about regardless of what the human agent decides to do. The moral of the simile is clearly that it is better to obey fate and attune one's intentions to what is preordained.

Bobzien argues that the simile is wrongly attributed to Zeno and Chrysippus.[18] In her view, it is an attempt to interpret Cleanthes' verses on following fate, probably by a first or second century AD Stoic, with Epictetus or another Roman Stoic as a likely guess. Among the numerous arguments Bobzien gives for her cause, the following two seem to me most noteworthy: (1) She argues that the reference to Zeno and Chrysippus ('they', referring to a mention of the two authors earlier in the text) should merely be seen as a general reference to orthodox Stoic doctrine in general. (2) She further argues that the simile contradicts Chrysippus' doctrine, since Chrysippus' reply to the Lazy Argument 'makes the point that even if everything is fated, action is *not* pointless'.[19]

As to Bobzien's first argument, the reference to both Zeno and Chrysippus is too pointed to be explained away. Bobzien has to admit that the reference to Zeno and Chrysippus means that the simile was orthodox Stoic doctrine, so why then should the simile not have been employed widely in the Stoic school and thus (perhaps among others) by Zeno and Chrysippus? Bobzien's second argument relies on a disputable interpretation of Cicero's *De fato* 30. Chrysippus' stance as reported in *De fato* 30 is that *not all* events are simple fated ones. There will be at least some events in respect of which purposive human action plays a decisive role in bringing about certain outcomes. Furthermore, what is determined according to the dog-and-cart simile and its picture of personal fate are the outcomes, not necessarily the paths that lead to these outcomes. Purposive human action is, therefore, not pointless. Since we do not normally know which outcomes are simply fated, trying for the outcomes one wants to see realized is always the best strategy.[20]

However, this is not to deny that Hippolytus or his source might have rephrased the simile.[21] It is remarkable that Hippolytus introduces the dog-and-cart simile with the words 'They too affirmed that *everything* is fated'. If the dog-and-cart simile served to illustrate a picture of personal fate, the pre-ordainment of some landmark events, then it is surprising to find it adduced as model for all causal structures.

I suggest, as best explanation of the surprising argumentative role attributed by Hippolytus to the dog-and-cart simile, that Chrysippus used two types or sets of rhetoric describing fate. He employed characterizations of fate which come down to a picture of personal fate alongside characterizations which point to fate as all-embracing. I also suggest that it is most likely that Chrysippus himself did not distinguish sufficiently between the two sets of rhetoric and that this accounts for the confusion we find in our sources. Perhaps the best way to show this is by analysing the following

polemic of Plutarch in which he attacks Chrysippus' theory of fate in relation to human agency (*Stoic. rep.* 1055F–1056D, trans. Cherniss, modified):

> But furthermore what he says about impressions is in violent contradic-
> tion to the doctrine of fate. For in his desire to prove that the impression
> is not of itself a sufficient cause of assent he has said that, if impressions
> suffice of themselves to produce acts of assent, sages will be doing injury
> when they induce false impressions, as in dealing with base men sages do
> often employ falsehood and suggest a specious impression, which is not,
> however, responsible for the assent, since in that case it would be respon-
> sible also for the false assumption and the deception. Then, if one trans-
> fers to fate this statement about the sage and says that not because of fate
> do acts of assent occur, since in that case erroneous assents and assump-
> tions and deceptions would be due to fate too and men would be injured
> because of fate, the argument that exempts the sage from doing injury
> proves at the same time that fate is not cause of all things. For, if it is not
> because of fate that men get fancies and suffer injuries, obviously it is
> not because of fate either that they perform right actions or are sensible
> or have steadfast conceptions or are benefited; and there is nothing left
> of the doctrine that fate is cause of all things. One who says that for these
> things Chrysippus considered fate not to be a cause sufficient of itself but
> only a preliminary cause will show him to be again at odds with himself
> there where he gives Homer extravagant praise for saying of Zeus 'There-
> fore accept, each and all, whatsoe'er he may send you of evil' or of good
> and Euripides for saying 'O Zeus, why should I say that wretched men /
> Take thought at all? For from thee we depend / And act such deeds as
> thou may'st chance to think.'
>
> He writes at length himself in agreement with these sentiments
> and finally says that nothing at all, not even the slightest, stays or moves
> otherwise than in conformity with the reason of Zeus, which is identical
> with fate. Furthermore, the preliminary cause is feebler than that which
> is of itself sufficient, and it falls short when dominated by others that
> obstruct it; but Chrysippus himself, declaring fate to be an invincible
> and unimpedible and inflexible cause, calls her 'swerveless' and 'inescap-
> able' and 'necessity' and, as setting a term for all things, 'determination'.
> So then, shall we say that we do not have control over acts of assent or
> over virtues or vices or right action of wrong-doing; or shall we say that
> fate is deficient and determination is indeterminate and the motions
> and stations of Zeus are frustrate? For the former is the consequence if
> fate is a cause sufficient of itself, and the latter if it is only a preliminary

cause, since, if it is of itself sufficient cause of all things, it abolishes the sphere of our control and volition and, if a preliminary cause, loses the character of being unimpedible and fully effective.

Before I can outline the support this text gives to the claim that Chrysippus himself was insufficiently clear about his entertaining two different characterizations of fate, I have to elucidate the main lines of Plutarch's argument. The concept of assent (συγκατάθεσις), which is so prominent in the text, is pivotal for the Stoic account of human agency. Human agency starts from having an impression (φαντασία), which a thing or event produces in us. The impression alone, however, cannot produce an action. We find several allusions to this in our text: for instance, Plutarch adduces Chrysippus' contention that the sage does induce false impressions yet does not deceive or lie.[22] Chrysippus' presumably maintained—admittedly, in a dark way— that the sage tries to influence morally inferior people for their own good by letting them believe what is, in fact, wrong. The sage does not, however, lie.

In order to produce action, the impression has to be accompanied by an act of assent (συγκατάθεσις), a decision about whether or not to 'accept' the impression. Only by giving assent does the human agent build up an impulse (ὁρμή) producing action.[23] Chrysippus maintains that assent is the pivotal factor for action, thereby making the assenting person fully responsible for what he does. It is precisely this point which Plutarch does not grant. His critique rests on the assumption that such a differentiation, between causal control over impressions and causal control over acts of assent, is not plausible. Plutarch extrapolates from the sage's control to the universal causal control of fate. To Plutarch's mind, it is inconceivable that fate's universal control could be limited to the production of impressions and could leave the human agent in control of his acts of assent. Obviously, if Plutarch were right, this would have enormous consequences for Chrysippus' project. If assent is not in the power of the agent, the action cannot be regarded as the agent's own in any substantive way. With this, praise or blame for human actions would be unjustified.

I shall evaluate Plutarch's argument against Chrysippus and the latter's resources to counter Plutarch's attack later on. For now, let us return to the more immediate question of what Plutarch's text can tell us about Chrysippus' maintaining two pictures of fate. Plutarch writes that 'Chrysippus considered fate to be not a cause sufficient of itself but only a preliminary cause' (Χρύσιππος οὐκ αὐτοτελῆ τούτων αἰτίαν ἀλλὰ προκαταρκτικὴν μόνον ἐποιεῖτο). The preliminary cause—or, as *prokatarktikē aitia* is sometimes rendered, the

'antecedent' or the 'triggering cause'—is explained by Plutarch a few lines
later as a cause that 'is feebler than that which is of itself sufficient (τὸ μὲν
προκαταρκτικὸν αἴτιον ἀσθενέστερόν ἐστι τοῦ αὐτοτελοῦς), and that [. . .] falls
short when dominated by others that obstruct it.' The preliminary cause
thus precedes an outcome, but it cannot necessitate the outcome on its
own.[21] We should bear in mind that the outcomes Plutarch has in mind are
human actions: he writes '*for these things* (τούτων) Chrysippus considered fate
not to be a cause sufficient of itself'. With 'these things' Plutarch refers back
to the discussion of human agency against the backdrop of the Stoic theory
of fate. Fate does not determine individual human actions; there is a range
of possible actions open for human agents. The description of fate as preliminary cause is, therefore, indicative of a picture of personal fate. Fate, so
understood, provides only the *situation* in which the agent has to make
choices; it might 'suggest' certain choices to the agent, but it does not
necessitate them. This is entirely compatible with the view that certain
outcomes of human actions (like Socrates' dying on the preordained day
anyway) are simple fated events.

The best way to account for Plutarch's report is to assume that Chrysippus
Plutarch, however, does not make explicit the link to a picture of personal fate. When it comes to mentioning that, according to Chrysippus, (at
least *some*) events are necessitated by fate, Plutarch claims that according
to Chrysippus *everything is fated* (just as Hippolytus did). This fits the picture
of an all-embracing fate. The picture assumes an inviolable sequence of
world states. Some of the typical descriptions of fate thus understood (see
above) are also enumerated by Plutarch in his polemic: fate is 'swerveless'
('Άτροπον), 'inescapable' (Άδράστειαν), 'necessity' (Άνάγκην), and as a summary
description, 'determination' (Πεπρωμένην).

The best way to account for Plutarch's report is to assume that Chrysippus
combined two ways of thinking about fate: one along the lines of the
picture of personal fate, the other along the lines of all-embracing fate.
Furthermore, even though inferences from the silence of our sources must
remain problematic, lack of clarity on Chrysippus' part as to the difference
between the two pictures he combined in his accounts seems the best
explanation of the fact that nowhere the two characterizations of fate
are differentiated. It would be very likely that the difference between the
two characterizations escaped Chrysippus' notice, since both originated
in the culture in which Chrysippus and his predecessors were writing.
Plutarch's polemic contains a clue that supports this interpretation. We
learn from him that Chrysippus saw what we identify as the picture of
the all-embracing fate expressed in Homeric and Euripidean verse. On
examining these quotations more closely, however, we find a characteristic

difference between them. While the verses from Euripides stress the universal control of Zeus and thus seamlessly fit the picture of all-embracing fate, the context of the quotation from the *Iliad* (15.109) points to a picture of personal fate. At *Iliad* 15.100–12, Hera calls on the Olympic gods to acknowledge Zeus' supremacy ungrudgingly and to accept whatever evil he sends to them, giving as an instance the death of Ascalaphos, Ares' son. This sounds far more like a characterization of fate according to which key biographical events are being predetermined than the universal determination of an all-embracing fate.

It seems, therefore, that Chrysippus simply overlooked the fact that the two texts evoked quite different pictures of fate. He must have been led by his well-attested admiration of the Greek literary tradition[25] to give these quotations in support of an all-embracing fate without noticing their different import. The picture of an all-embracing fate and the picture of personal fate condense two (quite different) lines of thought about fate which were equally present in Greek literature and could easily be mixed up even in philosophical discussions of fate.

That Chrysippus appreciated Greek literature and was constantly referring to it, is attested by reports that his writings abounded with literary quotations. Since Zeno had combined the same two lines of thought, it is even more likely that the difference between the two ways of describing fate just escaped Chrysippus' notice.[26]

However that may be, for students of Stoic thought nowadays it must be far easier than it was for Chrysippus and his contemporaries to see the difference between the two pictures of fate. After all, the picture of personal fate is culturally quite alien to us, whereas the picture of all-embracing fate seems familiar, by its apparent closeness to the Laplacean formulations of determinism. Such inklings of familiarity, however, can also be bad guides. I suspect that a concomitant 'embarrassment of hindsight' may be at work when contemporary scholars are reluctant to credit the 'strikingly modern' Chrysippus with an archaic picture of fate.

So far, I have pointed out that attributing to Chrysippus two different pictures or concepts of fate is the best way to make sense of our sources. Moreover, it credits Chrysippus with a realistic stance to take, considering the cultural context in which he wrote. In what follows, I shall broaden my argument by suggesting that the attribution of two different pictures of fate to Chrysippus also helps us to make sense of his solution to the problem of how human responsibility remains possible in a world governed by fate.

The picture of personal fate relies on a separation of two spheres: a sphere of human decisions and actions and a sphere external to the agent (with situational parameters). In the picture of personal fate, it is due to the external sphere that certain events are fated, regardless of what the agent is going to do. I suggest that this was the separation of spheres which Chrysippus employed when explaining how the necessitation of events according to the picture of all-embracing fate is compatible with genuine human action and therefore with human responsibility. The separation of spheres enabled Chrysippus to hold that all events are necessitated by an all-embracing fate, but that it makes sense to speak at the same time about human actions as being (in another sense) non-necessary or contingent.[27]

We find the separation of spheres in a lengthy report of Chrysippus' doctrine from Cicero (*De fato* 39–45). Here, I quote part of that report (*De fato* 41–3, trans. LS 62C):

> But Chrysippus, disapproving of necessity and at the same time wanting nothing to happen without antecedent causes, distinguishes between kinds of cause, in order to escape necessity while retaining fate. 'Of causes', he explains, 'some are complete and primary, others auxiliary and proximate. Hence when we say that all things come about through fate by antecedent causes, we do not mean this to be understood as "by complete and primary causes", but "by auxiliary and proximate causes". If these latter are not in our power, it does not follow that not even impulse is in our power. If, on the other hand, we said that all things come about by complete and primary causes, it *would* follow that, since these causes were not in our power, impulse would not be in our power either.' Therefore against those who introduce fate in such a way as to import necessity, the earlier argument will be valid. But it will have no validity against those who will not speak of the antecedent causes as complete and primary. He thinks that he can easily explain the statement that acts of assent come about by prior causes. For although assent cannot occur unless it is prompted by an impression, nevertheless, since it has that impression as its proximate, not its primary cause, Chrysippus wants it to have the rationale which I mentioned just now. He does not want assent, at least, to be able to occur without the stimulus of some external force (for assent must be prompted by an impression). But he resorts to his cylinder and spinning-top: these cannot begin to move without a push; but once that has happened, he holds that it is thereafter through their own nature that the cylinder rolls and the top spins. 'Hence,' he says, 'just as the person who pushed the cylinder gave it its beginning of motion but not its capacity for rolling, likewise, although the impression

encountered will print and, as it were, emblazon its appearance on the mind, assent will be in our power. And assent, just as we said in the case of the cylinder, although prompted from outside, will thereafter move through its own force and nature. If something were brought about without an antecedent cause, it would be untrue that all things come about through fate. But if it is plausible that all events have an antecedent cause, what ground can be offered for not conceding that all things come about through fate? It is enough to understand what distinction and difference obtains between causes.'

Cicero presents in this passage Chrysippus' theory of how genuine human action and universal fate are compatible. According to Cicero, Chrysippus wanted to defend a position midway between the two extremes of either admitting universal necessity (*necessitas*) or of embracing the view that some events occur without antecedent causes (*praepositae causae*), which would mean a thoroughgoing indeterminism. Chrysippus' attempted to show how a range of contingency which is presupposed in accounts of human agency remains conceivable in spite of the existence of universal fate. Chrysippus did so by differentiating between kinds of cause (*causarum genera distinguit*). For our present purposes, we need not go into the intricate and much-disputed details of Chrysippus' theory of causation. In Stoic analysis, a cause is a body and that which is caused is something incorporeal, namely a 'predicate' (κατηγόρημα).[28] Apart from this general characterization of 'cause', Chrysippus distinguished between a bewildering number of types of cause. Full of contempt, Alexander of Aphrodisias speaks of a 'swarm of causes'.[29] Among the distinctions proposed is also that between 'complete and primary causes' and 'auxiliary and proximate causes' employed in the Cicero passage. It is a matter of scholarly dispute whether 'complete and primary' and 'auxiliary and proximate' designate epexegetically two classes of causes or regroup four different types of cause into two classes. Our sources make it impossible to reach clarity on this any more than on other aspects of the Stoic doctrine of causation. It is perhaps best to tread lightly and see the distinctions of the types of causes as ad hoc distinctions proposed in order to explain in different concrete cases the complex network of relevant causal factors. Be that as it may, in the example at hand it is obvious that complete and primary causes are causes which necessitate the outcome, whereas auxiliary and proximate causes do not necessitate, but are necessary conditions, i.e. the circumstances for a determining cause. According to Chrysippus, the initial push and the body's capacity for

rolling are two different things. The former is the necessary condition of
the movement. The initial push plays the role of the auxiliary and proximate cause. The latter is responsible for the fact that the body continues to
move after being pushed. It illustrates Chrysippus' concept of a complete
and primary cause.

The simile is designed to explain the possibility of responsible human
agency in a world governed by fate. Earlier in this chapter I have referred
to the Stoic concept of assent. The Stoics held that human agency starts
from an impression (the necessary condition). However, assent is needed
to give the impression a driving power, so that an impulse is built up to
produce the action. In *De fato* 39–45 we find the same analysis of human
agency. There could be no human agency if assent were necessitated by
antecedent causes (i.e. by the external circumstances in which—according
to Chrysippus—the assent is given or withheld). Chrysippus maintained
that the situation provides necessary causal factors, but that it does not
necessitate the act of assent. The act of assent is dependent on the causal
sphere internal to the agent. It is the agent's character that determines
how he deals with circumstantial factors. In Chrysippus' analogy, this is
indicated by the description of the movements of the cylinder and spin-
ning-top. Cicero writes 'that the cylinder rolls and the top spins' (*cylindrum
volvi et versari turbinem*), to indicate that the two bodies roll along a specific
path because of their form. The phrase illustrates the irreducible causal
role played by human character in agency, a role circumstantial factors
cannot replace.[30] This is precisely the separation of causal spheres evoked
by the picture of personal fate.

It is likely that Chrysippus underpinned his defence of human action
and responsibility by an understanding of modal terms that allows for
counterfactual possibilities even in a completely deterministic world. Again,
a polemic of Plutarch's will serve as our starting point. He writes (*Stoic. rep.*
1055D–F, trans. Cherniss, modified):

And how does his [*sc.* Chrysippus'] theory of possibilities not conflict
with his theory of fate? For if 'possible' is not defined in the manner of
Diodorus as that which either is or will be true but if everything is possible
that is susceptible of coming about, even if it is not going to come about,
many of the things that are not in accordance with fate will be possible.
[Consequently, either] fate loses her invincible and ineluctable and
all-prevailing force; or, if she is what Chrysippus maintains, that which is
susceptible of coming about will often fall into the category of the impossible, and everything true will be necessary, being constrained by the most

sovereign necessity of all, and everything false impossible, since the mighti-
est cause is adverse to its becoming true. For how can he whose death at
sea has been determined by fate be susceptible of dying on land, and why
is it possible for the man at Megara to go to Athens when he is prevented
by fate from doing so?

Plutarch suggests that Chrysippus' theory of the modalities is inconsistent
with his theory of fate, because Chrysippus maintained that there is contingency in a world governed by fate. Chrysippus attempted to achieve
that with a definition of the possible which leaves room for contingency
even in a deterministic world. For Chrysippus, 'everything is possible that is
susceptible of coming about, even if it is not going to come about' (πᾶν τὸ
ἐπιδεκτικὸν τοῦ γενέσθαι, κἂν μὴ μέλλῃ γενήσεσθαι, δυνατόν ἐστιν). This definition
of the possible is part of Chrysippus' definitions of the modalities. We have
reports of Chrysippus' definitions in Diogenes Laertius and Boethius. This
is what Diogenes writes (7.75, trans. LS 38D):

> Further, some propositions are possible, some impossible, and some
> necessary, some non-necessary. Possible is that which admits of being true
> and which is not prevented by external factors from being true, such as
> 'Diocles is alive.' Impossible is that which does not admit of being true,
> [or admits of being true but is prevented by external factors from being
> true], such as 'The earth flies.' Necessary is that which is true and does
> not admit of being false, or admits of being false but is prevented
> by external factors from being false, such as 'Virtue is beneficial.' Non-
> necessary is that which both is true and is capable of being false, and
> is not prevented by external factors from being false, such as 'Dion is
> walking.'[31]

Note that the definitions each consist of two parts. The first part contains
the criterion of a proposition's (not) admitting of being true. This criterion
mirrors the internal capability of a thing to be in a certain state (or of an
agent to perform a certain type of action). The danger of such a criterion is
that it admits implausibly many things as possible. Therefore, the restricting
second parts of the definitions are important. They invoke the criterion of
(permanent) preventing external factors, factors which immediately qualify
the claim to a capability. It is pivotal that the definitions do not aim at an
epistemic understanding of the modalities. The existence of open counterfactual possibilities is not defended by reference to limitations of our knowledge that lead us to call certain things possible which in fact are not.[32]

Rather, Chrysippus' modal system should be understood as underpinning the existence of counterfactual possibilities by reference to capabilities that are not discounted by external factors. Unless I am held imprisoned or am very ill, it makes perfect sense even in a deterministic world to say that I have the capability to play hide-and-seek with my children. Of course there may be causal factors which make it impossible for me to do this today (for instance, my resolution to finish writing this chapter). But these factors are internal to me, in the sense that they lie in my character, in my way of reacting to external stimuli. Thus understood, Chrysippus' theory of the modalities draws on the differentiation between internal and external causal spheres. It relies on an argumentative pattern and a rhetoric made available by the picture of personal fate.

In the above argument, I have supported my claim that the attribution of two pictures of fate to Chrysippus helps us to better understand his answer to the problem of human responsibility in a world completely determined by fate. I want to go on to suggest that the polytheistic thought upon which these pictures must have drawn can also offer an explanation of the attitude felt by the Stoics towards universal determination.

In modern thought, the prospect of universal determinism has often provoked reactions of fear. In a Laplacean world-view human beings can hardly avoid feeling subjected to an anonymous and uncontrollable power. The Stoics did not conceive determinism in that way, and this must have been due to their conception of nature as controlled by a divine force. This divine force is not seen merely as a causal structure of the world, as the physico-theological analysis of the divine element would suggest; it is also interpreted as something external to the human agent, something which can be identified and appealed to by categories developed in (poly-)theistic thought. For the Stoics, the divine element can thus be represented as a positive power that has all the virtues.[33] The divine element is the *benevolent* administrator of the world, providentially arranging the world for the best of mankind. The divine element is not a hostile power that man has to be frightened of. Thus, the Stoic lives in a world where man can feel at home.[34] Moreover, it must have been pivotal for the broader appeal of the Stoic system that one could relate positively to the divine principle. The Stoics expressed this idea in the famous imagery of the 'cosmic city'.[35] Witness the following description in Eusebius (*Praeparatio Evangelica* 15.15, trans. Schofield 1999: 66f.):

The universe is said to be an organization of heaven and air and earth and sea and the natures within them. The universe is called also the habitation of gods and men and the organization of gods and men and the things which have come into being for their sake. For just as city is spoken of in two ways, as the habitation and as the organization of the inhabitants along with the citizens, so also the universe is as it were a city consisting of gods and men, the gods exercising the leadership, the men subordinate. Community exists between them because they partake in reason, which is natural law; and all else has come into being for their sake. In consequence of which it must be believed that the god who administers the whole exercises providence for men, being beneficent, kind, well-disposed to men, just and having all the virtues.

We see in this passage that men and gods form a genuine community in which the gods take the lead and human beings are subordinate. In the imagery, the subordination to the divine administration of the world which man encounters in the deterministic world process is thus brought back to human proportions, stripped of its threatening potential; the divine administration of the world is much like the government of a city.

The city is conceived of as a 'natural' community, based on a common characteristic: rationality. Schofield has rightly pointed out that we have to think here of a 'substantive conception of reason', in the sense that the common 'attachment to certain values, namely those prescribed by reason' is presupposed.[36] Those who share reason are thus understood to hold the same views; this is what makes them form a community, a community of values, as one could say. This is corroborated, among other texts, by a passage in Stobaeus (2.94.1–4):

> Agreement [ὁμόνοια] is the knowledge of common goods, and therefore all the wise agree with each other because they hold the same opinions on the questions of life.

Prescriptive reason has to be considered the exclusive property of the virtuous. Yet, it seems that the Stoics wanted to appeal also to ordinary men and allowed therefore that every human being (as a being intended by nature for this substantive rationality) is to be counted as a member of the cosmic city. Whereas only sages are full members, non-wise persons are members by the same token that children are considered citizens of a city, even though they cannot (yet) fulfil the duties of an adult citizen.[37] This mitigating interpretation, in which we may hear Chrysippus' voice, makes the Stoic imagery of the cosmic city appeal reassuringly to everyone among the Stoic audience. Anyone attending a Stoic lecture could learn that the

Stoic cosmos is deterministic, but that this is no reason to be frightened. Determinism allows for the maximal control of the divine principle, which benevolently administers the world. Man does well in following that benevolent rule and should know that in doing so, he is in a world where he can feel at home.

Part Two

Virtue and the Virtues

Chapter 4

Definitions of Virtue

In writings on ancient ethics, it has become a convention to stress the broad meaning of the Greek word *aretē*. Indeed, *aretē* ('excellence' or 'virtue', as I shall translate) is an unusually broad concept. Denoting 'some sort of excellence' (τελείωσίς τις), as Aristotle summarizes general usage,[1] the concept applies to very different items. A knife, farmland, a horse as well as human beings can have 'virtue'. Paradoxically, it may well be that the broadness of meaning of *aretē* was a decisive factor in shaping Greek ethics. When philosophers wanted to talk about specifically human virtue, or more specifically still, about the virtue of a citizen, they had to offer an analysis of what differentiated human beings (or citizens) from other items that could have *aretē*. In short, it may have been the breadth of meaning of the word *aretē* that triggered thinking about human nature or human 'functionings' that undergirds so much of Greek virtue ethics.

I shall show that the Stoic definitions of virtue bear witness to the triggering role of the broad Greek concept of *aretē*. The Stoics took for granted the general meaning of *aretē* as 'some sort of excellence'. In the case of human beings, however, the Stoics restricted the scope of excellences by claiming that rationality is a specific characteristic defining a nature of its own, the nature of rational being. Rationality gives rise to a specific set of virtues. The possession of these virtues is an all-or-nothing affair. You can only be completely virtuous or not virtuous at all. If you have one virtue, you have all the virtues. Since gods and men are rational, they have the same virtues. I shall argue that Chrysippus' theory of virtue paradigmatically exemplifies the Stoic restriction of human virtue to rational excellence, but that, some time after Chrysippus, a more inclusive understanding of virtue was advanced which acknowledged also other human virtues not directly defined by rationality.

The task of analysing the Stoic definitions of virtue is complicated by the fact that the Stoics used the word 'virtue' in the singular, in two interrelated but quite distinct meanings. When we encounter in our sources

the word 'virtue' in the singular, it can be either of two things: first, it can
be the overall excellent state of a human being. This is usually translated as
'honestum' in Latin texts; I shall render it as 'virtue *tout court*'. However,
'virtue' in the singular can also be a generic term of which virtues like
courage or justice are species. We lack evidence that the Stoics addressed
this difference and it is possible that they failed to see it. This would be
quite natural, given that for the Stoics the two meanings of 'virtue' in the
singular were closely related. The Stoics regarded rationality as defining a
specific unitary nature, and they saw the different virtues as interdepen-
dent to such a degree that having virtue was an all-or-nothing affair.[2] In
addition, the task of distinguishing between the two meanings of 'virtue' in
the singular must have been complicated by the Stoic usage. In what must
have become the standard Stoic view, Chrysippus used the term 'generic' to
characterize the four virtues of practical wisdom, temperance, courage and
justice, to which numerous specific virtues were subordinated.[3]

However this may have been, 'virtue' in the second sense (as a generic
term) had a number of more specific (Chrysippean 'generic') virtues subordinated to it. In analysing 'virtue' in the second sense we arrive at 'virtues'
in the plural.

This part of the book is devoted to an analysis of the Stoics' definitions
of virtue in the singular and their theories about virtues in the plural.
In this chapter I discuss two characterizations of virtue: virtue (in the
singular) is a 'perfect state' and a 'consistent character'. Both characterizations refer to the Stoic description of virtues as forms of knowledge.
The Stoic conception of virtues as *epistēmai* is dealt with in Chapter 5. In
Chapter 6 I analyse how virtues in the plural retain their separateness
while being inextricably interconnected. Chapter 7 presents and analyses
the Stoic table of virtues.

Chrysippus' Characterization of Virtue as 'Perfect State'

The most convenient starting point for our discussion is a polemic of
Galen's against Chrysippus. The text reads (*PHP* 5.5.38–40, trans. De Lacy):

> Chrysippus, however, committed a major blunder, not in failing to make
> any virtue a power—that kind of error is of little consequence, and we
> are not attacking it—but in saying that there are many kinds of knowl-
> edge and many virtues, yet that the power of the soul is single. For it is
> impossible that a single power have many virtues, since it is impossible

that a single thing have many perfect states. The perfect state of each thing that exists is single, and virtue is the perfect state of the nature of each, as he himself agrees. Ariston of Chios did better: he said that the soul does not have a plurality of virtues, but only one, which he called knowledge of things good and evil; and in his account of the affections he did not contradict his own presuppositions, as Chrysippus did.

To Galen, Chrysippus' position seems incoherent. Galen claims (1) that Chrysippus recognized only one (rational) power of the soul and (2) that he accepted a definition of virtue according to which virtue is the single perfection of the thing in question.[1] (3) Therefore, Chrysippus should have recognized only one excellence of the soul, not many. (4) Aristo, who embraced the conclusion that there is just one virtue, did not fall prey to inconsistency on that count and thus offers the model Chrysippus should have adopted.

We learn from Galen's polemic that Chrysippus accepted and employed a definition of virtue which captured the broad meaning of the word *aretē*: virtue is a 'perfect state'. More specifically, Chrysippus thought that each thing can have only *one* characteristic excellence: 'virtue is the perfect state of the nature of each'. In the case of human beings, rationality is the property which comes on top of, and transforms, the characteristics of animals and which defines the place of human beings on the *scala naturae*.[5] Rationality is thus the single characteristic which defines the nature and thus the excellence of human beings.[6] The excellence characteristic of rationality must be thought of in terms of 'knowledge'.[7] That human virtue is a form of knowledge is a matter on which both Chrysippus and Aristo of Chios are agreed. What is at issue is whether or not there can be more than one virtue defined as knowledge. Whereas Aristo claimed that the unity of the rational state made it inevitable that there is only one virtue, defined as 'knowledge of things good and evil', Chrysippus (deploying arguments to be reviewed in Chapter 6) contended that the fact that human virtue is the unitary state of excellence of the unitary rational nature does not preclude the fact that there are different forms of knowledge which identify as many different virtues. For our present purposes it is relevant that Chrysippus' understanding of virtue in terms of knowledge was interpreted more leniently at a later stage of the Stoic school. So much can be inferred from a passage in Diogenes Laertius (7.90–1):

Virtue in a general sense is a sort of perfection of each thing, [more specifically it is, for instance, the perfection of an artefact], say of a statue;

and then there is non-intellectual virtue, like health, and there is intellectual virtue, like practical wisdom. For Hecato says in his first book *On the Virtues* that some virtues are forms of knowledge and are intellectual, namely those which have a systematic structure of theoretical principles, like practical wisdom and justice; others are non-intellectual, namely those that are understood by extension from those which have a systematic structure of theoretical principles, like health and strength. For health is found to follow on and be an extension of temperance, an intellectual virtue, just like strength supervenes on the building of an arch. They are called non-intellectual, because they do not involve assent, but they supervene and occur even in bad men, like health and courage.

Since the passage presents major textual and interpretive difficulties, I quote the Greek text in full and explain more about the nature of the difficulties and the best way to resolve them:

Ἀρετὴ δέ τοι ἡ μέν τις κοινῶς παντὶ τελείωσις, <ἡ δὲ ἰδίως οἷον τεχνήματος [or: σκευαστοῦ] τελείωσις> ὥσπερ ἀνδριάντος, καὶ ἡ ἀθεώρητος, ὥσπερ ὑγίεια· καὶ ἡ θεωρηματική, ὡς φρόνησις. Φησὶ γὰρ ὁ Ἑκάτων ἐν τῷ πρώτῳ Περὶ ἀρετῶν ἐπιστημονικὰς μὲν εἶναι καὶ θεωρηματικὰς τὰς ἐχούσας τὴν σύστασιν ἐκ θεωρημάτων, ὡς φρόνησιν καὶ δικαιοσύνην· ἀθεωρήτους δὲ τὰς κατὰ παρέκτασιν θεωρουμένας ταῖς ἐκ τῶν θεωρημάτων συνεστηκυίαις, καθάπερ ὑγίειαν καὶ ἰσχύν. Τῇ γὰρ σωφροσύνῃ τεθεωρημένῃ ὑπαρχούσῃ συμβαίνει ἀκολουθεῖν καὶ παρεκτείνεσθαι τὴν ὑγίειαν, καθάπερ τῇ ψαλίδος οἰκοδομίᾳ, τὴν ἰσχὺν ἐπιγίνεσθαι. Καλοῦνται δ' ἀθεώρητοι, ὅτι μὴ ἔχουσι συγκαταθέσεις, ἀλλ' ἐπιγίνονται καὶ περὶ φαύλους γίνονται, ὡς ὑγίεια, ἀνδρεία.

Von Arnim indicates that there is a lacuna after Ἀρετὴ δέ τοι ἡ μέν τις κοινῶς παντὶ τελείωσις.[8] It is significant that other scholars attempting to fill the lacuna have not inserted words after τελείωσις, but after ὥσπερ ἀνδριάντος. This indicates that these scholars have found fault with the transition from a general definition of virtue, exemplified by the excellence of a statue, to specifically human forms of excellence (ἀθεώρητος . . . θεωρηματική). Their attempts agree in seeing ὥσπερ ἀνδριάντος as an explanation of virtue in the broadest sense and in trying to render acceptable the transition to specifically human virtues. In this vein, Philippson has suggested ἡ δὲ τῆς ψυχῆς διττῶς λέγεται, von Arnim preferred ἡ δέ τις ἀνθρώπῳ ἰδίως τοῦ λόγου τελείωσις, and Marcovich (1999) suggested ἡ δέ τις ἰδίως ἀνθρώπου. Apart from being paleographically less likely (since they add words where no lacuna is indicated), these attempts also gloss over the crucial point: Diogenes Laertius (or his source) struggles to synthesize two different Stoic discussions of 'virtue'. He first quotes the standard Stoic (Chrysippean) definition of virtue as 'some sort of perfection' which does no more than repeat common Greek usage.[9] This concept of virtue can be applied to very different things, for instance to artefacts, but it also applies to human virtue *tout court*. Diogenes then informs us that, in addition to this very general concept of virtue, there was another Stoic discussion of virtue that differentiates two *generic* virtues (more particularly, human virtues): intellectual and non-intellectual virtues.[10] Diogenes' source had drawn this differentiation from the first book of *On the Virtues*, a work of Hecato of Rhodes.[11] Diogenes can hardly have had more to go by than the bare outline of a differentiation between the two (generic) virtues. He does not relate this differentiation to the general definition of virtue that he has just quoted.[12] With Diogenes apparently having had very little information at his disposal, we cannot be certain whether Hecato was the inventor of the division or merely an influential spokesman explaining a division that had obtained prominence within the Stoic school some time earlier. However, I shall argue that the division of virtues into intellectual and non-intellectual ones was alien to Chrysippus and reflects the concerns of the 'Middle' Stoa.[13]

From the two Galen passages discussed above it has become clear that Chrysippus used the general definition of virtue as 'the perfect state of the nature of each' to argue that there is a single overall state of human virtue defined by rationality. Rationality is the characteristic property defining the (ideal) nature of human beings. In consequence also the Chrysippean definitions of specific virtues are phrased so that the virtues are identified as 'rational' excellences. For instance, courage is defined as 'the *epistēmē* of what is terrible and not terrible and what falls under neither heading' in Chrysippus' catalogue of virtues.[14] The division into two generic virtues which Diogenes' source found in Hecato is in effect an extension of the range of virtues found in Chrysippus' catalogue of virtues. Virtues defined in terms of knowledge are apparently subordinated to the genus of 'intellectual virtues'. In addition to these intellectual virtues, another genus of virtues is recognized, the non-intellectual virtues. The non-intellectual virtues are virtues in a more lenient understanding of the word, to be understood 'by extension' from the intellectual virtues. The class of non-intellectual virtues seems to contain two very different sorts of characteristics: (1) it contains qualities like (psychological) strength which are not themselves intellectual virtues, but are concomitants of (or 'supervene on') intellectual virtues. (2) Something entirely different (and something that Chrysippus could by no means have granted) is the occurrence of health and courage in inferior people. Their possession of non-intellectual virtues cannot be a concomitant of intellectual virtues since they do not have any; intellectual virtues are an all-or-nothing affair. In the case of inferior people, health and courage appear to be rather like animal traits, which do not presuppose intellectual virtues.

This extension of the range of human virtues to non-intellectual virtues could hardly have originated with Chrysippus. As our discussion of Galen's critique of Chrysippus[15] for acknowledging a plurality of virtues has shown, Chrysippus understood human virtue as the single state of perfection of the unitary rational human nature. It is hard to see how Chrysippus could have squared this view with an acknowledgement of 'animal-like' virtues in human beings. As to an acknowledgement of non-intellectual virtues as concomitants of intellectual virtues, it seems to me that Chrysippus certainly would have granted that a quality like (psychological) strength adequately describes the state of virtue, but there was no need for him to make this non-intellectual virtue supervene on the intellectual virtues. He would have declared that psychological strength is already *contained* in his conception of the virtues as forms of knowledge.[16] This interpretation is supported by the fact that wherever we can trace the definition of a (human) virtue to Chrysippus, the link between virtue and the rational nature of human beings is evident. Not only are all definitions in the list of specific virtues[17] attributed to Chrysippus formulated in terms of 'knowledge', but the same link between virtue and the rational nature of human beings is also borne out by other definitions attributed to him. Take Chrysippus' definitions of courage as quoted in Cicero's *Tusculan Disputations* 4.53: 'Courage is, says he [Chrysippus], the knowledge of things one has to endure or a character of the soul which is obedient to the highest law without fear in suffering and enduring.' Although the two definitions differ from the definition given in the catalogue of the virtues, they agree in presenting courage as an essentially rational excellence.[18] The definition in terms of knowledge is given first; the second definition of courage, as a 'character of the soul (*affectio animi*) which is obedient to the highest law without fear in suffering and enduring', merely adds another dimension to the first definition. The Latin words *affectio animi* translate the Greek διάθεσις ψυχῆς which we find in a Chrysippean characterization of virtue *tout court*.[19] The term '*diathesis*' ('character') expresses the non-graduality of virtue and thus indicates that the possession of virtue-knowledge is an all-or-nothing affair. The second definition is not used independently of the first. It 'locates', as it were, the definition in terms of knowledge by showing that the particular virtues are aspects of the unitary virtue *tout court*. Had Chrysippus wished to attribute a non-intellectual virtue of courage to human beings, we should find clear proof of it, in particular at so convenient a point as Cicero's enumeration of definitions of courage. Furthermore, an acknowledgement of non-intellectual courage, a virtue that even bad men can have, would contradict Chrysippus' well-attested conviction[20] that virtue in gods and human beings is the same.

While a division of virtues into intellectual and non-intellectual ones does not square with the basic tenets of Chrysippus' theory of virtue, it fits the teachings of the Middle Stoa. The acknowledgement of non-intellectual virtues, which even bad men can have, betrays a tendency to make the difference between virtuous men and bad men appear blurred. It is likely that the conception of non-intellectual virtues in inferior people relies on a non-monistic psychology. Bi- and tripartite psychologies allowing for non-rational functions of the soul were advanced by two leading figures of the Middle Stoa, Panaetius and Posidonius.[21] Hecato could have been influenced by these theoretical developments, but nothing is known about his own stance on the question of a monistic versus a non-monistic psychology.[22]

In all likelihood, therefore, the differentiation between intellectual and non-intellectual virtues originated with the Middle Stoa. We can perhaps be more specific and argue for Hecato as its most probable author. In Diogenes Laertius 7.92, a division of virtues into theoretical and practical ones is attributed to Panaetius. This seems to be incompatible with the division into intellectual and non-intellectual ones—intellectual virtues like justice must be supposed to be 'practical'. In the same context, a theory of four (generic) virtues is attributed to Posidonius. Since an explanation of the distinction between intellectual and non-intellectual virtues is attributed to Hecato at Diogenes Laertius 7.90, it is most probable that Hecato was also its author.

Having argued that the differentiation between intellectual and non-intellectual virtues was probably an innovation of Hecato, we are now in a position to ask how Chrysippus would have accounted for qualities like psychological health or strength. It seems probable that he would not have wished to deny that the virtuous soul has such qualities. In Cicero's *Tusculan Disputations* we find a text that displays different strategies to account for such qualities within the framework of Chrysippean intellectual virtues. While we cannot be sure that the strategies stem from Chrysippus, they are certainly indicative of the options available to him. The passage at *Tusculan Disputations* 4.30–31 reads as follows:

As with bad things the similarity with the body touches upon the nature of the soul, so it is with good things. For there are not only excellent qualities of the body, like beauty, forcefulness, strength, firmness, quickness, they exist also with regards to the soul. For, just as the good balance of the body, when what we consist of is in agreement with each other, is health, so one also talks of the health of the soul, when the judgements and opinions of the soul agree, and that is the virtue of the soul which some call temperance, whereas others say that it is obedience to the precepts of temperance and is a result of it and does not have a specific class it belongs to. However that may be, it is only in the sage. However, there is also a certain health of the soul which also occurs in fools, namely when by medical treatment a mental disorder is taken away.

The text reports three strategies to account for health of the soul. We can be short about the last one. A 'certain health of the soul which also occurs in fools, namely when by medical treatment mental disorder is taken away' accounts for the undemanding common usage of the word 'health'. Health in this sense signifies the absence of grave disorders. This is a quality that the Stoics could also attribute to fools, since it is not a virtue. However, the text shows that two different views on health as a virtue were proposed: (a) health, understood as psychological excellence, was integrated into the schema of intellectual virtues by identifying it with temperance; and (b) health was connected to the schema of intellectual virtues by making it supervene on the virtue of temperance. The denial that health is not a specific virtue among other virtues could indicate that health should be understood as a descriptor of the virtuous life as a whole. We lack the evidence to attribute either option to Chrysippus, but it seems obvious that both strategies would have been equally open to him. In the following section I discuss some material that will show that the Stoic definition of virtue as a consistent character points towards qualities like psychological health as key descriptors of the virtuous life as a whole.

Virtue as 'Consistent Character'

The definition of virtue as 'consistent character' (διάθεσις ὁμολογουμένη) is not easy to understand. To begin with, the translation is contested. Does the word *homologoumenē* merely point to the consistency of the rational thoughts of the sage and is it, therefore, merely an internal standard of rightness, or should *homologoumenē* be taken to mean that the rational thoughts of the sage agree with an external standard, the will of God as manifest in nature?[23] I shall argue that this is a mistaken alternative. The definition of virtue as *diathesis homologoumenē* points to both an internal and an external standard of rightness.

At the outset of our discussion of *diathesis homologoumenē* it is important to realize that the words *diathesis homologoumenē* are only part of the complete definition of virtue. In Diogenes Laertius we find the following (7.89, trans. LS 61A):

> Virtue is a consistent character (διάθεσις ὁμολογουμένη), choiceworthy for its own sake and not from fear or hope or anything external. Happiness consists in virtue since virtue is a soul which has been fashioned to achieve consistency in the whole of life.

The definition of virtue as 'a *soul* which has been fashioned' does not provide anything surprising. The definition focuses on the physical basis of virtue. Virtue is nothing else than the soul-*pneuma* qualified in a specific way.[24] What is relevant for our present purposes is that the definition determines the range of things virtue is about. Consistency must be achieved 'in the whole of (one's) life'. That this is an important qualification is proven by other reports on Stoic virtue theory. In Stobaeus 2.60.7–8, for instance, we find the characterization that 'virtue is generally speaking a character of the soul consonant with itself concerning the whole life' (διάθεσιν . . . ψυχῆς σύμφωνον αὑτῇ περὶ ὅλον τὸν βίον). Virtue's focus on the whole life is repeated a little later, at 2.66.20–2.67.1, where virtue is described as 'a technique concerning the whole of life' (ἀρετήν, περὶ ὅλον οὖσαν τὸν βίον τέχνην). The Stoic definition of virtue in terms of 'consistent character' must therefore be completed with the qualification 'in (concerning) the whole of one's life'. In order to understand the precise meaning of this definition, I shall discuss its three elements in turn: what is a 'character', what does 'consistency' mean, and what can we learn from the qualification 'in (or: concerning) the whole of one's life'?[25]

Character. The term 'character' was used not only to define virtue *tout court*; as Chrysippus' definitions of courage show, 'character' could also be used to define specific virtues.

The Stoics used the term 'character' to indicate that a property is non-gradual. This is clearly brought out by the sixth-century philosopher Simplicius. In his commentary on Aristotle's *Categories*, Simplicius contrasts Stoic terminology with Aristotle's.[26] At *Categories* 8b25–9a13 Aristotle differentiates between two sorts of traits, 'tenors' (ἕξεις) and 'characters' (διαθέσεις). Tenors are more stable and persistent. Aristotle, therefore, classes knowledge and the virtues as 'tenors' on the grounds that they are stable psychological traits of the knowledgeable and virtuous. Simplicius reports that the Stoic terminology was understood to be a reaction against Aristotle in that it took character to be more stable than tenor, but he

immediately points out that this was a misapprehension. The Stoic terminological choice is expressive of an entirely different criterion. For the Stoics,
'character' denotes a non-gradual property, whereas 'tenors' can intensify
or slacken. Thus the Stoics referred to the straightness of a stick as its
'character', even though the straightness of a stick is a property which can
easily be destroyed. The example was carefully chosen. Whereas common
sense might say that the straightness of a stick is a gradual property (some
sticks are straighter than others), we learn from mathematicians that this
is wrong. In fact, straightness is not a matter of degree; only the entirely
rectilinear stick is straight at all. We cannot even expect to find such a stick
out there during our walks. So too the Stoics attempt to make us understand that common sense is mistaken in claiming that virtue is a matter
of degree and that many people are, to a greater or lesser degree, virtuous.
In fact, virtue is an extreme: it does not allow for variation and it is extremely
rare; perhaps no human being has ever been virtuous.[27]

Consistency. As announced above, I shall argue that the alternative between
an external standard of rightness (the will of God) and a merely internal
standard of rightness is mistaken. In fact, both aspects are part of the meaning of *diathesis homologoumenē*.

In order to show this, let us first look at D.L. 7.84–9. This is the first
part of a detailed report on Stoic ethical doctrines. Diogenes begins with
an enumeration of the topics discussed in Stoic ethics. Diogenes names
the following eight: (1) impulse, (2) things good and bad, (3) passions,
(4) virtue, (5) the end, (6) primary value,[28] (7) appropriate functions,
(8) persuasions and dissuasions to act.

It is possible that in this enumeration Diogenes harmonizes two different
types of exposition used within the Stoic school.[29] However that may be,
Diogenes' beginning of his exposition of Stoic ethics with the topic of
impulse offers him the possibility of pointing out the underpinnings
of Stoic virtue theory in the Stoic account of human nature. The account of
impulse is, therefore, primarily an analysis of appropriation (οἰκείωσις) that
terminates in an account of how a transformation of impulse is effected
by human rationality (D.L. 7.85–6).[30]

Diogenes Laertius' exposition does not slavishly follow the list of topics
that he has given at the outset. The discussion of how human rationality
transforms human nature leads seamlessly to a discussion of the Stoic
conception of the end of human life (τέλος): for rational entities, living
according to nature is living according to reason (7.86) and virtue is
the perfection of reason (as will be explicitly stated later in Diogenes'
text, at 7.94).

Diogenes Laertius attributes the definition of the end as 'living in agreement with nature' (ὁμολογουμένως τῇ φύσει ζῆν) to Zeno.[31] According to Zeno, living in agreement with nature is also living according to virtue. Diogenes notes that Cleanthes, Posidonius and Hecato agreed with Zeno's definition. The next Stoic he mentions is Chrysippus. His elaboration of the Zenonian theory must have been felt to be an important clarification,[32] since it is presented in some detail (D.L. 7.87–8, trans. LS 63C):

> Further, living in accordance with virtue is equivalent to living in accordance with experience of what happens by nature, as Chrysippus says in *On Ends* book 1: for our own natures are parts of the nature of the whole. Therefore, living in agreement with nature comes to be the end, which is in accordance with the nature of oneself and that of the whole, engaging in no activity wont to be forbidden by universal law, which is the right reason pervading everything and identical to Zeus, who is this director of the administration of existing things. And the virtue of the happy man and his good flow of life are just this: always doing everything on the basis of the concordance of each man's guardian spirit with the will of the administrator of the whole.

The standard of rightness described in this passage is clearly external; it is, moreover, characterized in terms of Stoic theology. Living in agreement with nature is living in obedience to the universal law, further described as 'right reason pervading everything'. Right reason is then identified with Zeus or 'the will of the administrator of the whole'. Only against this background of Stoic theology can we understand why Chrysippus could characterize living in accordance with virtue as 'living in accordance with experience of what happens by nature': nature is structured by, and thus expresses, God's will. Human beings must, therefore, turn to nature in order to find the normative standard of action.

However, this characterization of *diathesis homologoumenē* in terms of an external, theologically interpreted standard of rightness is not the only account that we find in the sources. We also find characterizations of *diathesis homologoumenē* which clearly imply 'internal coherence'.[33] A good example is Stobaeus' report quoted above that Stoic 'virtue is generally speaking a character of the soul consonant with itself concerning the whole life' (διάθεσιν . . . ψυχῆς σύμφωνον αὐτῇ περὶ ὅλον τὸν βίον).[34] Another example is the definition of virtue as *logos homologoumenos*.[35] Here, *homologoumenos* is not followed by a dative to indicate what reason should agree with. 'Agreement with itself' or 'consistency' is clearly the meaning of the unsupplemented *homologoumenos*: virtue is 'consistent reason'. Moreover, the Stoics' emphasis on the *systematicity* of virtue-knowledge indicates a concern with consistency.[36]

In short, there is no reason to discard consistency as part of the meaning of *diathesis homologoumenē*. There is, therefore, no reason to choose between the two interpretations. It is precisely because human nature is part of the nature of the whole[37] that the consistency of one's psychology depends on one's aspirations being in tune with the divine normative guidelines implicit in the nature of the world at large.

The whole of one's life. The qualification 'in (or concerning) the whole of one's life' is an important addition to the definition of virtue as 'coherent character'. The qualification facilitates an understanding of some of the concerns motivating Stoic virtue ethics. The claim that virtue concerns the whole of one's life is reflected in the three Stoic teachings on the range and application of virtue.

First, Stoic virtue is about the shape of human life, understood in the broadest possible sense. This means that virtue should shape all human actions, including the most minute and seemingly trivial ones.[38] The Stoics even held that the shaping influence of virtue extended to the sage's sleep.[39] Thus the focus of virtue is not limited to certain key situations in life, like cases of extreme hardship to be overcome, great temptations to be faced, or particularly difficult moral questions to be resolved. The Stoics believed that even a trivial action like bending one's finger could be shaped by virtue and, in the case of the sage, is indeed expressive of his virtue.[40] This is not to deny that the Stoics recognized that certain key situations made the sage's virtue particularly *visible* to others, perhaps even that such situations demanded the practice of virtue in a 'peak-performance sense',[41] but the Stoics maintain that all actions alike, even the most trivial ones, are shaped by all the specific virtues.[42]

Second, the qualification 'in the whole of one's life' is reflected in the Stoics' insistence that virtue, once it is acquired, is a stable trait. Virtue cannot (normally) be lost. This seems to have been the bottom line of the Stoic theory, in spite of what were clearly different emphases placed by Cleanthes and Chrysippus. Since some of our sources make more of the difference than is in my view warranted, I shall elaborate my claim.[43] Diogenes Laertius reports (7.127, trans. Hicks, modified) that

Chrysippus holds that virtue can be lost, Cleanthes maintains that it cannot. According to the former, it may be lost in consequence of drunkenness or melancholy; the latter takes it to be inalienable owing to the certainty of our cognitions.

As far as this passage is concerned, it seems that Chrysippus flatly contradicted Cleanthes. This, however, is misleading, since only a few sentences later, at 7.128, Diogenes presents 'Cleanthes and his followers' as holding that '[the sage] always uses virtue . . . for virtue cannot be lost and the sage always uses his perfect soul', as if the inalienability of virtue was not a contended position at all. Compare also the following text (Simplicius *In Arist. Cat.* 401.34–402.26 = *SVF* 3.238):

> The reverse [sc. that virtuous agents turn into vicious ones] the Stoics do not grant. For they say that virtue cannot be lost. (. . .) In addition to this it is easy to say that he [sc. Nicostratos] takes a simplistic opinion by saying that virtue cannot be lost. For Theophrastus has shown sufficiently much about its change and this also seems so to Aristotle, namely that inalienability does not belong to human beings. Also the Stoics agree that by melancholy, by loss of consciousness, by lethargy and by taking drugs virtue itself can be lost, together with the whole state of reason (μεθ' ὅλης τῆς λογικῆς ἕξεως), yet that it does not turn into vice, but that the strength relaxes and that it turns into a state which the old [philosophers] called a medium state.

Simplicius' text also implies the existence of a standard Stoic view, only this time the generally held opinion is that virtue can be lost under certain extreme circumstances.[44]

The textual evidence can best be accounted for if we assume that Chrysippus' contribution was seen as an elaboration of Cleanthes' position and not as a flat contradiction. What must have happened is that Cleanthes stressed the extraordinary stability of the sage's virtue. Cleanthes would have detailed the strength of the sage's virtue in different adverse circumstances and he may even have argued that the sage proves this stability by not completely losing control over himself after imbibing large quantities of alcohol.[45] The question which springs to mind is, of course, if (and in what circumstances) the sage's extraordinary strength and self-control will collapse. For extraordinary as the sage's psychological strength may be, it would be utterly implausible to postulate that he must be entirely immune to any, even the most extreme, physical influences. Chrysippus, I suggest, attempted to elaborate Cleanthes' position with respect to these obvious problems when he explained that the sage's virtue, although extraordinarily stable, could be lost in some, albeit extreme, circumstances. These circumstances had to be so extreme as to simply 'switch off' the rationality of the agent and make the possession and exertion of virtue (temporarily) impossible. Chrysippus would have hastened to add that such extreme circumstances are very rare indeed and do not arise as the result of the sage's choice, but must rather be considered unfortunate accidents.[46] To the doxographers, the views of Cleanthes and Chrysippus must have appeared complementary: Chrysippus elaborated Cleanthes' position by answering an obvious question not addressed by his predecessor. Nevertheless, so much difference of emphasis was apparent that it remained worthwhile to quote both Cleanthes and Chrysippus as having pronounced differently on the question whether virtue could be lost.

If this reconstruction is correct, we can identify the general Stoic position to be that virtue is an extraordinarily stable trait. The sage cannot lapse from virtue into vice. However, the stability of virtue is not absolute. The sage is not immune to a temporary loss of reason or to its destruction. In case of an affliction so severe that the rationality of the agent is temporarily suspended or, worse, completely destroyed, no virtue can remain. The general Stoic position would thus stress both the extraordinary (although not absolute) stability of the sage's virtue and the vulnerability of human beings. However, in circumstances which leave the agent's rationality intact, the sage has acquired virtue at some point in the course of his life and continues to have it until the periodic conflagration puts an end to the pneumatic power of his soul.[47]

At this point, another inconsistency seems to threaten the Stoic position, but once more, as I shall argue, the inconsistency is merely apparent. The sage, so the Stoics held, acquires virtue at some point in the course of his life. Since virtue is an extreme, an unsurpassable maximum, the sage is not more or less happy by having virtue for a longer or shorter time. When it comes to virtue and happiness, length of time does not matter. This conviction is part of the assumptions leading the Stoics to claim that the sage's virtue and happiness equal the divine. However, this conviction appears to be in stark contrast to claims made by Chrysippus that a momentary acquisition of virtue is not worthwhile. Plutarch writes (*Stoic. rep.* 1046C–E, trans. Cherniss, modified):

> Although in many passages he [*sc.* Chrysippus] has said that the happy are no more happy for being longer happy, but are happy in the same manner and degree as those who have had happiness for an instant, yet again in many places he has said that one ought not even to extend a finger for the sake of practical wisdom that is momentary like a fleeting flash of lightning. It will suffice to cite what he has written on this matter in the sixth book of the *Moral Questions*, for after remarking that neither does joy apply to every good in the same degree nor glorification to every

right action he has proceeded as follows: 'For in fact, if it should be that a man would get prudence for only an instant or for his final moment, it would not behove him even to stretch out his finger on account of such possession of prudence'—and yet the happy are supposedly no more happy for being longer happy and everlasting happiness when compared with that which is momentary turns out not to be more an object of choice. Now, if he had held practical wisdom to be a good productive of happiness, as Epicurus did, only the mere absurdity and paradoxicality of the doctrine would have had to be attacked; but, since practical wisdom according to him is not different from happiness but is happiness, how is it other than inconsistent to say that momentary happiness is an object of choice in the same degree as that which is everlasting and yet that momentary happiness is worthless?

Certainly, had Chrysippus indeed claimed outright that different durations of the possession of virtue produce different degrees of happiness and that a very brief possession of virtue is (on the grounds of being of short duration) not worthwhile, he would be guilty of self-contradiction. However, Chrysippus' derisory remark about an instantaneous possession of virtue need not be understood in that way. The remark should rather be taken as heaping scorn on the idea of virtue not being practical, not being useable in concrete actions. Practical wisdom is defined as knowledge of the things to do and not to be done;[48] the idea of such a virtue being unemployable in action is ridiculous. In a parallel text, *Comm. not.* 8, Plutarch mentions a change from vice to virtue while being, like Lichas, hurled to one's death by Heracles.[49] Chrysippus would have used such examples in which virtue is acquired for an instant only (or at the last moment of one's life) as describing situations in which virtue cannot be operative: the time is too short for the agent to realize that he has become virtuous, and his possibilities are so confined as to make action according to virtue impossible. In such cases, Chrysippus must have doubted the usefulness of virtue. Virtue aims at realization, at shaping all the actions of an agent. Since this is not possible in such cases, virtue is a less attractive aim than in situations where it can be operative. Chrysippus seems to have expressed his opinion with strong words and talked of the complete unattractiveness of such a non-operative virtue. Rather than presenting a self-contradiction, Chrysippus' contention probably relied on and strengthened the point that virtue is directed to *shaping* the whole life of the agent, in all his actions. This aspect of virtue is so important that, unless it can be employed, virtue does not seem an attractive goal at all.

Chapter 5

The Virtues as *Epistēmai*

Chrysippus' definitions of specific virtues employ the Greek term *epistēmē*. Justice, for instance, is 'the *epistēmē* of distributing what is due to each'.[1] It is extremely difficult to translate *epistēmē* into English. The English word 'knowledge', for instance, is an uncountable noun, whereas the Greek *epistēmē* takes the plural form (*epistēmai*). 'Science' would be a good shot at translating *epistēmē* (particularly if taken to express the systematic and certain character of *epistēmē*), were it not for the misleading association with modern natural science which the word inevitably triggers. In what follows I shall leave the word *epistēmē* untranslated in most instances. In the few cases where a translation is inevitable, I use the word 'knowledge'.

In this chapter I attempt to clarify what the Stoics meant when characterizing virtues as *epistēmai*. In order to do so it will prove pivotal to understand the relation between *epistēmē* and another Greek term which was used confusingly in our sources. The word *technē* ('technique'), I shall argue, was used in two different senses without our sources clarifying this ambiguity.

The following definitions of *epistēmē* are listed by Stobaeus (2.73.19–74.3, trans. LS 41H, modified):

(According to the Stoics) (1) *epistēmē* is a cognition (κατάληψις) which is certain and irrefutable by argument. (2) Secondly, *epistēmē* is a system of *epistēmai*, for example the specific argumentative [*epistēmē*] which is present in the good agent. (3) Thirdly, *epistēmē* is a system of expert *epistēmai* which has firmness by itself, like the virtues. (4) Fourthly, it is a tenor for the reception of impressions, which is irrefutable by argument, consisting, as some people say, in a tension and power.

At first sight, it seems that these definitions of *epistēmē* divide into two pairs expressing two unrelated concepts of knowledge. Definitions (1) and (4) characterize *epistēmē* as a specific quality of the cognitive state of the agent.

The knowledge of the agent is 'certain', it is 'irrefutable by argument', and it is explained in terms of physics as 'tension and force'. Definitions (2) and (3), by contrast, characterize *epistēmē* as a body of knowledge to be found, say, in a scientific textbook. Using two labels that have become customary, the two pairs of definitions exemplify the contrast between the 'what' and the 'how' of knowledge.[2] Definitions (2) and (3), by highlighting the systematic nature of the body of knowledge, express an aspect of *what* the agent knows, whereas definitions (1) and (4) describe the state of the person who knows, and thus say something about *how* he is. Phrased in these terms, one could doubt that the pair of characterizations illustrating the 'how' side and the pair illustrating the 'what' side of knowledge have any connection, at least insofar as virtue is concerned. In support of this view, one could point to the fact that only definition (3) links knowledge explicitly to virtue. Yet, the 'what' and the 'how' aspects of knowledge are not so unconnected as it might seem. This becomes obvious when we examine one of the generic virtues, namely dialectic.[3] Diogenes Laertius 7.46–7 writes (trans. LS 31B, modified):

> They [the Stoics] take dialectic itself to be necessary, and a virtue which incorporates (περιέχουσαν) specific (ἐν εἴδει) virtues. Non-precipitancy (ἀπροπτωσία) is the *epistēmē* of when one should and should not assent. Uncarelessness (ἀνεικαιότης) is a strong rational principle against the plausible, so as not to give in to it. Irrefutability (ἀνελεγξία) is strength in argument, so as not to be carried away by argument into the contradictory [of one's own thesis]. Non-randomness (ἀματαιότης) is a tenor/disposition that refers impressions to the correct rational principle. And *epistēmē* itself, they say, is either secure cognition or a tenor in the reception of impressions which is unchangeable by reason. Without the study of dialectic the wise man will not be infallible in argument, since dialectic distinguishes the true from the false, and clarifies plausibilities and ambiguous statements. Without it, too, it is impossible to ask and answer questions methodically.

Without any doubt, knowledge of argumentative figures is an indispensable ingredient of dialectical abilities. In that sense, the 'what' side of knowledge is implicit in the text. However, dialectic is more than a system of argumentative figures and stratagems. This is shown by the definitions of the specific virtues subordinated to dialectic. They are unmistakeably about the 'how' side of the virtuous agent's knowledge. The virtuous agent, according

to the definitions, has a disposition which stabilizes and rectifies his reception of potentially misguiding impressions. It is no coincidence that the
characterization of *epistēmē* given in this context is a combination of the
definitions which figure as (1) and (4) in Stobaeus' list, the definitions
dealing with the 'how' side of knowledge.

The 'how' side of knowledge plays a pivotal role in the ethical virtues,
too. As in dialectic, there is the danger of being misguided by impressions.
Courage, for instance, is the '*epistēmē* of what is terrible and not-terrible and
of what falls under neither heading'. In order for the agent to act coura-
geously, more is needed than knowing lists of things which are terrible and
of things which are not. The agent has to have a stable disposition of receiving and judging impressions. He must not be tempted by the force of
impressions to assent mistakenly to the judgement that death is something
genuinely terrible. A stable cognitive disposition is needed in order to
inhibit the misleading force of certain impressions (see definition (4) in
Stobaeus' list). Moreover, the agent will only be able to act with unfailing
courage over a long period of time if his grasp of what is fearful and what is
not is absolutely certain. The agent must not waver, but this does not mean
that he is acting like an automaton, imperceptive of argument. The clause
'irrefutable by argument' in definitions (1) and (4) in Stobaeus' list should
be understood as meaning that the agent has thought matters through and
reached a certainty which is final in the sense that an argument cannot
take him by surprise and undermine his certainty.

The stress on stability as characteristic of the 'how' side of knowledge was
part of the Stoic doctrine right from the beginning of the school. It was
introduced by Zeno.[4] The following report shows that Zeno must have done
so in the context of his theory of assent (συγκατάθεσις). The text is Sextus
Empiricus *Adversus Mathematicos* 7.151. Sextus relates the critique that
the sceptical Academy under Arcesilaus brought forward against the Stoic
doctrine of cognitive impressions (trans. LS 41C, modified):

> The Stoics say that there are three things which are linked together,
> knowledge (ἐπιστήμη), opinion (δόξα) and cognition (κατάληψις) stationed
> between them. Knowledge is cognition which is secure and firm and
> unchangeable by reason. Opinion is weak and false assent. Cognition in
> between these is assent belonging to a cognitive impression; and a cogni-
> tive impression, so they claim, is one which is true and of such a kind that
> it could not turn out false. Of these, they say that knowledge is found only
> in the wise, and opinion only in the inferior, but cognition is common to
> them both, and it is the criterion of truth.

In this text the concepts of knowledge, opinion and cognition are distinguished. 'Cognition' (κατάληψις) is a common element in both opinion and knowledge. Cognition consists in assenting to the content of the so-called 'cognitive impression' (φαντασία καταληπτική). According to a Stoic definition, a cognitive impression 'is one which arises from what is and is stamped and impressed exactly in accordance with what is, of such a kind as could not arise from what is not'.[5] Thus the cognitive impression is 'a type of impression which gives its recipient an absolute guarantee that it represents the object with complete accuracy and clarity.'[6] It is an impression which is necessarily true, and the recipient of the impression can, if he is in the right frame of mind, *know* that it is a true impression. The wise and the ignorant differ in that they assent differently to an objectively true ('cognitive') impression: The ignorant and hence bad agent (φαῦλος) gives 'weak and false assent' (ἀσθενὴς καὶ ψευδὴς συγκατάθεσις), whereas the wise agent (σοφός) gives certain, firm and unchangeable assent (ἀσφαλὴς καὶ βεβαία καὶ ἀμετάθετος ὑπὸ λόγου κατάληψις).[7]

It seems that Zeno taught a cognitive hierarchy ranging from impression (*visum*), assent (*adsensus*), and cognition (*comprehensio* = κατάληψις) to knowledge (*scientia*) as the highest level. Witness Cicero's report in *Academica* 2.145 (trans. LS 41A, modified):

> Zeno used to clinch the wise man's sole possession of knowledge with a gesture. He would spread out the fingers of one hand and display its open palm, saying 'An impression is like this.' Next he clenched his fingers a little and said, 'Assent is like this.' Then, pressing his fingers quite together, he made a fist, and said that this was cognition (and from this illustration he gave that mental state the name of *katalēpsis*, which it had not had before). Then he brought his left hand against his right fist and gripped it tightly and forcefully, and said that knowledge was like this and possessed by none except the wise man.

In this model, the difference between the wise agent and the bad consists in their way of assenting to the truth of cognitive impressions. And this in turn rests on the frame of the mind of the agent: his moral quality, his being wise or not wise, determines the way he is going to react to the cognitive impressions, his assent or non-assent. The Stoics expressed this thought in the fourth definition of *epistēmē* quoted above. They considered *epistēmē* 'a tenor for the reception of impressions, which is irrefutable by argument' (ἕξιν φαντασιῶν δεκτικὴν ἀμετάπτωτον ὑπὸ λόγου) and which ultimately consists in some physical qualities. The sage is characterized as having such a tenor.

He is not deterred by the manifold impressions he receives. The sage is able to recognize those impressions which, being cognitive, are necessarily true and he unfailingly assents only to them. Equally unfailingly, he recognizes those impressions which do not have the status of cognitive impressions and withholds (or at least qualifies) his assent accordingly.

By contrast, the inferior agent does not have the stable moral knowledge of the sage. His assent is characterized in *Adversus Mathematicos* 7.151 as 'opinion', that is, 'weak and false assent'. This means that the inferior agent lacks precisely the stability of unfailingly sorting out impressions and assenting to the cognitive ones and withholding (or qualifying) his assent to other impressions. The inferior agent might thus happen to assent to exactly the same cognitive impressions as the wise person, but the crucial difference is that the fool's reception of impressions does not rest on a stable and irrefutable disposition. Hence, it depends more or less on circumstantial factors whether or not he assents to those impressions to which he should assent. The agent is therefore *prone* to assent to false impressions and to withhold his assent to cognitive impressions. This is a shortcoming that will have its impact in the course of events, for genuine knowledge is needed to produce results regularly and skilfully.[8] The 'how' side is thus an indispensable element of knowledge in general and hence of virtue.

At this point, the following problem has to be addressed: our sources on Stoic virtue theory speak not only of the virtues as forms of 'knowledge' (ἐπιστήμη); they also use the term *technē* ('technical knowledge' or 'techniques') in order to characterize the status of the virtues as *epistēmai*. Stobaeus, for instance, lists definitions of individual virtues which use the term *epistēmē* (Stob. 2.60–62), but he uses the term *technē* as well[9] and even uses both jointly.[10]

It would be a convenient way out of the difficulty if it could be shown that no contrast can be drawn between the two terms and that those ancient authors who, like Philo of Alexandria, did so were simply mistaken. This has in fact been suggested[11] but it seems unlikely, given indications in our sources that the two terms do indeed differ. On the other hand, it is not easy to point to the exact difference between the two terms. In my view, this is due to the fact that the Stoics use the term *technē* (as well as the term *hexis* which they use to explain an aspect of *technē*) in two distinct senses, without saying so explicitly.

In Simplicius' *In Arist. Cat.* 237.25–238.2, *technē* is characterized as 'tenor' (ἕξις) but not as a 'character' (διάθεσις), because it is a gradual property. Virtues, by contrast, are non-gradual properties and therefore 'characters'.[12] Later in the same commentary (*In Arist. Cat.* 284.32–285.1 = *SVF*

2.393), Simplicius credits the Stoics with an opinion which is strangely out of tune with this terminological choice:

> The third school is the school of the Stoics, who distinguish these virtues (τὰς ἀρετάς) from the middle techniques (τῶν μέσων τεχνῶν) and say that they cannot be intensified nor relaxed. But the middle techniques, they say, allow of intensification and relaxation. Of the tenors (τῶν . . . ἕξεων) and qualities which result from these, some allow neither intensification nor relaxation, some allow both.

Here we see, in apparent contrast to the earlier passage, that tenors cannot be neatly distinguished from characters on the basis of their being or not being gradual properties. Only one subclass of tenors consists of gradual properties, whereas another subclass does not. If we do not want to resort to the assumption of gross self-contradiction, it is necessary to assume that two different senses of 'tenor' (ἕξις) are at issue in the two passages. In the first passage, Simplicius refers to *hexis in a narrow sense*, which refers to a gradual quality. In the second passage, Simplicius uses *hexis* as a *generic term*, which covers both *hexis* in the aforementioned narrow sense and *diathesis*. Thus, *hexis* as a generic term could be, and was in fact, used to refer to a *diathesis* (at least in a rather loose way of talking).

A similar terminological ambiguity, I argue, can be found in the definition of the terms *technē* and *epistēmē* by means of the notions *hexis* and *diathesis*. Without such an ambiguity, the joint use of the words *technē* and *epistēmē* in Stobaeus' report (2.63.6–7, see above) cannot be explained. Moreover, Stobaeus quotes a definition of virtue as technique to do with life as a whole (ἀρετὴν, περὶ ὅλον οὖσαν τὸν βίον τέχνην),[13] and a definition of *epistēmē* in terms of *hexis* (Stob. 2.74.1–3) and a definition of justice (δικαιοσύνη) as a '*hexis* to distribute what is due to each' (Stob. 2.84.16–17), after having defined the same virtue as an *epistēmē* before (Stob. 59.9–10).

Stobaeus' report would be overtly inconsistent unless one assumes that two different meanings of *technē* are presupposed. There is, first, *technē* in a narrow, specific sense, which covers those disciplines traditionally understood as techniques, and there is, second, *technē* in a generic sense, which covers the aforementioned specific *technai* as well as *epistēmai*. Hence, the Stoics could use the term *technē* in its generic sense to talk loosely about something more strictly to be defined as a form of *epistēmē*.

Technai in the narrower sense, which correspond to *hexeis* in the narrower meaning, are sometimes called 'middle techniques' (μέσαι τέχναι). These middle techniques are clearly differentiated from virtue (understood as knowledge) by their allowing intensification and relaxation.[14] The name 'middle techniques' is not explained in the sources, but we can assume that the following two associations played a role: first, middle techniques could have gained their name from being gradual properties which could be elevated to something 'like a virtue' (as well as, presumably, being misused and thus degraded to something 'like vice'). Second, the middle techniques are directed at obtaining the preferred (προηγμένα) among morally neutral things (ἀδιάφορα), which form a third class as it were 'in between' morally good and bad things.

Let us now compare the concepts of *technē* (in the narrower sense) and *epistēmē*. One of the central ideas expressed by the concept of *technē* is the idea of systematicity: technical knowledge is a system of cognitions.[15] These cognitions are acquired by training (συγγεγυμνασμένος);[16] they are organized to serve a practical end, 'to further what is useful for the things in life',[17] an aim which technical knowledge achieves in a methodical way.[18]

Whereas *technē* and *epistēmē* are both instrumental towards an end, it is a different end to which they are subservient: *technē* furthers 'what is useful for the things in life'; the end of *epistēmē* is to live in accordance with nature.[19] The latter is superior to the former; it is one thing to be able to do or produce useful things, but quite another thing to know what is truly useful in life. Without such knowledge, the techniques can serve good as well as bad ends; their employment can ultimately harm the agent more than that it helps him. The possession of virtue integrates the techniques in a stable framework of knowledge; they find in it their place and an unwavering orientation towards the good. Techniques possessed by the sage are therefore, as it were, something beyond themselves; they become 'like virtues', sharing in their irrefutability. Witness Stobaeus 2.73.1–10 (trans. LS 61J):

Of goods, some are 'in process' (ἐν κινήσει), others are 'in state' (ἐν σχέσει). Of the former type are joy, delight, modest socializing; of the latter type are well-organized leisure, undisturbed stability, manly concentration. And of those that are 'in state', some are also 'in tenor' (ἐν ἕξει), e.g. the virtues; but others, like those mentioned above, are 'in state' only. 'In tenor' are not only the virtues but also the other expertises in the virtuous man which are modified by his virtue and become unchangeable, since they become like virtues ('Εν ἕξει δὲ οὐ μόνας εἶναι τὰς ἀρετάς, ἀλλὰ καὶ τὰς ἄλλας τέχνας τὰς ἐν τῷ σπουδαίῳ ἀνδρὶ ἀλλοιωθείσας ὑπὸ τῆς ἀρετῆς καὶ γενομένας ἀμεταπτώτους, οἱονεὶ γὰρ ἀρετὰς γίνεσθαι).

The Stoics also distinguish a class of techniques, the so-called 'pursuits' (ἐπιτηδεύματα). Pursuits are techniques which can be seamlessly integrated into the virtuous life. The above report continues as follows (Stob. 2.73.10–15):

> They [the Stoics] also say that goods 'in tenor' include the so-called 'pursuits' as well, like love of music, love of literature, love of geometry and the like. For there is a method for selecting in these techniques what has an affinity with virtue, by referring it to the end (τέλος) of life.[20]

These techniques are the exclusive property of the sage. Yet their integration into the sage's life does not change the character of the pursuits into full-blown *epistēmai* (Stob. 2.67.5–12, trans. LS 26H, modified):

> 'Pursuits', rather than '*epistēmai*', is the name they [the Stoics] give to love of music, love of literature, love of horseriding, and love of hunting, both in general and with reference to the 'curricular' expertises as they are called. The Stoics include these in virtuous tenors, and accordingly say that only the wise man is a lover of music and literature etc. This is their outline account of a pursuit: a method which by means of expertise or a part of expertise is conducive to the domain of virtue.

So far I have sketched the difference that Stoic sources draw between techniques and *epistēmai* and have begun to comment on the characteristics that our sources allude to by calling the virtues *epistēmai*. In particular, I have attempted to show that the 'how' side and the 'what' side of knowledge are intimately connected in the concept of virtue. It is now time to take the discussion of the 'what' side one step further and turn to the extent of the sage's knowledge. According to definition (3) in Stobaeus' list, the sage must have a 'system of expert *epistēmai* which has firmness by itself'. Does not this require the impossible, that the sage is omniscient?

The Stoics based the sage's knowledge on correct assent to so-called 'cognitive impressions'. According to the Stoics, cognitive impressions are impressions which have the guarantee of truth in them. The sage justly assents to these cognitive impressions, but withholds assent in all other cases. Thus the sage cannot be mistaken since he knows about the limitations of his knowledge. Stobaeus reports (2.111.18–21):

> They [the Stoics] say that the sage never assumes anything wrong, and does not assent to anything non-cognitive at all, because he never holds

a mere opinion and never is in ignorance. For ignorance is refutable and weak assent.

Thus, the Stoics did not have to make the implausible claim that the sage is aware of all possible facts. The pivotal characteristic of his knowledge is the infallibility and firmness of his assent, which is given only to cognitive impressions.

Seen in this light, the Stoic claim that the sage has infallible knowledge is far more limited than appears at first. For instance, there can be many areas of research about which the sage does not have secure knowledge, since many theorems of a particular branch of research might not be cognitive impressions after all.[21] As we shall see, to the Stoics' mind it is most important that the sage possesses a fundamentally correct perspective in viewing the world and his own position in it. Although this presupposes a wide range of knowledge, the Stoics need not attribute omniscience to the sage.[22]

Chapter 6

The Virtues—Different yet Inseparable

In our discussion in Chapter 4 of virtue as a perfect state we took our cue from Galen's polemic against Chrysippus in *PHP* 5.5.38–40. The text is of interest in the present context as well, since it takes issue with Chrysippus' complex view of the unity and plurality of the virtues. In Galen's eyes, Chrysippus was guilty of inconsistency, because—in tune with his monistic psychology—he defined virtue as single state of perfection of the rational human nature but postulated at the same time a plurality of virtues. Galen's polemic suggests that the apparent self-contradiction had escaped Chrysippus' notice. Yet, as we shall see presently, this cannot have been the case. The question of the plurality and unity of the virtues was pivotal for Chrysippus. In fact, he designed an elaborate theory to make it plausible that there is a plurality of virtues while at the same time supporting the unity of the virtues with seemingly counterintuitive assertions of their complete interconnectedness. In the following section I shall discuss Chrysippus' view of the difference between the virtues. Thereafter, I shall turn to the issue of the complete interconnectedness of the virtues. A discussion of Chrysippus' arguments will allow us to understand better the philosophical debate which formed the backdrop to Chrysippus' theory of the virtues as forms of knowledge. Moreover, it will prepare the discussion of Chrysippus' catalogue of virtues in the next chapter.

The Difference between the Virtues

Our sources show that the issue of the plurality of the virtues and their interconnectedness was contended at the early phase of the Stoa. According to Plutarch, our main but unfavourable witness,[1] Zeno had simply followed Plato's lead in recognizing the four virtues of practical wisdom, courage, temperance and justice and in regarding these virtues as different yet inseparable. In Plutarch's view, Zeno's definitions of the four virtues did not match up with his conviction that the virtues are different from one another. Zeno defined the virtues in terms of practical wisdom (*phronēsis*) being applied to different fields of actions, thus giving the impression that there is really only one virtue which is merely called by different names according to the different fields of action on which it is exercised. We cannot be certain whether this was in fact what Zeno intended or whether Zeno simply failed to state unambiguously that he thought of different *types* of practical wisdom being employed in different fields of action. However, if we can take our cue from the way Cleanthes formulated the Stoic position, the former alternative looks far more likely. In his *Physical Treatises* Cleanthes presented the different virtues as constituted by the application of a unitary property[2] of the soul in different fields of action. On this interpretation it appears that the question of how the virtues can be different from one another was not resolved satisfactorily by Zeno or Cleanthes. It was Aristo, a pupil of Zeno's, whose radical affirmation of a single unitary virtue must have triggered Chrysippus' development of a model intended to resolve the issue of the plurality and interconnectedness of the virtues once and for all. Chrysippus devoted a whole treatise, entitled *On (the Doctrine) that the Virtues are Qualities* (Περὶ τοῦ ποιὰς εἶναι τὰς ἀρετάς), to the question.[3] Since this treatise seems to have been Plutarch's main source, we must expect that his accounts of Aristo's and Chrysippus' positions reflect Chrysippus' but not necessarily Aristo's terminology.[4] According to Plutarch, Aristo considered the virtues different and plural only 'by relativity'. This phrase invokes the fourth Stoic genus, 'relative disposition' (πρός τί πως ἔχον). The genus 'relatively disposed' expresses an extrinsic relation in which a thing *x* is standing. The relation can cease to exist without any material change in *x*. For instance, if *x* is sitting to the right of person *y*, the relative disposition of *x* to sit to the right of *y* ends the moment *y* leaves.[5] This would imply that the virtuous agent has only a general unitary virtue all the time. The specific virtues come into existence by applying that general unitary virtue to particular fields of activity: Plutarch quotes what must have been Aristo's own account of his theory: 'just as if someone wanted to call our vision "white-seeing" when it apprehended white things, "black-seeing" when it apprehended black things, and so on . . . as the knife, while being one thing, cuts different things on different occasions, and fire acts on different materials although its nature is one and the same'.[6] Ultimately, however, there is only one unitary virtue Aristo called 'health' and, as Galen reports (*PHP* 5.5.40), 'knowledge of things good and evil'.

Recent scholars have emphasized the degree to which Aristo was critical of Zeno, and perhaps also his virtue theory was a deliberate attempt to shift the consensus of Zeno's followers towards a more Cynic stance.[7] Be that as it may, Aristo's virtue theory did not deliver a genuine plurality of different virtues, which, in Chrysippus' view, had been Zeno's goal, however imperfectly realized. Chrysippus rejected Aristo's virtue theory outright. According to Plutarch, Chrysippus invoked the 'qualified'—i.e. the second Stoic genus—which meant that a virtue was 'constituted by its own quality'.[8] The specific quality that a thing has is brought about by the formative presence of the divine principle in the shape of *pneuma*. Since the *pneuma* is itself a body, this leads to claims that two bodies are present at the same place simultaneously and to speculations about virtue being itself a 'living being'.[9]

Presenting his own theory as the correct interpretation of Zeno, Chrysippus had to explain away the impression of a fundamentally unitary virtue made plural only 'by relativity', which was produced by Zeno's description of the four virtues in terms of the practical wisdom applied to different fields of action. Chrysippus claimed that Zeno really meant *epistēmē* when defining the virtues in terms of *phronēsis*. The different virtues are different *epistēmai*.

Chrysippus' reading of Zeno presented him with a double task: he had not only to show how the different virtues represent different *epistēmai*, but he also had to explain how the virtues, as different *epistēmai*, can be completely interconnected so that a virtuous agent has all the virtues and acts with all the virtues simultaneously.

The Inseparability of the Virtues

The most detailed account of how Chrysippus attempted to fulfil this double task is given by Stobaeus (2.63.6–24, trans. LS 61D and LS 63G, modified)[10]:

[A] All the virtues which are *epistēmai* and *technai* share their theorems (θεωρήματα) and, as already mentioned, the same end. Hence they are also inseparable (ἀχωρίστους). For whoever has one has all, and whoever acts in accordance with one acts in accordance with all.

[B] They differ from one another by their own primary considerations (τοῖς κεφαλαίοις). For the primary considerations of practical wisdom are, primarily the theory and practice of what should be done; and secondarily the theory also of what should be distributed, [what chosen, and what endured] for the sake of unerringly doing what should be done.

Of temperance the special primary consideration is, primarily, to keep the impulses healthy and to grasp the theory of them; but secondarily, the theory of what falls under the other virtues, for the purpose of conducting oneself unerringly in one's impulses. Likewise courage primarily grasps the theory of everything that should be endured; and secondarily, that of what falls under the other virtues. And justice primarily studies individual deserts: but secondarily, the rest too. For all the virtues focus upon the range of objects that belongs to all of them and upon each other's subject-matter.

[C] For Panaetius said that what happens in respect of the virtue is similar to a single target set up for many archers, which contains within itself lines of different colours. In that case each archer would aim to hit the target, but one would do so, if he were successful, through striking into the white line, and another through striking into the black line, and another through doing so into a line of different colour. For just as these people make hitting the target their highest end, but propose to achieve it in different ways, so all the virtues make being happy their end, which consists in living in agreement with nature, but they achieve this in different ways.

The passage falls into three parts. The first part (A) shows why the virtues are inseparable (ἀχωρίστους). The second part (B) provides an explanation as to how the virtues can still be considered different from one another. The third part (C) adduces in support of these theories a simile formulated by Panaetius. In what follows I shall discuss the parts in turn.

In part (A) the argument begins with the claim that the virtues which are *epistēmai* and *technai* share their theorems and their ultimate goal.[11] A parallel report in Diogenes Laertius 7.125 uses the definite article with *theorēmata*, thus confirming that the virtues share *all* their theorems. The virtues are bodies of knowledge which contain exactly the same theorems. This explains why the virtues form a coherent whole, a unitary virtuous state, and are thus inseparable. The radical unity of the virtues is supported by two different interentailment theses: (a) whoever has one virtue has all the virtues, and (b) whoever acts in accordance with one virtue acts in accordance with all the virtues. The theses differ in strength. Since using a virtue implies having it, but not vice versa, the interentailment thesis about *using* all the virtues is stronger than the interentailment thesis concerning the *possession* of virtues.

The weaker interentailment thesis finds direct support in the claim that all the virtues consist in the knowledge of the same theorems. Since the virtues consist in knowing the same theorems, somebody who acquires the knowledge of one virtue has thereby acquired the knowledge of all the virtues.

It seems that there is no such straightforward argument for the stronger interentailment thesis. Since the virtues are knowledge of the same theorems, why is more than one virtue necessary for a single virtuous act? An account is called for in how far the virtues differ from one another so that the different virtues provide different perspectives necessary for any virtuous action. This account is given in the second part (B) of our Stobaeus passage, which deals with the differences between the virtues.

The second part announces its content with the first word, the Greek verb *diapherein* ('to differ'). The difficulty for Chrysippus was to provide a model that made both claims plausible, the claim that the virtues differ from each other as well as the claim that they all entail knowledge of the same set of theorems. His solution was that although the set of theorems is the same for all virtues, the virtues differ by having their own *kephalaia*, their own 'primary considerations', as I propose to translate.[12] Although the set of theorems is the same, each virtue consists of a different arrangement of the set of theorems: each orders the theorems differently. Each virtue puts, as it were, 'some things first' and considers others to be secondary. The primary consideration for each virtue is the specific 'sphere of action' it is directed at.[13] Practical wisdom is directed at the theory and practice of what should be done, temperance deals with the good quality of our impulses, courage with cases of endurance and justice studies individual deserts and, with it, distributions.[14] While each virtue takes its own primary considerations first, it is also, secondarily, about the considerations of the other virtues.

But why should a virtue also have to cover (secondarily) the considerations of the other virtues? Long and Sedley have suggested that this is necessary in order to avoid, for instance, a moderate act's being at the same time performed with cowardice, injustice or folly.[15] While undoubtedly true, this statement is in my opinion a very negative way of expressing what Chrysippus suggested. Undoubtedly the virtues form a unitary virtuous state so that no virtue combines with vices in other fields, but we should also look for a positive contribution towards virtue and virtuous action from the considerations primarily associated with other virtues.[16]

That we should look for a positive contribution of these considerations is confirmed by the emphasis placed in part B on 'unerringly' (ἀδιαπτώτως) fulfilling the task of a virtue. The adverb 'unerringly' (ἀδιαπτώτως) occurs twice. At the first occurrence, the text explains that *phronēsis* has to attend to the *kephalaia* of the other (generic) virtues, 'in order to unerringly do what has to be done' (χάριν τοῦ ἀδιαπτώτως πράττειν ὃ ποιητέον). This alludes to the definition of practical wisdom (φρόνησις) as the 'theory and practice of what should be done', which had been given immediately before. The meaning of the text is clearly that each (generic) virtue can only do its own job unerringly, if it attends to the *kephalaia* of the other (three generic) virtues.[17] The second occurrence of 'unerringly' is a repetition of the argument in respect of temperance (σωφροσύνη). Temperance has the *kephalaion* 'to keep the impulses healthy and to grasp the theory of them'. Temperance has to attend to the *kephalaia* of the other virtues for the sake of 'conducting oneself unerringly in one's impulses', which means 'for the sake of unerringly doing the job of temperance'. The occurrences of 'unerringly' show that a virtue's attending (secondarily) to the *kephalaia* of the other virtues enables that virtue to do its own job in the right way, it is a positive contribution to the workings of that virtue.[18]

Can we say more on the relationship between the virtues? I suggest that the key to understanding the relationship between the virtues is Panaetius' archer simile in part C. The simile describes how different archers set themselves the task of hitting the same target, but that each does so by aiming at (and hitting) a different line of the target. We would certainly misconstrue the simile if we assumed that the different lines of the target represent different scores, thus awarding different ranks to different virtues. The simile must be understood as assuming that the lines represent the same value; each virtuous activity is equally valuable and adequate. The simile suggests that there are separate areas of conduct—the differently coloured lines. A map can be drawn of human practice which identifies actions that are the issue of a specific virtue. The separateness of the virtuous is represented by different archers: a specific virtue enables the archer to hit a specific line, to get his action 'right', which asks for a specific virtue. The simile also makes us understand the interconnectedness of the virtues. An archer can only propose to hit a specific band, if he is able to hit whatever line he wants. The archer has to employ his good grip and steady hand, trained to send the arrow wherever he wants. Thus, not only generally to get his whole life (an unspecified range of practices) 'right', but also specifically to perform a specific action well, the sage has to possess and to practice all the virtues. The archer simile shows that possession of all the virtues is needed to enable the sage to perform 'perfect' actions. It shows that the performance of such perfect actions depends on the perfection of the sage's psyche, characterized by the synchronous presence of all the virtues.

Chapter 7

A Catalogue of Virtues

Having discussed the precarious balance between the unity and the plurality of the virtues in the previous chapter, we are now in a position to compile an inventory of the virtues that Chrysippus recognized. In extending the scope of the discussion, I shall first consider Chrysippus' particularization of the four generic virtues of practical wisdom, temperance, courage and justice by recognizing a number of more specific subordinated virtues. Then I shall examine the evidence of Chrysippus' and other Stoics' having acknowledged apart from these 'ethical' virtues two other generic virtues, (understanding of) logic and (understanding of) physics, again with a number of virtues subordinated to them. I shall conclude this chapter with a discussion of the question whether the Chrysippean catalogue of virtues was 'closed', a definitive complete list, or whether it was an open list which allowed additions.

Ethical Virtues

For the first step of our inquiry, we are in the fortuitous position of having a veritable catalogue of virtues recognized by Chrysippus. The catalogue is reproduced in Stobaeus (2.59.4–62.6), without any mention of its author. However, for about half of the catalogue we have an exact parallel[1] in Pseudo-Andronicus of Rhodes' *De passionibus* (Περὶ παθῶν), where the title—'According to Chrysippus' (Κατὰ Χρύσιππον)—explicitly attributes the catalogue to Chrysippus.[2] The Stobaeus text reads as follows (2.59.4–62.6):

Practical wisdom is the *epistēmē* of what one ought to do and ought not to do and of what falls under neither heading. Or the *epistēmē* of good things and of bad things and of what falls under neither heading for a living thing which is by nature political [and rational]—and [the Stoics] demand that in the case of the other virtues [the definitions] should be understood in the same way. Temperance is the *epistēmē* of things to be chosen and things to be avoided and of what falls under neither heading. Justice is the *epistēmē* of distributing what is due to each. Courage is the *epistēmē* of what is terrible and not-terrible and what falls under neither heading. (. . .) Some of the virtues are primary; the other [virtues] are subordinated to the primary. Primary are the following four: practical wisdom, temperance, courage, and justice. Practical wisdom is about appropriate actions; temperance is about the impulses of man; courage is about cases of endurance: justice is about distributions. Of the class of virtues which are subordinated to these some are subordinated to practical wisdom, some to temperance, some to courage, and some to justice. Subordinated to practical wisdom are: good judgement, good practical overview, quick moral sense, discretion, [shrewdness], inventiveness in difficulties; to temperance: good ordering, propriety, sense of honour, self-control; to courage; perseverance, confidence, magnanimity, mental stoutness, industry; to justice: piety, kindness, sociability, blameless companionship. Good judgement, the Stoics say, is the *epistēmē* of what we can do—and how we can act—advantageously.[3] Good practical overview is the *epistēmē* which balances and sums up what is happening and what is performed. Quick moral sense is the *epistēmē* which finds the appropriate action at the moment. Discretion is the *epistēmē* [of what is worse and better. Shrewdness is the *epistēmē*] which is able to achieve the aim in every case. Inventiveness in difficulties is the *epistēmē* which is able to find a way out of difficulties. Good ordering is the *epistēmē* of when [something] should be done, and what after what, and in general about the order of actions. Propriety is [the *epistēmē*] of seemly and unseemly behaviour. Sense of honour is the *epistēmē* which is careful to avoid just blame. Self-control is the *epistēmē* of not transgressing the bounds of what appears to be correct according to right judgement. Perseverance is the *epistēmē* of sticking to what has been judged correctly. Confidence is the *epistēmē* according to which we know that we do not fall prey to anything terrible. Magnanimity is the *epistēmē* which makes one be above those things whose nature it is to happen to good and bad persons alike. Mental stoutness is the *epistēmē* of the soul that represents it to itself [i.e. the soul] as unconquerable. Industry is the *epistēmē* which is able to accomplish what is due to be dealt with, undeterred by trouble or pain.[4] Piety is the *epistēmē* of service to the gods. Kindness is the *epistēmē* of doing good. Sociability is the *epistēmē* of equality in social intercourse. Blameless companionship is the *epistēmē* of socializing blamelessly with one's neighbours.

This catalogue starts with the four generic virtues: practical wisdom (φρόνησις), temperance (σωφροσύνη), courage (ἀνδρεία) and justice (δικαιοσύνη). As Plutarch reports, these four virtues were acknowledged by Zeno who thereby followed Plato's lead.[5] It is certainly right to see continuity in the recognition of a group of specifically important virtues. Prior to this, Socrates seems to have discussed a group of five virtues so frequently that Gregory Vlastos termed them 'Socrates' five canonical virtues'.[6] In the *Republic*, Plato singled out the four, later so-called 'cardinal', virtues of wisdom (σοφία), temperance (σωφροσύνη), courage (ἀνδρεία) and justice (δικαιοσύνη). In spite of the continuity, however, there seems to be an obvious difference between the Stoic group of primary virtues and Plato's four cardinal virtues, in that the Stoics name 'practical wisdom' (φρόνησις) instead of 'wisdom' (σοφία). In the absence of direct evidence, it seems likely that the Stoics were reluctant to use *sophia* as a name for a particular virtue since they prominently called the exemplar of Stoic virtue, the agent who possesses all the virtues, 'wise' (σοφός). In any case, trading 'wisdom' for 'practical wisdom' was most probably just a terminological difference, since Plutarch, usually not shy of pointing out Stoic innovation, did not avail himself of it.

Each of the four generic virtues has its own sphere. Each is related to a distinct area of conduct. In this way, practical wisdom is 'about' proper functions (καθήκοντα), temperance in respect of impulses (ὁρμαί), while courage deals with cases of endurance (ὑπομοναί) and justice with distributions (ἀπονεμήσεις).[7] These virtues are considered 'primary' (πρῶται); others are 'subordinated' (ὑποτεταγμέναι), yet dealing with the same area of conduct.[8] They characterize in more detail what it means to possess the primary virtue. For instance, having practical wisdom (φρόνησις) entails that one also has good judgement (εὐβουλία); that is, one knows in a given situation what is and is not advantageous. In general, if one possesses a generic virtue, it implies that one also has the subordinated virtues. And, vice versa, one cannot have a subordinated virtue (for instance, good judgement) without having the generic virtue (practical wisdom) and thereby—see the previous chapter—also the other generic virtues and the virtues subordinated to them.

Perhaps the idea of subordinating secondary virtues to primary ones was stimulated by Plato. For instance, in the *Euthyphro* (12E9–10) piety is said to be a 'part' (μέρος) of justice, and in the *Republic* Plato has Socrates argue that the hypothetically constructed city is wise *because* it is resourceful (εὔβουλος γάρ: 428B). For the discussants in the *Republic*, resourcefulness is an integral part of, or subsumed under, wisdom, so that having resourcefulness implies being wise. Obviously Plato was prepared to integrate other publicly recognized virtues under the headings of his virtues. Chrysippus thus seems to have followed Plato's lead—we cannot be certain how far Zeno considered the possibility—in drawing a list of more specific virtues subordinated to the four primary ones.

The whole catalogue reflects Chrysippus' intellectualistic stance: all definitions, without exception, are formulated in terms of *epistēmē*. Having virtue is quintessentially knowing something.[9] In the remainder of this chapter, I shall not attempt a detailed discussion of the range and practical import of the virtues contained in Chrysippus' catalogue. A discussion of these virtues can be found in Appendix 2. For now, I turn to a discussion of the evidence of Chrysippus' having recognized additional (generic) virtues.

Additional (Generic) Virtues

In a report by Aetius (*Placita* 1 *Prooem.* = *SVF* 2.35) we read that

> The Stoics said that wisdom is the *epistēmē* of things divine and human and philosophy the exercise of a useful technique. Useful in the highest sense is only virtue. There are three virtues on the highest generic level (γενικωτάτας): physical, ethical, logical. For this reason philosophy consists of three parts, namely physics, ethics, logic. And [we exercise] physics when we do research on the world and the objects in the world, ethics is the occupation with the human life, logic is the occupation with the logos. This they [the Stoics] also call dialectic.[10]

The text describes a superstructure of highest generic virtues (γενικωτάται), which is explicitly linked to the differentiation of philosophy into three parts. The superstructure is presented as a general Stoic position. While it is unclear if Chrysippus himself advocated the tripartite superstructure and described the generic virtues of practical wisdom, temperance, courage and justice as falling under the highest genus of 'ethical virtue',[11] the conception is certainly compatible with his position. Chrysippus advocated the differentiation of philosophy into these three parts, and we shall see shortly that there is good reason to attribute to him the recognition of other virtues than those listed in the catalogue of ethical virtues reproduced in Stobaeus and Pseudo-Andronicus.

That the Stoics recognized virtues in addition to the ethical ones is confirmed by Cicero's *De finibus* 3.72–3. Cicero has the Stoic spokesman

Cato vigorously defend the status of dialectic and physics as virtues. He writes:

> To the virtues discussed so far they also add dialectic and physics, both of which they call virtues, the former because it ensures that we do not assent to something false or are ever deceived by deceptive appearance of truth and that we are able to keep and preserve what we have learnt about the things good and evil. For without this technique, they hold, everyone can be led away from truth and be deceived. It is therefore right, if in all things rashness and ignorance is bad, that the technique which prevents this is called virtue.
>
> To physics the same honour is attributed, and equally not without reason, since he who wishes to live according to nature must take the whole world and its administration as his starting point. Nor can anyone judge correctly about things good and evil unless one knows the complete reasonable order of nature and of life—also of the gods—and knows whether or not the nature of man is in agreement with nature as a whole. Also, without physics one cannot grasp the force—and indeed they have immeasurable force—of those old precepts of the wise, commanding to consider the circumstances, to follow God, to know oneself and not to exceed the limitations set by nature. And also the influence which nature has on the cultivation of justice, on the keeping of friendships and other special relationships only this single discipline of knowledge can teach. Nor can the piety towards the gods and the amount of gratitude owed to them be understood without an explanation of nature.[12]

We can supplement the information given by Cicero on dialectic as a virtue with two passages in Diogenes Laertius. At D.L. 7.83 we read (trans. LS 31C):

> The reason why the Stoics adopt these views in logic is to give the strongest possible confirmation to their claim that the wise man is always a dialectician. For all things are observed through study conducted in discourses, whether they belong to the domain of physics or equally that of ethics. As to logic, that goes without saying. In regard to 'correctness of names', the topic of how customs have assigned names to things, the wise man would have nothing to say. Of the two linguistic practices which do come within the province of his virtue, one studies what each existing thing is (τί ἕκαστόν ἐστι τῶν ὄντων σκοπεῖ), and the other what it is called (ἡ δὲ τί καλεῖται).

This passage seems to reflect Chrysippus' view of dialectic. For Chrysippus, dialectic has two areas of enquiry: signifiers (σημαίνοντα) and things signified (σημαινόμενα),[13] the latter being about semantic considerations and thus about the truth-functional aspect and ontological commitments of language. This bipartition is reflected in Diogenes Laertius 7.83 by the differentiation of two spheres of dialectical virtue: 'what each existing thing is (τί ἕκαστόν ἐστι τῶν ὄντων σκοπεῖ) and what it is called (ἡ δὲ τί καλεῖται)'.

Diogenes Laertius 7.83 puts a strong emphasis on the indispensability of dialectic for physics and ethics and thus spells out an aspect which remains implicit in Cicero's *De finibus* 3.72. The slight difference of emphasis is also reflected in two different ways of describing the contribution of dialectic. Whereas *De finibus* 3.72 describes the benefit of dialectic negatively as avoidance of error, Diogenes Laertius 7.83 describes it in a positive way as attainment of truth. These are, however, differences of presentation rather than differences in substance. In both accounts dialectic is linked to the attainment of truth, save that Cicero puts the role of dialectic in terms of prohibiting error and Diogenes puts it more positively in terms of attaining truth. Both are aspects of Stoic dialectic.[14]

The second passage which can supplement *De finibus* 3.72 is Diogenes Laertius 7.46–8 (trans. LS 31B, modified):

(1) They [the Stoics] take dialectic itself to be necessary, and a virtue which incorporates (περιέχουσαν) specific (ἐν εἴδει) virtues. (2) Non-precipitancy (ἀπροπτωσία) is the *epistēmē* of when one should and should not assent. Uncarelessness (ἀνεικαιότης) is a strong rational principle against the plausible, so as not to give in to it. Irrefutability (ἀνελεγξία) is strength in argument, so as not to be carried away by argument into the contradictory [of one's own thesis]. Non-randomness (ἀματαιότης) is a tenor that refers impressions to the correct rational principle. (3) And *epistēmē* itself, they say, is either secure cognition or a tenor in the reception of impressions which is unchangeable by reason. (4) Without the study of dialectic the wise man will not be infallible in argument, since dialectic distinguishes the true from the false, and clarifies plausibilities and ambiguous statements. Without it, moreover, it is impossible to ask and answer questions methodically. (5) Precipitancy in argument extends to what actually happens; so people who do not have their impressions trained veer into states of disorder and carelessness. (6) Only in this way will the wise man show himself to be penetrating, sharp-witted and someone who, quite generally, is formidable in argument. For the person whose job it is to discuss and to argue correctly is the very person whose

job it is to discuss debating topics and to respond to the questions put to him; and these are functions of the man experienced in dialectic.

As it stands, the passage is a rapid succession of Stoic formulae, unfortunately somewhat less organized than we would wish. We can distinguish six different parts[15]: (1) The status of dialectic as indispensable generic virtue is asserted. (2) Then the virtues subordinate to dialectic are named and defined. The definitions indicate that the importance of dialectic and the virtues subordinate to it lies in the attainment and preservation of knowledge. (3) It is not clear what role *epistēmē* is supposed to play. The formulation is very much in line with the enumeration of the virtues so far. It appears as if *epistēmē* was presented as another virtue subordinated to dialectic. Yet, this would be utterly unsatisfactory since the first subordinate virtue was already defined in terms of *epistēmē*. It is also possible (even if less likely as far as the formulation is concerned) that *epistēmē* is not meant to be considered a virtue but that a need was felt to define *epistēmē* at this point, since the previously-defined virtues focus on the attainment and preservation of knowledge. (4) It is affirmed that dialectic, by making judgement stable and true, is indispensable for the sage, the personification of knowledge. Part (5) interrupts the train of thought by stating *ex negativo* the relevance of dialectic to the good life in general (for the possession of the ethical virtues, as one might say): the vice of precipitancy impedes one's dealing adequately with one's impressions, resulting in 'states of disorder and carelessness'. Part (6) continues the train of thought begun in (4) by claiming that the wise man must be considered a shrewd discussant, which is the same as to say that he must be an experienced dialectician.

To sum up, the text as it stands is a hodgepodge, and it seems problematic to attribute its content to any one author alone. Undoubtedly some formulations in the passage are in line with Chrysippus or might even originate with Chrysippus: (a) the first subordinated virtue, non-precipitancy, is defined as an *epistēmē*, just as Chrysippus defined the ethical virtues listed in his catalogue; (b) the argument for the indispensability of dialectic for the sage is very similar to the arguments in Cicero *De finibus* 3.72 and Diogenes Laertius 7.83, which reflect Chrysippus' view; and finally (c) the definition of *epistēmē* as secure cognition (κατάληψις ἀσφαλής) could also be taken from Chrysippus. Other formulations, however, cannot be linked to Chrysippus with any certainty; they seem to derive from an un-Chrysippean virtue theory: (a) the three subordinated virtues following non-precipitancy (uncarelessness, irrefutability and non-randomness) are characterized in turn as 'a strong rational principle', 'strength' and 'a tenor', but not as *epistēmai*; (b) the subordination of more specific virtues is described with a participle of the verb *periechein*, 'to incorporate', but not with a form of the verb *hypotassein*, 'to subordinate', as in the Chrysippean virtue catalogue in Stobaeus and Pseudo-Andronicus. That this is probably more than just an innocent linguistic variation, is evident from Diogenes Laertius 7.126, where a deviant description of the relationship between generic and subordinated virtues (characterized with the verb *hepesthai*, 'following') coincides with a list of subordinated virtues different from the Chrysippean catalogue in Stobaeus and Pseudo-Andronicus.[16]

I suggest, therefore, that Diogenes Laertius 7.46–8 should be seen as the result of a process of addition to, and reformulation of, a Chrysippean schema of dialectic as a generic virtue. While it is likely that the status of dialectic as a generic virtue originated with Chrysippus, and while it is quite possible that he subordinated the virtue of non-precipitancy to it, it is hard to see how he could have authored the definitions of the other subordinate virtues. The extant schema seems a later and much abbreviated handbook synthesis, which would also explain how the awkwardly positioned definition of *epistēmē* could have slipped in.[17]

The discussion so far might make it appear as if dialectic was *the* logical virtue. This is, however, not entirely accurate. While 'dialectic' could be used in a broad sense to signify the whole field of logic, there is also a more limited understanding of dialectic according to which it is only a part of logic. The other part is rhetoric, for even rhetoric was considered a virtue by the Stoics. Defined as the '*epistēmē* of talking well' and the '*epistēmē* of talking correctly', rhetoric seems to have played an integrative role, combining the practical ability to deliver perfect orations with the perfection of the character of the orator. One of our main witnesses, Quintilian, explicitly ascribes this understanding of rhetoric to Chrysippus who seems to have followed Cleanthes' lead.[18] According to Quintilian, Chrysippus brought out different aspects of rhetorical virtue in other definitions,[19] but we do not have information on whether or not he recognized specific subordinated rhetorical virtues, systematized in the same style as the ethical virtues.

As to physics, our evidence is once more quite limited. We have no material whose significance equals *De finibus* 3.73. *De finibus* 3.73 argues that physics is an indispensable virtue since living according to nature is dependent on knowing the rational order of the world, created and maintained by the divine principle. The passage portrays humans as being allotted a specific position in the order of creation. By studying nature, human beings learn to understand their place in nature and with it also how they should act.[20] But not only is the study of physics imbued with theological motifs; it is also presented as a pivotal preparation or ingredient of an accurate theology and good religious practice.[21] However, important as the passage is, it does not provide information in respect of our present questions of whether or not physics was considered a *generic* virtue, and if so, which virtues were subordinated to it. Other texts do not allow us to settle the question with any certainty: for instance, in a curious passage (*De ebrietate* 88–92), Philo of Alexandria describes that the sage's wisdom will also show in fields like meteorology.[22] However, the *De ebrietate* passage does not allow us to determine if meteorology was considered a virtue which is subordinated to physics or rather a quality which is not itself a virtue but still betrays the unique grasp of the sage (if he chooses to devote himself to the kind of theorizing that meteorology is about).

Reviewing the results so far, we can conclude that the Stoics recognized *non-ethical* virtues in addition to the *ethical* virtues listed in the Chrysippean catalogue in Pseudo-Andronicus and Stobaeus. The additional virtues belong to the other two disciplinary fields of Stoic philosophy, namely logic and physics. As a part of logical virtue, rhetoric was considered a virtue, and the evidence allows us to trace the status of rhetoric as a virtue back to Chrysippus. We have no evidence as to whether rhetoric was considered a generic virtue with several more specific virtues subordinate to it. As regards the other part of logic, dialectic was considered a generic virtue with several subordinate virtues. It is likely that Chrysippus proposed a schema of dialectical virtue(s), but it seems that the schema we have in Diogenes Laertius 7.46–8 is the result of later additions or reformulations. Physics was considered a virtue as well, but the jury must remain out on the question whether or not it was conceived as a generic virtue with several virtues subordinate to it.

The whole schema of virtues in the three fields of Stoic philosophy powerfully brings home an intellectualistic conception of virtue as knowledge. The ethical and non-ethical virtues are closely connected: in order to know what to do, the agent has to know the place in nature allotted to human beings. The agent needs dialectical virtue in order to deal correctly with his impressions and attain correct judgements. And the ability to talk well or correctly presupposes the perfection of the agent's character.

Having established that a number of non-ethical (generic) virtues were recognized both by Chrysippus and by other Stoics, it is an intriguing question to ask why the additional virtues were not listed in the Chrysippean catalogue in Stobaeus and Pseudo-Andronicus. Simply to say that the doxographers to whose work we owe the Chrysippean catalogue focused on ethics will not do, since in the Stoic view the additional virtues are clearly relevant to the possession of the ethical virtues.

Even if the answer must remain speculative, it is attractive to attribute the exclusion of the non-ethical virtues to the context in which the virtue catalogue seems to have been drawn up by Chrysippus. In Stobaeus' report, Chrysippus' virtue catalogue is reproduced in the context of a discussion of the togetherness of, and difference between, the virtues (2.63.6–67.4).[23] Chrysippus' theory of the unity and difference of the virtues was a pivotal element in his attempt to steer the interpretation of Zeno's virtue theory free from Aristo's unitarian virtue theory.[24] However, if the correct interpretation of Zeno's theory was at stake, then it is likely that Chrysippus detailed his view by drawing up a catalogue of the different specific virtues subordinate to the four ethical virtues recognized by Zeno, but that Chrysippus would have left out virtues which he himself recognized but which were not at issue in the struggle against Aristo's theory.

The Openness of Chrysippus' Catalogue of Virtues

Was the Chrysippean catalogue of virtues 'closed', a definitive complete list, or was it an open one which allowed additions? It has been suggested that the number of virtues in Chrysippus' catalogue was fixed and the catalogue thus a closed one, reflecting the 'harmonics' of Stoic virtues.[25] This, however, seems quite unlikely. Not only do the numbers of subordinate virtues fail to show a clear pattern,[26] but the claim that the Chrysippean catalogue is a closed one does not square with other evidence.

Plutarch criticizes Chrysippus as follows (*De virtute morali* 441B, trans. Helmbold, modified):

> But Chrysippus, invoking the 'qualified' and claiming that a virtue is constituted by its own quality, unwittingly stirred up a 'swarm of virtues', as Plato has it, which were not familiar nor even known; for as from the adjective 'courageous' he derived courage, from 'mild' mildness and justice from 'just', so from 'charming' he derived charmingnesses, from 'virtuous' virtuousnesses, from 'honourable' honourablenesses, postulating also the other qualities of the same sort, dexterousnesses, approachablenesses, adroitnesses, as virtues, and thus filled philosophy, which needed nothing of the sort, with many absurd names.

Quite independent of its questionable worth as an accurate report of Chrysippean virtues, Plutarch's polemic certainly indicates that Chrysippus pursued the strategy of deriving virtues from adjectives signalling laudable characteristics of the agent. Plutarch's switch to the use of plural forms ('charmingnesses' etc.) is an important hint. It is, of course, a rhetorical device to mark his contempt, but a valuable one for our present concerns. I suggest that the use of plural forms reflects Plutarch's disdain for what he perceives to be an extremely messy 'list'—if indeed he would have chosen to call it a list—of virtues recognized by Chrysippus. Like a swarm of bees, new and unknown virtues seem to fly in and out, confusing the reader's sense of order and stability. Plutarch's polemic, in short, is a clear indication that the list of virtues recognized by Chrysippus was far more open to the inclusion of new virtues than the seemingly definite shape of the virtue catalogue reproduced in Pseudo-Andronicus and Stobaeus could induce us to believe.

However, Chrysippus did not consider every laudable characteristic of the sage to be a virtue. There are characteristics fully possessed only by the sage, which are not *epistēmai* and thus not virtues. This is the case with a class of distinguished techniques, the so-called 'pursuits' (ἐπιτηδεύματα). While not full-blown *epistēmai* themselves, they play an important role in the acquisition of the virtues, even if only the sage possesses them fully.[27] Since the full possession of such characteristics was considered to be exclusive to the sage, they play an important role in Stoic descriptions of him. Their occurrence in exalting characterizations of the sage, where they stand alongside virtue terms, makes it extremely difficult if not impossible to distinguish which characterizations were meant as virtues and which characterizations were merely other laudable qualities exclusive to him. The lengthy characterizations of the sage in Stobaeus are a case in point, and a modern reader cannot help feeling that even among the Stoics the boundary between virtues and other characteristics exclusive to the sage was not always clear or uncontroversial. The key considerations in placing a characteristic on either side of the boundary must have been the perceived centrality of a characteristic to the best human life as well as the number of theoretical concerns connected with it. Inevitably, such considerations would have differed between the Stoics. We still find traces of all that in Stobaeus, perhaps most prominently at 2.67.13–68.17, immediately after a discussion of pursuits. At the beginning of the passage, five characteristics exclusive to the sage are enumerated: Only the sage is a good prophet, poet, rhetorician, dialectician and critic. Whereas the context of the passage seems to indicate that all of these abilities are thought of as pursuits, two of them (rhetoric and dialectic) are presented as virtues elsewhere (see above). However, straying from the outline of the discussion offered at the beginning, the remainder of the passage discusses in fact four (partly different) qualities exclusive to the sage: the abilities to be a prophet, to be a priest, to be holy and to carry out religious rites. Again, while the context makes the reader expect that all four qualities are pursuits, the first of them is characterized in the style of a Chrysippean virtue: *mantikē* is the 'theoretical *epistēmē* of signs from gods or demons having an application to human life', embracing several subdisciplines (or subordinate virtues). However, to regard *mantikē* as an *epistēmē* (and hence, presumably, also as a virtue) was not the only stance taken in the Stoic school, since *mantikē* is listed explicitly as a 'pursuit' in a later passage (at 2.71.3).

Such inconsistencies show that the boundary between virtues and non-virtue characteristics exclusive to the sage was unclear or controversial. The lack of clarity or unanimity enabled different Stoics to inscribe their own views on the relative centrality of human qualities into the list of Stoic virtues. The hodgepodge appearance of much of the characterization of the sage that we find, for instance, in Stobaeus shows that ample use was made of this possibility. Unfortunately, more often than not there is no knowing whose views are reflected in the definition and praise of a particular quality of the sage. For instance, at Stobaeus 2.65.15–66.13 the following four virtues are ascribed to the sage (to illustrate the thesis that the sage acts on the basis of all the virtues): discretion (νουνέχεια), dialectic (διαλεκτική), conviviality (συμποτική) and erotic virtue (ἐρωτική). As we have seen above, discretion made part of Chrysippus' table of ethical virtues and it is likely that he recognized dialectic as a virtue. However, in the schema of dialectical virtues (see above) we found clear evidence for a process of enlargement or reformulation of the Chrysippean conception. Such a process is also evident in the discussions of conviviality and erotic virtue in our Stobaeus passage.[28] The beginning of the discussion of erotic virtue is marked by a reflection on the label 'erotic man', in effect amounting to no more than a distinction between a positive and a negative meaning of this label. Two definitions of erotic virtue are offered, but only after a brief interlude on conviviality, a virtue apparently closely related to erotic virtue. Conviviality is defined as an *epistēmē*. As it is about the behaviour appropriate at a symposium, it is said to be the *epistēmē* of 'how one should run symposia and how one should drink at them'.[29] While the definition could stem from Chrysippus, we have no clear proof that in fact it does stem from him. Moreover, of the scarce mentions of conviviality in the sources at least one shows that the differentiation between virtues and other characteristics exclusive to the sage was not always clear.[30]

Erotic virtue is defined as the *epistēmē* of 'hunting for well-bred young men, preparing them for what is in agreement with virtue'[31] and, more broadly, as the *epistēmē* of 'loving in a good way'. Erotic love occupied a central place in Zeno's Republican political thought, as Schofield has shown. Erotic love had the educational function of raising young people of promise to virtue. Erotic love would have secured the concord in the city and thus its security from internal strife. While erotic love characterized the sage's role in the asymmetrical relation to the progressing young people of promise, the relationships among sages are characterized by friendship, *philia*.[32]

The definitions of erotic love in Stobaeus clearly square Chrysippus' other definitions of virtues as *epistēmai*, and it is therefore attractive to picture him as their author. Perhaps Chrysippus attempted to capture Zeno's emphasis on erotic love and to integrate it in his schema of virtues. All this, however, is speculation. There is no guarantee that Chrysippus himself proposed the two definitions. The end of the Stobaeus passage points, in connection with other evidence, to a broad discussion within the Stoic school of erotic love and it may well be that the definitions stem from a later author who was emulating Chrysippus' definitions.[33]

Thus we cannot trace the recognition of conviviality and erotic virtue unequivocally to Chrysippus or to any other specific Stoic. We should not be too concerned about it. As the example of dialectical virtue shows, we should rather see the extant lists of virtues as a collective Stoic enterprise, as a process of continuous enlargement and reformulation of a Chrysippean (and, ultimately, Zenonian) nucleus. With the far-reaching flexibility of his recognition of virtues, Chrysippus laid the foundations for successive generations of Stoic philosophers to extend and reformulate his systematization of the virtues a Stoic should acknowledge.[34]

Part Three

Becoming Virtuous

Chapter 8

Vice and the Attainability of Virtue

This part examines Stoic accounts of how to become virtuous. Chapter 8 asks how virtue is attainable in principle, since by the enormously demanding standards of the Stoics it is an extremely rare possession—if it is ever realized at all. A pivotal role in arguing in general terms that virtue is attainable was played by the Stoic theory of 'appropriation' (οἰκείωσις). Chapters 9 and 10 analyse the religious language employed by the Stoics in describing the acquisition and possession of virtue. Chapter 9 studies the Stoic outline of the philosophical training necessary to acquire virtue and in particular the description of theological training as 'initiation', whereas Chapter 10 analyses descriptions of the possession of virtue as taking God's point of view. I suggest (and shall elaborate further in Part Four) that this religious outlook is the key element in the Stoic theory of virtue as knowledge. The precedence of the religious outlook can help to explain why wherever Stoic accounts of virtuous practice tackle more specific problems, they point to a surprising versatility and contentiousness without endangering the unity of the Stoic school.

The analyses in Part Two—of the Stoic characterizations of virtue, the definitions of the specific virtues and the thesis that the possession of, and action in agreement with, the specific virtues is an all-or-nothing affair—have made it abundantly clear that the Stoics set high the standards for the possession of virtue. Accordingly, the Stoics held that virtue was an extremely rare possession. Hardly anyone, perhaps even no human being, had ever been a sage.[1] The Stoics were not even prepared to claim that one of the foremost members of their own school deserved this title.[2] Furthermore, for the Stoics there was no intermediate state between virtue and vice (κακία): a sharp dichotomy separates the wise and the vicious.[3] Whereas the possession of virtue is tantamount to happiness, the possession of vice makes an agent utterly unhappy.[4] The Stoics describe the vicious with insulting terms: they are 'stupid', 'foolish', 'impious', 'lawless', or even 'mad'.[5]

The contrast between virtue and vice becomes particularly visible in characterizations of vice as 'lack of knowledge' (ἄγνοια)[6] and as 'tenor or character which is inconsistent in the whole of life and out of harmony with itself (*habitus aut adfectio in tota vita inconstans et a se ipsa dissentiens*)',[7] which are obviously analogous to the standard definitions of virtue. The contrast between virtue and vice was marked even further by tables of *generic vices* and more specific *subordinate vices* which were designed in analogy to the Chrysippean schema of ethical virtues.[8] Moreover, the Stoics held that all vices are equal,[9] and that whoever has one vice, has all the vices and that the fool acts in accordance with all vices.[10]

The Stoic dichotomy between virtue and vice is not easily understood. Its black-and-white radicalism, which seems to relinquish the grey 'middle ground' of moral progress, piqued the Stoics' ancient critics.[11] We should nevertheless, resist the temptation to tone down or limit the contrast between virtue and vice.[12] The evidence points rather to the Stoics' *playing up* the contrast between virtue and vice by choosing the least conciliatory formulations imaginable. For instance, the definition of vice quoted above is 'a tenor or character which is inconsistent in the whole of life and out of harmony with itself'. Less antagonizing ways of conceiving the contrast are readily available: why not 'a habit or disposition *not entirely* consistent and in harmony throughout life'? An explanation for the particularly stark way of formulating the contrast has been sought in the Stoics' insistence that '"to act rightly" means *always* to act in accordance with *orthos logos*'. Thus, one failure would be 'sufficient to falsify the "always"'.[13] This explanation, however, will not do. The maximizing radicalism of the characterization of vice ('*throughout life* inconsistent and out of harmony with itself') indicates that a quantitative assessment—the frequent, occasional or even single failure to act rightly—was not what interested the Stoics primarily; on the contrary, the emphasis must have been put on how (in what 'frame of mind') something is done.[14] This is consistent with the fact that it was the 'how' side of human action which marked for Chrysippus the pivotal difference between virtue and vice.[15]

I want to suggest here that the Stoic dichotomy between virtue and vice is informed by a religious conception of virtue as knowledge. The possession of virtue is linked to taking a unique perspective, namely God's perspective on the world. If something can be seen from one position only, then approximation to that position brings us closer to seeing that thing, but nevertheless we cannot see it until we have taken that position. This renders understandable why the Stoics viewed the possession of virtue as an all-or-nothing affair and maximized the contrast between virtue and vice: one either takes that unique position and sees completely or one does not take it and in consequence does not see things 'straight'. Moreover, the claim that all vices are equal is understandable against the background of this religious conception: in failing to take the divine perspective, all vices are expressive of the same fault, and are equally expressive of the corruption of the agent's rationality. Likewise, if happiness consists in taking the divine standpoint, then not having taken it means that one is unhappy, however far advanced one is on the way towards taking that standpoint.

While a detailed defence of this interpretation must be deferred to Chapter 10, two obvious problems for the Stoic position can already be discussed in the remainder of this chapter. The first is the need to account for the presence of vice in a world which the Stoics claimed to be benevolently administered by God. The second problem is the need for a theory as to how, in the face of extremely high Stoic standards for virtue and the consequent rarity of the sage, human beings can become virtuous at all.

The Stoics attempted to solve the first problem by arguing that nature provides the newborn with starting points sufficient for the acquisition of virtue. If human beings turn out bad, as they in fact do, this must be ascribed to corrupting influences outside the original design of nature.

At the beginning of their lives, newborn human beings are not in a state of vice. As a defect of rationality, vice presupposes that the vicious agent has developed reason. Since young children are not yet rational, the initial state that human beings are in is not a state of vice and therefore not bad.[16] By nature human beings are designed for the acquisition of virtue: man has the natural inclination to develop perfect rationality and thus to become virtuous.[17] However, the development of perfect reason—which would happen if everything went according to nature's design—is interfered with by corrupting influences from the outside.[18] Nature, the Stoics held, cannot be blamed for that.[19]

In order to confirm the goodness of nature's starting points, and thereby the benevolent design of the divinity, Chrysippus named two corrupting factors: the deceptiveness of things and the teachings of other people.[20] These two factors are presented in more detail in Calcidius' *Commentary on Plato's Timaeus*, where it is explained that the Stoics proposed a theory of two corrupting influences, one 'from things themselves' (*ex rebus ipsis*), the other 'from dissemination' (*ex divulgatione*).[21] The corrupting influences 'from things themselves' begins as early as immediately after birth. Newborn babies acutely feel the change from the warm and humid womb of the mother to the dry and cold air to which they are exposed. The customary remedy to immerse newborn children into warm water to counteract the temperature shock induces the belief that unpleasant things are bad and pleasant things are good. An example of the corrupting influence 'from dissemination' is that wrong ideas are passed on by mothers and nurses.

These two factors induce human beings not to follow the inclinations towards virtue given by nature.[22] Instead, human beings regard pleasure and things productive of pleasure as (the) good. Corrupted by the two factors, human beings are guided in their choices by pleasure.[23]

The Stoics' claim that pleasure is not the end intended by nature, but that mistaking it for the end is the result of a corrupted human development, had to be backed up by an analysis of what (if not pleasure) was the uncorrupted starting point of human development. This analysis was given with the wide-ranging Stoic theory of 'appropriation' (οἰκείωσις).[24] I cannot discuss the details of the theory of *oikeiōsis* here, and have to restrict the following short remarks to its import on the general accessibility of virtue.[25] The theory of *oikeiōsis* explains that nature appropriates every animal to its own constitution, so that the animal 'rejects what is harmful and accepts what is appropriate'.[26] The first impulse is thus directed towards self-preservation but not towards pleasure. Pleasure is only a by-product of the adequate state an animal is in. The important thing is that the object of appropriation changes during the development. This is particularly visible in the case of human beings, whose first impulse is directed towards self-preservation (in a very limited way, of course, owing to the limited abilities of the newborn). However, the development of reason changes the maturing human being's constitution. Several of our sources emphasize the transformative role of reason. At Diogenes Laertius 7.86, for instance, reason is said to 'supervene as the craftsman of impulse' (τεχνίτης . . . τῆς ὁρμῆς).[27]

When human beings acquire reason at a certain age, the appropriation is directed towards the altered constitution of a rational being: rationality now shapes the impulses and thus transcends the narrowly confined sphere of self-preservation. That the egocentricity of self-preservation can and must be transcended (or at least reduced) is also underlined by the famous Stoic simile of the concentric circles. In the second century AD the Stoic philosopher Hierocles, to whom we owe the simile, described individuals as encompassed by concentric circles which contain—in declining degree of supposed closeness—the individual's own body and bodily concerns, and different groups of relatives, local residents, fellow-tribesmen, fellow-citizens, members from neighbouring towns, fellow-countrymen and the whole human race. The individual should attempt to 'contract' the circles and to promote those from a more distant circle to a nearer one.[28]

While these accounts of *oikeiōsis* seem to describe to some extent not what is in fact going on in ordinary human beings, but an exceptional process which should take place (or in fact does take place) during the acquisition of virtue, it is still clear that the texts attempt to show the acquisition of virtue to be possible in principle.

The acquisition of virtue is dependent on the interplay of natural talent and conscious efforts to acquire the knowledge that virtue consists in. This is stressed, for instance, in an illuminating comparison between the Aristotelian and Stoic concepts of virtue (*Anecdota graeca* = SVF 3.214):

> Aristotle [thought that human beings become virtuous] by nature (φύσει), by habit (ἔθει) and by reason (λόγῳ); and so also the Stoics, since virtue is a technique (τέχνη). Every technique is a system of theorems acquired by training. Concerning the theorems, there is reason involved; concerning training, habit; and by nature we are all created to acquire virtue, insofar as we have impulses . . . [which lead us towards virtue].

The attempt made in this text to assimilate a Chrysippean intellectualistic concept of virtue to the framework of Aristotelian moral philosophy certainly introduces elements alien to the early Stoics. The differentiation between reason and habit in particular has its proper place in the context of Aristotelian (and Platonic) moral psychologies that acknowledge the existence of different parts or functions of the soul. There, habituation was needed to render an independent emotive part or function of the soul subservient to the rational part or function. In the context of the Chrysippean monistic moral psychology this differentiation between reason and habituation does not make sense. Reason is developed by means of training, which consists in the acquisition of a systematically organized system of cognitions.[29] Yet habituation, and with it sustained effort, does play a role in the Stoic as well as in the Aristotelian conception of virtue. In the case of Stoic virtue, habituation is conceived as the perfection of human reason. Accordingly, Chrysippus as well as other Stoics emphasized that virtue 'can be taught'. In fact, the teachability of virtue was a standard ingredient of Stoic ethics, as the wide array of names listed in Diogenes Laertius shows:

> That it, virtue, can be taught is laid down by Chrysippus in the first book of his work O*n the End*, by Cleanthes, by Posidonius in his *Protreptica*, and by Hecato; that it can be taught is clear from the case of bad men becoming good.[30]

In addition to the agent's conscious efforts, natural talents were held to play a role in the acquisition of virtues, but it is difficult to gather from the sources exactly how important this role was. Since human beings were held to have a natural tendency towards virtue and to possess certain yardsticks for truth, the necessary starting points should be within everybody's reach in principle.[31] The multifarious abilities, however, which would be needed to put these starting points to adequate use and to successfully pursue a long and strenuous training were certainly considered to be far scarcer. A short passage in Stobaeus indicates that there was some disagreement among the Stoics as to how far natural giftedness was indispensable and in how far training could make up for deficiencies of talent:

> As to natural ability and noble birth, some members of this [the Stoic] school were led to say that every wise man is endowed with these attributes; but others were not. For some think that men are not only endowed with a natural ability for virtue by nature, but also that some are such by training, and they accepted this proverbial saying: 'practice, when aged by time, turns into nature.' And they made the same supposition about noble birth, so that natural ability is a condition congenial to virtue which comes from nature or training, or a condition by which certain men are prone to acquire virtue readily. And noble birth is a condition congenial to virtue which comes from birth or training.[32]

The key issue behind this debate was presumably the attempt to combine two stories which inevitably counteracted each other: on the one hand, the Stoics wanted to stress the enormously high standards of virtue and the consequent rarity of the sage; on the other hand, they wanted to maintain that virtue was accessible in principle and that their invitation to embark on the path to virtue was not vain.

Chapter 9

Initiation

According to Galen, Chrysippus never offered a concrete plan for the education necessary for the acquisition of virtue and 'did not even leave his successors a starting point for investigation'.[1] This remark seems grossly unfair, however, given the well-attested efforts of Chrysippus and other Stoics to theorize the attainability of virtue. Moreover, in the sources we find evidence of Stoic discussions on the philosophical curriculum. In this chapter I analyse Chrysippus' ideas on the philosophical curriculum in general, and in particular I analyse the religious language employed by Chrysippus to describe the crowning role of theology in the Stoic curriculum.

The fullest statement of Chrysippus' ideas on the philosophical curriculum is Plutarch's *Stoic. rep.* 1035A–D (trans. Cherniss, modified):

Chrysippus thinks that young men should hear lectures on logic first, on ethics next, and after that on physics and should get theology last as the termination for these studies. He says this in many places, but it will suffice to quote the statement in the fourth book on *Ways of Living*, which runs word for word as follows: 'Now I believe in the first place, conformably with the correct statements of the ancients, that the philosopher's speculations are of three kinds, logical, ethical, and physical; then that of these the logical must be put first, the ethical second, and the physical third; and that of physical speculations theology must be last, which is why its transmissions have also been called *teletai*.' Yet this very doctrine, theology, which he says must be put last he habitually puts first and makes the preface to every ethical enquiry, for it is plain to see that, be the subject goals or justice or good and evil or marriage and child-rearing or law and government, he makes no remark about it at all unless in the same fashion in which the movers of public decrees prefix the phrase 'Good Fortune' he has prefixed Zeus, Destiny, Providence and the statement that the universe, being one and finite, is held together by a single power—none of which can carry any conviction for anyone who has not been thoroughly steeped in physical theory. Hear what he says about this in the third book *On the Gods*: 'It is not possible to discover any other beginning of justice or any source for it other than that from Zeus and from the universal nature, for thence everything of the kind must have its beginning if we are going to have anything to say about good and evil.' Again in his *Physical Propositions* he says: 'For there is no other or more suitable way of approaching the theory of good and evil or the virtues or happiness [than] from the universal nature and from the dispensation of the universe.' And further on once more: 'For the theory of good and evil must be connected with these, since good and evil have no better beginning or point of reference and physical speculation is to be undertaken for no other purpose than for the discrimination of good and evil.' According to Chrysippus, then, physical theory turns out to be 'at once before and behind' ethics, or rather the whirligig of the arrangement is utterly bewildering if the former must be placed after the latter, no part of which can be grasped without it; and the inconsistency is obvious in the man who, while asserting that physics is the beginning of the theory about good and evil, still orders it to be taught not before but after the latter. Still, Chrysippus, it may be said, in the treatise on *Use of Discourse* has written that one taking up logic as the first subject is not to abstain altogether from the rest but is to take such part of them also as opportunity offers.

Plutarch claims that Chrysippus advocated and practised the teaching of philosophy in the order logic, ethics and physics, with theology as the crowning part of physics. Interestingly, we find Chrysippus credited with a different curricular order in Diogenes Laertius. Diogenes reports (7.39) that the differentiation of the three disciplines physics, ethics and logic in the Stoic school went back to its founder Zeno, and was, as Diogenes shows by mentioning a whole list of names, generally accepted within the Stoic school. Diogenes continues (7.40, trans. Hicks):

Philosophy, they say, is like an animal, logic corresponding to the bones and sinews, ethics to the fleshy parts, physics to the soul. Another simile they use is that of an egg: the shell is logic; next comes the white, ethics; and the yolk in the centre is physics. Or, again, they liken philosophy to a fertile field: logic being the encircling fence, ethics the crop, physics the soil or the trees. (. . .) No single part, some Stoics declare, is independent of any other part, but all blend together. Nor was it usual to teach them separately. Others, however, start their course with logic, go on to physics, and finish with ethics; and among those who so do are Zeno in his treatise *On Exposition*, Chrysippus, Archedemus and Eudromus.

We should not attach too much value to Diogenes' report. It is not only inconsistent—the examples unwittingly support the order 'logic, ethics, physics', which makes one suspect that this was the received Stoic order after all—but also Diogenes' primary interest seems to have been to show that some Stoics, among them Zeno and Chrysippus, supported a curriculum in which the three parts of philosophy were taught separately and consecutively. The actual sequence of subjects taught, however, seems to have been of lesser interest to Diogenes, and it appears that he did not bother to verify his account. It is possible that the sequence 'logic, physics, ethics' stems from Zeno, whose treatise *On Exposition* is mentioned, but it is by no means certain.

As far as Chrysippus is concerned, we should follow Plutarch's report. Plutarch specifically targets Chrysippus and supports his case by quotations from specific publications of his opponent. Although one has to allow for *some* polemical distortion as far as fundamental philosophical tenets are concerned, one can surely trust him on minor, purely factual points like the order of the Stoic curriculum. Another point in question is Plutarch's claim that Chrysippus required theology to be taught last, but at the same time 'puts [it] first and makes [it] the preface to every ethical inquiry'. As far as the report goes, this seems a well-informed and accurate statement of Chrysippus' idea about the place of theology in the Stoic curriculum as well as of the structure of Chrysippus' ethical treatises. Polemic distortion only gains the upper hand when Plutarch draws from it the conclusion that Chrysippus is guilty of inconsistency. Plutarch ignores the pivotal difference between the systematic structure of philosophical argument and the pedagogically optimal sequence of philosophical subjects, which the continuation of Plutarch's report suggests as a more benevolent way of understanding Chrysippus: Plutarch notes (*Stoic. rep.* 1035E) that Chrysippus declared in his work on the *Use of Discourse* that 'one taking up logic as the first subject is not to abstain altogether from the rest but is to take such part of them also as opportunity offers' (κατὰ τὸ διδόμενον). This suggests that Chrysippus was concerned with the pedagogically optimal ordering of subjects in teaching philosophy, but not with the optimal systematic arrangement of the arguments. While upholding the disciplinary sequence of logic, ethics and physics, Chrysippus advocated showing the systematic interconnection between the subjects by teaching, for instance, *capita selecta* of ethics and physics already in the course on logic.

The systematically most adequate structure of Stoic philosophy was an entirely different matter. Chrysippus did not tire of pressing the point that ethics is dependent on *theological* doctrines: according to Plutarch, he invariably introduced his ethical treatises with theological statements (*Stoic. rep.* 1035B) and was convinced that ethical reasoning has to begin with a reflection on Zeus and universal nature (*Stoic. rep.* 1035C). Plutarch's para- phrases and quotations prove that Chrysippus was convinced that ethical doctrines must be systematically established on the basis of *theological* doctrines. Chrysippus identified the constitutive role of a divine *pneuma*, the divine providential administration of the world and determinism—in short: the theological world-view explored in the first part of this book—as systematic basis of ethics. This squares with the role of physics as a virtue analysed in Chapter 7. I shall say more on the foundational role of the Stoics' theological world-view for their more specific ethical precepts in Chapter 11.[2] In the remainder of this chapter I shall analyse the import of religion for the acquisition of virtue by another route.

At *Stoic. rep.* 1035B, Plutarch attributes to Chrysippus the characterization of theological teaching as *teletai* (the plural of *teletē*): Chrysippus claimed 'that of physical speculations theology must be last, which is why its transmissions have also been called *teletai*'. This is repeated a little later, when Plutarch unfolds his critique in more detail: 'Chrysippus is at odds with himself here in ordering theology to be taken up as last and terminal, on the ground that for this reason it is called *teletē* also, and elsewhere again saying that part of this too should be taken along with the first subjects' (1035E, trans. Cherniss, modified). So far I have left the transcribed Greek words untranslated, because they contain a wordplay.

The noun *teletē* is connected with *telos* and the verb *telein*. Taken straight- forwardly, *teletē* could be translated as 'fulfilment', 'completion' or 'end'. As a subject which was taught last[3] and completed the education by offering the foundational doctrines for ethical treatises, theology could justly be called *teletē*. Yet, the word *teletē* would also have, apart from this straight- forward meaning, a specific religious meaning in the Greek of Chrysippus' as well as of Plutarch's times. Whilst the word originally denoted the fulfil- ment of religious duties and the performance of rites,[4] it was used in a more specific meaning from the fifth century onwards, namely 'with special reference to the initiatory parts of mysteries or to initiation in general'[5] and with reference to the Eleusinian mysteries in particular.[6] That Chrysippus used the word *teletē* in the specific meaning of 'initiation into mystery cults' is suggested in the anonymous twelfth century *Etymologicum magnum*. According to the lemma on *teletē*,

> Chrysippus says that the theological doctrines are rightly called *teletai* because one uses them last (τελευταίους) and they are taught on top of everything else, when the soul commands of support and has achieved self-control and is able to keep silence against the non-initiated. For it is a big privilege to hear, and master, correct teachings about the gods.[7]

So far, this is not novel; a plethora of commentators has observed as much.[8] What I propose to do here is to follow this hint further than has so far been done and to show what the allusion to mystery cults would mean against the background of ancient religious practice.[9]

Ancient mystery cults, for all their diversity, can perhaps best be typified as forms of 'personal religion, depending on a private decision and aiming at some form of salvation through closeness to the divine'.[10] Within the framework of ancient polytheistic civic cults, which were for a good part governed by social expectations, mystery cults were an area of individual, 'optional activity', comparable to what nowadays is 'a pilgrimage to Santiago di Compostela within the Christian system'.[11] The Eleusinian mysteries, dedicated to Demeter and Kore (Persephone) were the oldest among the mystery cults.[12] The age, but also the 'untouchable purity of the cult' and surely also the dominant cultural position of Athens, where the cult was located, determined its fame.[13] The rough outlines of what happened at the Eleusinian mysteries are described by Jan Bremmer as follows:

> After a procession from Athens to Eleusis along the (still existing) Sacred Way and more individual rites of fasting and purification, the climax of the ritual took place collectively in the main building, the *telestērion*. Here, at night, the hierophant showed 'a single harvested ear of grain' and called out at the top of his voice: 'the Mistress has given birth to a holy child, Brimo to Brimos'. The mention of the corn ear seems to confirm Isocrates' words that Demeter was well disposed towards Attica 'because of benefits which only the initiated may hear' (*Panegyr.* 28). It also suggests that the mysteries did not conceal an esoteric wisdom. In fact, the *Homeric Hymn to Demeter*, the oldest source (late seventh century BC) to relate the institution of the mysteries by Demeter during her search for her kidnapped daughter, explains the secrecy from the 'awesomeness' of the rites and states that 'a great reverence of the gods restrains utterance'

(478f.). The *Homeric Hymn to Demeter* singles out two gains for initiates: prosperity in this life and a blessed state in the life hereafter (480–9).[14]

I suggest that the traits of an initiation into a mystery cult provide an important standard of comparison with Stoic characterizations of the role of theological teaching. The following similarities are particularly striking:

1. The Eleusinian and most other mystery cults did not restrict admission to a class or sex.[15] Also the Stoic school was open to all.
2. The initiation is prepared and completed by the transmission of knowledge: 'Speech, *logos*, had an important role to play, and the injunction "not to tell" the uninitiated was taken so seriously because verbalization was central to the proceedings.'[16] Likewise, the transmission of knowledge, and in particular theological knowledge, was the central activity of Stoic philosophical training leading to virtue. The Stoic lecture theatre was effectively the philosophical counterpart of the hall of initiation, the *telestērion*.
3. At first sight, the mention of secrecy seems difficult to place. Stoic teaching was—as far as we know—conducted publicly and without any secrecy. However, the mysteries' demand of secrecy in respect of the uninitiated did not serve to exclude a specific group (see 1), but emphasized rather the commitment necessary to obtain initiation. Likewise, in the context of Stoic philosophy the learner's commitment would have been thought necessary. In addition, the demand of secrecy would have served to stress the comparative difficulty of acquiring the necessary knowledge.[17]
4. A certain dissimilarity seems to lie in the fact that the *logoi* in the mysteries would not have taken the form of systematic theological reasoning,[18] whereas Stoic theology, of course, was a systematic, argumentative enterprise. However, we shall see below (Ch. 10) that Cicero's account suggests that the acquisition of virtue crucially relied on a change in perspective, on taking the divine point of view. In many ways, this change would have stood closer to a religious experience than to doctrinal theological teaching.
5. The purpose of initiation was a happy and successful life by divine protection as well as a blessed afterlife.[19] The initiates were to lose, also by the ritual enacting of terrible situations, the natural fear of death.[20] Generally, the initiates learned to put common human anxieties at a distance and could therefore be called happy.[21] For the Stoics, the possession of virtue was tantamount to being happy. The sage does not

have fear or other unreasonable emotions and is the exclusive owner of certain characteristics: for instance, the sage is the only wealthy person.

6. The cults were also intended to have a 'moral impact'. The initiated were to promise to abjure evil as a condition of initiation.[22] Likewise, Stoic philosophical training, crowned by the discipline of theology, was intended to provide a stable foundation to the precepts, with right action as an invariable consequence of knowledge.[23]

7. The cults attempted to achieve 'closeness to the divine' and even—at least in the case of the Bacchic cult as witnessed by the so-called 'Thurii gold leaves'—apotheosis.[24] This was an inner change that—far more than any doctrinal teaching—determined the self-perception of the initiated.[25] Closeness to the divine was also the focus of Stoic ethics. The sage was elatedly described as being a companion of the gods, as God-like, and even as taking the divine point of view.[26]

8. The people who received initiation together were considered a community. The term 'brother' was used among fellow initiates.[27] The close circle of initiates and their common closeness to the divine resembles the close connection between gods and sages postulated by the Stoics. The closeness to the divine and close connection between gods and sages received vivid expression in the Stoic simile of the 'cosmic city', a community of gods and sages.[28]

So far, our comparison between the initiation into ancient mystery cults and the role of theological teaching for Stoic ethics has shown a number of striking structural similarities. In the next chapter I shall elaborate the analysis of the fourth trait included (perhaps surprisingly) in the above list of structural similarities. Initiation is more than the reception of doctrines, it is at root a personal experience leading to an inner change. I shall argue in more detail that a comparable trait played a key role in Stoic virtue theory. The religious language used to describe the sage's *eudaimonia* suggests that a change of perspective, coming to share God's perspective on the world was a pivotal ingredient of the Stoic conception of virtue as knowledge.[29]

Chapter 10

Virtue and Happiness

The ancient mystery cults were by no means unique in attempting to achieve a 'closeness to the divine' and even apotheosis. Metaphors like drawing close to the gods, being a companion of the gods, and becoming like God occur in a number of ancient philosophical authors, with Plato as a particularly rich source.[1]

In the *Phaedrus*, in a language imbued by the terminology of mystery cults, the philosopher is cast as role model for those wishing to imitate the divine. Only the philosopher grasps the ultimate idea-realities and is thereby 'alone [among men] truly perfect' (τέλεος ὄντως μόνος γίγνεται: 249C). The sight of the idea-realities forms the 'highest form of initiation' (τελέους ἀεὶ τελετὰς τελούμενος: 249C). This state is described as *eudaimonia* and is further characterized as 'standing above human concerns' (ἐξιστάμενος . . . τῶν ἀνθρωπίνων: 249C–D) and as 'being travel-companion of a god' (θεῷ συνοπαδός: 248C; ψυχὴ συμπορευθεῖσα θεῷ: 249C) and 'drawing close to the divine' (πρὸς τῷ θείῳ γιγνόμενος: 249D). Although Plato's formulations imply a closeness, a companionship between man and the divine, there remains a marked gap between man and the gods: only the gods have an unimpeded and effortless sight of the idea-realities, taking 'their stand on the high ridge of heaven, where its circular motion carries them around as they stand while they gaze upon what is outside heaven'.[2] Human beings cannot see the idea-realities in such an unimpeded and effortless way. 'As for the other souls, one that follows a god most closely, making itself most like that god, raises the head of its charioteer up to the place outside and is carried around in the circular motion with the others. Although distracted by the horses, this soul does have a view of Reality, just barely.'[3]

In the *Theaetetus*, Plato has Socrates advise man to avoid evil by making haste 'to escape from earth to heaven; and escape means becoming as like God as possible; and a man becomes like God when he becomes just and pure, with understanding'.[4] Man can imitate the divine by acquiring the virtues. There is a compelling motive for making virtue one's object: the possession of virtue is decisive for man's happiness. By being virtuous, man follows the divine pattern and becomes thereby 'supremely happy'. If one follows the opposite pattern, by contrast, one becomes utterly unhappy.

The Stoics, too, employ a number of metaphors expressing the sage's closeness to the divine. Man should 'contemplate and imitate the world', identified with God.[5] Man is invited to view himself as a tiny part of divine nature and thus to see things from the perspective of the divine administrator of the world. Owing to his limitations, the agent does not know what the divine administration of the world has in store for him, so he has to strive and act with reservation and will thus be prepared for unexpected turns.[6]

The Stoics describe a closeness to the divine which goes further than anything we find in Plato. Instead of the philosopher's being a remote witness of the idea-realities, impeded by the imperfections of the human soul and therefore a travel-companion of the gods only in a weak sense (as Plato has it), the Stoic sage is a *citizen* of the cosmic city.[7] This simile implies a closer relationship between man and the divine than thought possible by Plato; in Stoic philosophy, the sage is, as it were, on equal footing with the divine. The Stoics claim that the virtue of God and the virtue of the sage are equal.[8] Cicero in his *De legibus* 1.25 offers a reason supporting such a claim:

> Virtue, however, in man and God is the same. Besides, it is not in a different genus. For virtue is nothing else than nature perfected and brought to a summit: it is, therefore, a point of similarity between man and God (*est igitur homini cum deo similitudo*).

Since virtue is sufficient for *eudaimonia*, also the happiness of God and the sage are held to be equal, as is stressed in Stobaeus (2.98.17–99.2):

> Therefore the good among the human beings are always happy, whereas the morally inferior are always unhappy. And the happiness [of the good] does not differ from the divine happiness, and the momentary—says Chrysippus—not from the happiness of Zeus, and the happiness of Zeus is by no means preferable or more beautiful or nobler than the happiness of the wise men.[9]

The radicalism with which Chrysippus does away with differences in virtue and happiness between God and the sage blurs the clear divide between God and mortal. This was scandalous to those who felt that such an unbridgeable difference was essential to the concept of the divine. Plutarch, for one, attacked the Stoics (and Chrysippus in particular) on this count. He felt that the Stoics 'began to upset from the very hearth and foundation, as it were, the established traditions in the belief about the gods and, generally speaking, have left no conception intact and unscathed' (*Comm. not.* 1074E, trans. Cherniss). In his view, one of the worst errors of the Stoics was their claim that the virtue and happiness of God and the sage are the same:

> The third feature for the conception about gods is the notion that the gods differ from men in nothing so much as they do in happiness and virtue. According to Chrysippus, however, they have not even this advantage, for Zeus does not excel Dion in virtue and Zeus and Dion, being sages, are benefited alike by each other whenever the one encounters a movement of the other.[10]

The closeness between God and the sage is also reinforced by the great distance between the sage and ordinary human beings. A large array of characteristics is the exclusive property of the sage; he is the only truly rich man, orator, poet, king and so on. These characteristics make the sage appear like a God among human beings.

Arguably the most vivid expression of Stoic ideas on the closeness to the divine can be found in book 5 of Cicero's *Tusculan Disputations*. Cicero argues there that the possession of virtue is sufficient for happiness. Even though Cicero judges the sufficiency of virtue for happiness a position held more widely in Greek philosophy,[11] he draws heavily on Stoic sources to support his argument; even if not entirely novel, the Stoics had provided the most elaborate defence of the sufficiency thesis. In this context, Cicero offers in *Tusculan Disputations* 5.68–72 a sketch of the acquisition of virtue which underlines why the possession of virtue is necessary and sufficient for happiness. His rhetorically charged description suggests that coming to share the divine point of view plays a pivotal role in the acquisition and possession of Stoic virtue and explains at the same time its motivational power. The text goes as follows (trans. King, modified):

> [68] But that we may not try by the use of argument alone to reach the truth we wish to reveal, we must set before our eyes certain as it were palpable inducements to make us turn more readily to the knowledge and understanding of its meaning. Let us assume a man pre-eminently endowed with the highest qualities and let our imagination play for a moment with the picture. In the first place he must be of outstanding intelligence; for virtue is not easily found to go with sluggish minds; secondly he must have an eager enthusiasm in the quest of truth; and from this springs the famous threefold progeny of the soul: one centred

in the knowledge of the universe and the disentanglement of the secrets of nature; the second in distinguishing the things that should be sought out or avoided and in framing a rule of life; the third in judging what is the consequence of each premise, what is incompatible with it, and in this lies all refinement of argument and truth of judgment.

[69] With what joy must then the soul of the wise man be thrilled when in such company he spends his life and passes his nights in their study! When he discovers the movements and revolutions of the whole heaven and sees the countless stars fixed in the sky in unison with the movement of the vault itself as they keep their appointed place, seven others preserving their several courses, though far remote from one another in the height or lowliness of their position, and yet their wandering movements mark the settled and regulated spaces of their course—no wonder the spectacle of all this stimulated those men of old and encouraged them to further search. Hence sprang the investigation into the beginnings and as it were the seeds from which all things got their origin, propagation and growth, to find out what was the beginning of each kind whether inanimate or animate, or mute or speaking, what life is, what death, and what the change and transmutation from one thing into another, what the origin of the earth, what weights preserve its equilibrium, what are the caverns in which the seas are upheld, what force of gravity makes all things tend to the world's centre which is also lowest in what is spherical.

[70] To the soul occupied night and day in these meditations there comes the knowledge enjoined by the god at Delphi, that the mind should know its own self and feel its union with the divine mind, the source of the fullness of joy unquenchable. For meditation upon the power and nature of the gods of itself kindles the desire of imitating his [sc. God's] immortality, nor does the soul think that it is limited to this short span of life, when it sees that the causes of things are linked one to another in an inevitable chain, and nevertheless their succession from eternity to eternity is governed by reason and intelligence.

[71] As the wise man gazes upon this spectacle and looks upward or rather looks round upon all the parts and regions of the universe, with what calmness of soul he turns again to reflect upon human affairs and what used to be nearer to him! Hence comes his knowledge of virtue; the kinds and species of the virtues break into blossom, discovery is made of what nature regards as the end in what is good and the last extremity in what is evil, the object of our duties and the rule for the conduct of life that must be chosen. And by the exploration of these and similar

problems the chief conclusion of all attained is the aim of this discussion of ours, that virtue is self-sufficient for leading a happy life.

[72] In the third place follows that which spreads freely over all parts of the field of wisdom, which gives the definition of a thing, distinguishes kinds, links up sequences, draws just conclusions, discerns true and false—the doctrine and knowledge of reasoning; and this, besides its supreme usefulness in weighing judgments, affords particularly a noble delight which is worthy of wisdom. But this is the occupation of leisure: let the wise man we have imagined also pass to the maintenance of the public weal. What course more excellent could he take, since his prudence shows him the true advantage of his fellow citizens, his justice lets him divert nothing of theirs to his own family, and he is strong in the exercise of so many different remaining virtues? Add to this the fruit which springs from friendships in which learned men find the counsel which shares their thoughts and almost breathes the same breath throughout the course of life, as well as the supreme charm of daily social intercourse. What, pray, does such a life require to make it happier? And to a life filled with joys so abundant and intense, fortune itself is bound to yield its place. If then it is happiness to rejoice in such goods of the soul, that is virtue, and all the wise men have full experience of such joys, we are bound to admit that they are all happy.

As much as the composition of the passage is Cicero's own doing, it is clear from numerous allusions that he relies on Stoic doctrine.[12] Attempts to pinpoint a specific Stoic as Cicero's source are doomed to failure. The allusions are to a generally Stoic position but cannot be traced back to one specific Stoic.[13] For all we know, we must suppose that Cicero attempted to sketch a common Stoic position.

One should not, however, underrate Cicero's role in organizing the Stoic doctrines that he wanted to relate. It would be mistaken to attribute to Cicero the wish to give a definitive Stoic outline of the acquisition of virtue proceeding along clear-cut successive steps.[14] Cicero begins (at *TD* 5.68) with a short description of the three disciplines of the Stoic curriculum: physics, ethics and dialectics (which describe as well the highest generic virtues). In his subsequent description Cicero follows this order (physics—ethics—dialectic). If the description had to be understood as outlining clear-cut successive steps, physics (and theology as its crowning part) would *precede* the acquisition of ethical virtue, whereas dialectic would only *follow* upon ethical virtue.[15] Yet, our sources, and among them Cicero himself, point towards the indispensable and fundamental role of dialectic and thus to dialectic virtue as necessary for, and inextricably connected with, ethical virtue. That suggests that Cicero did not intend the order of the disciplines to be important in this context. Rather than presenting a definitive number of clear-cut steps, Cicero wanted to give an explanation of the motivational force of the Stoic ideal of virtue and thereby of the sufficiency of virtue for happiness.

Cicero attributes a crucial role to theology. The prospective sage's quest for knowledge of nature is crowned by theological reflections (5.70). Nature is represented as divinely administered and the prospective sage recognizes the divine administration, the rational design in nature. Appreciation of this design engenders the realization of a connectedness or even (as King translates) 'union' with the divine mind and creates the desire to imitate the divine immortality. Immortality was not a goal envisaged by the Stoics.[16] The mention of immortality should be understood as a metaphor preparing the description of the sage's way of looking at the world (which, as we shall see, amounts to sharing the divine perspective).[17]

In Cicero's description, the sage has obtained a position removed from the ordinary human perspective on the world. He does not look upward (the Latin text has *suspiciens*, 'looking upward') any more, as would be the ordinary human perspective, but rather 'looks around' (*circumspiciens*). With this Platonic, *Phaedrus*-like evocation of the celestial view of the gods, Cicero indicates that the sage has come to share the divine point of view. Yet, in contrast to the *Phaedrus*, no mention is made of a somewhat inferior or impeded view allotted to the mortal human being, attributable to the composite structure of his soul and the consequent struggle between its parts. It seems that there is no difference between the ways in which the gods and the sage look at things. They take the same perspective. By sharing the divine perspective, the sage finds that ordinary human affairs have lost their sharpness and urgency. As Cicero writes at 5.71: 'with what calmness of soul he turns again to reflect upon human affairs and what used to be nearer to him (*humana et citeriora*).' The former point of view, self-centred or at best well-embedded in a wider social stratum, loses its momentum. The sage has learned to look adequately at the world and at his own place in it. From this perspective, the sage can grasp (fully) that virtue is 'self-sufficient for leading a happy life' (5.71).

In effect we have long left the sphere of doctrinal theological teaching. Cicero's account suggests that taking the divine point of view is the key ingredient of the acquisition of virtue and explains at the same time the motivational force of the Stoic ideal of virtue. Just as initiation into mystery cults was a personal experience, at best a life-changing event, so

in Cicero's representation the Stoic acquisition of virtue seems to be
dependent on a profound personal change, coming to take or share
the divine perspective on the world. The sage's quasi-divine role—or, as we
could say, his sharing the divine standpoint—in the world is the quintes-
sential expression of the sage's happiness. In sharing the divine standpoint,
he shares in the divine invulnerability and freedom of anxieties; this is precisely what the mystery cults attempted to achieve in their way. It explains
why the Stoic ideal of *eudaimonia* could have been a supremely motivating
conception.

So far, I have claimed only that Cicero accounted for the motivational
force of Stoic virtue and for the sufficiency of virtue for happiness by pointing to the sage's sharing the divine perspective on the world. We have in
fact no other source analysing this aspect of Stoic virtue theory in comparable detail. How seriously should we take Cicero's account in *Tusculan
Disputations* book 5? Undoubtedly Cicero synthesized his account with
Greek literary models, foremost perhaps Plato, in mind.[18] Yet, I want to
argue that Cicero's account is more than mere literary convention and that
it deserves to be taken very seriously. If taking or sharing the divine point
of view was indeed, as Cicero suggests, a key ingredient of the acquisition
of virtue, it would explain a number of structural features of Stoic virtue
theory which otherwise must remain inexplicable: (1) There is a radical
difference between virtue and vice, both of which are non-gradual properties. If one does not have virtue, one is utterly unhappy, and progress
towards virtue does not change anything about it. (2) The change from vice
to virtue is radical and sudden, yet the change can take place without the
sage's noticing it directly. (3) The Stoics placed considerable emphasis
on the 'how' side of virtue-knowledge: virtue is more than knowing a well-
ordered system of propositions; it is a specific way of knowing and making
use of that knowledge. (4) For all their elated claims about the sage, the
Stoics did not claim the sage to be omniscient. Yet they held that the virtue
and happiness of God and the sage do not differ. (5) Things ordinarily held
to be goods were demoted to 'indifferents' by the Stoics, yet the sage was
held to deal expertly with such indifferent things and to have a detached
form of motivation concerning them.

All these features, I suggest, are readily explicable if we allow the taking
of the divine point of view to have played a pivotal role in the Stoic
account of virtue as knowledge. Taking the divine perspective is conceived
of as taking or sharing a unique perspective; one sees straight only from
that perspective and from no other. Approximation towards the divine

perspective brings us closer to seeing straight, but we do not actually see straight before we have taken the right perspective. In the light of this metaphor, it becomes understandable why the Stoics considered the possession of virtue an all-or-nothing affair and maximized the contrast between virtue and vice: one either takes that unique position and sees completely or one does not take it and in consequence does not see things straight. Also, the claim that all vices are equal is understandable against the background of this religious conception: through failure to take the divine perspective, all vices are expressive of the same fault, and are equally expressive of the corruption of the agent's rationality. If taking the divine perspective is tantamount to being happy, then not having taken it as yet means that one is unhappy, however far advanced one is on the way towards taking it:

> [J]ust as in the sea the man an arm's length from the surface is drowning no less than the one who has sunk five hundred fathoms, so even those who are getting close to virtue are no less in a state of vice than those who are far from it. And just as the blind are blind even if they are going to recover their sight a little later, so those progressing remain foolish and vicious right up to their attainment of virtue.[19]

The motif of sharing the divine standpoint can also serve to explain the Stoics' emphasis on the 'suddenness' of the acquisition of virtue:

> [T]he wise man has changed in a moment from the greatest possible worthlessness to an unsurpassable virtuous character, and has suddenly shed all the vice of which he failed to remove even a part over a considerable time.[20]

Sharing the divine point of view is an all-or-nothing affair so that taking this standpoint can only be characterized as an instantaneous occurrence. By the same token we can understand why the Stoics posited that the sage may not immediately realize that he has become virtuous:

> What you would find most extraordinary . . . is their [the Stoics'] belief that, having got virtue and happiness, a man often does not even perceive them, but it eludes him that he has now become both prudent and supremely happy when a moment earlier he was utterly wretched and foolish.[21]

Taking the divine standpoint is to be understood foremost as a change on the 'how' side of knowledge. It is less about the number of propositions one knows than about looking from the right perspective on the knowledge one has. In the Stoic view, the sage's taking the right perspective presupposes much natural ability and knowledge, but he need not be omniscient to have the same virtue and happiness as the gods.

If the change from vice to virtue was primarily a question of coming to acquire a new piece of knowledge, the change could hardly elude the progressing agent. By contrast, a change of perspective will primarily bear on future perceptions of one's own place in the world. It is conceivable that the agent will only notice such a change after some time.[22]

Against the background of Greek philosophy (particularly Plato) and the mystery cults, happiness was identified with drawing close to the gods and even sharing the divine point of view. The divine life was characterized in terms of epistemic stability and freedom of anxiety. If this ideal explains the motivational force of Stoic virtue, as Cicero suggests, it becomes understandable why things ordinarily regarded as important must have appeared indifferent to the Stoics and why at the same time the sage was held to deal expertly and detachedly[23] with things considered indifferent.[24] While the human condition of the sage makes it inevitable for him to deal with things that are, to a Stoic, indifferent, his actions are informed by the view from the divine perspective. Taking this perspective detaches the sage from the ordinary human concerns without making him lose his ability to act in a perfectly adequate way.

Part Four

Practices of Virtue

Chapter 11

Law and Rules

The last part of this book focuses on the practices of Stoic virtue. The plural 'practices' indicates what is a major—in my view even the single most important—interpretive puzzle about the practical application of Stoic ethics. We find in our (admittedly rather scarce) sources not only evidence of a far-reaching flexibility and sensitivity to context of the Stoic practical prescriptions, but we also find opposite courses of action explicitly prescribed by leading Stoics without any indication that the unity of the teaching of the Stoic school was perceived to be endangered. It is not easy to see how the flexibility and the contentiousness of practical prescriptions square with the stress in our sources on the concept of a natural moral law that leads us to expect a deduction of exceptionless rules from general first principles and a rigid prescription of Stoic practice rather than flexible and contended prescriptions of divergent practices. In consequence of this difficulty it seems that, in the recent literature, readings of Stoic ethics that give the notions of natural law and deduced rules a weaker, procedural interpretation and play down their overall importance have got the upper hand. Although such interpretations have reminded us of hitherto neglected problems in the traditional natural law interpretation of Stoic ethics, they fail to make sense of the whole range of available evidence. In the remaining two chapters of this book I shall defend the more traditional interpretation that ascribes a far stronger role to the concepts of natural law and deduced rules, and I shall attempt to show how these concepts could have worked within the framework of Stoic ethics.

In this chapter I shall examine the evidence for the Stoic concepts of a natural law and action-guiding rules prescribing what is appropriate (the *kathēkon*), and I shall offer my view of how the concepts could have worked in Stoic practical deliberation. In Chapter 12 I shall analyse our evidence for the versatility and contentiousness of Stoic practical prescriptions. I shall argue that the interpretation of Stoic ethics as a fundamentally religious system can help us to understand why the contentiousness of Stoic practice did not undermine the unity of the teaching of the Stoic school.

Law

A convenient starting point for an analysis of the Stoic concept of a (natural moral) law is Diogenes Laertius 7.87–8. The passage situates the discussion of 'the law', as the Stoics call what we refer to as 'natural law', 'moral law' or 'divine moral law' (as I shall argue, with some danger of distorting the Stoic meaning), in the context of a discussion of the end (*telos*). After presenting as the received Stoic view the claim that the end was 'living in agreement with nature', Diogenes focuses on Chrysippus' formulation of the Stoic position:

> Again, living virtuously is equivalent to living in accordance with experience of the actual course of nature, as Chrysippus says in the first book of his *On Ends*; for our individual natures are parts of the nature of the whole universe. And this is why the end may be defined as life in accordance with nature or, in other words, in accordance with our own nature as well as that of the universe, a life in which we refrain from every action forbidden by the law common to all things, that is to say, the right reason which pervades all things, and is identical with this Zeus, lord and ruler of all that is.[1]

The 'law common to all things' can be read out of the 'actual course of nature'. The experience of what actually happens by nature can discover the reasonable structure in nature. This structure is the result of the formative influence of the divine principle. It is no coincidence that the right reason pervading all things is explicitly identified with Zeus. By employing the name of Zeus, the Stoics evoked the theistic imagery of an individual, personal God. A personal God could act as a lawgiver. The theistic imagery could thus undergird the characterization of the reasonable structure in nature as a 'law'. The order of the world and the way the world develops are presented as the result of Zeus' administration, as his design. His intentions can be read in the course of natural events. Nature is not merely displaying an order, this order receives the status of a normative standard, something one should follow. Human beings are called on to reconstruct the normative standard in their own minds and thus share in the divine right reason.[2]

It has been suggested in the literature that the divine moral law is merely the abstract idea of a normative standard and thus quite ineffective in concrete human deliberations about what is or is not an appropriate course of action.[3] Although we have to address the issue in the context of the larger question of whether the Stoics thought that (rules prescribing) appropriate actions were deducible from ultimate principles (see below), I want to make clear at this point that our sources do not warrant that suggestion, at least not as a description of what the Stoics themselves thought they were doing. Our sources' rhetoric shows clearly that, however much head-way they actually made or even wanted to make, the Stoics *meant* the divine natural law to prescribe human actions in a detailed way. Take for instance the beginning of Chrysippus' book *On Law*, quoted by the Roman jurist Marcian in the third century AD (Marcian *ap.* Justinian *Digesta* 1.3.2, trans. LS 67R):

> Law is the king of all things human and divine. Law must preside over what is honourable and base, as ruler and as guide, and thus be the standard of right and wrong, prescribing to animals whose nature is political what they should do, and prohibiting them from what they should not do.

Clearly, law prescribes what to do and what not to do, thereby forming 'the standard (κανών) of right and wrong'. It deals with the affairs of rational beings and covers all aspects of life ('all things human and divine'). Chrysippus must have thought that *every* question as to which course of action is right can in principle be answered by recourse to natural law.[1]

With the long history of Christian natural law tradition and the natural science interpretation of natural laws standing between us and the Stoics, we can be easily misled into misrepresenting the Stoic concept of law. Stoic natural law was not primarily about establishing a definitive list of ultimate commands and it had little to do with the sort of exceptionless principles modern science attempts to formulate. We shall see presently that the Stoics were indeed convinced that general rules expressing the content of natural law could be formulated and that such rules could aid the agent's progress towards virtue as well as guiding the sage's decisions.[5] However, the Stoic concept of natural law does not stop at this level of generality. The standard of natural law is the standard of right reason that has to read in the course of natural events. It prescribes what the divine administrator of the world wants to see done—down to specific actions in concrete circumstances. We shall see that Seneca's account of rules reflects this position by attributing the status of rules even to concrete instructions. However, Stoic natural law not only prescribes courses of action. It is crucially about the right attitude to take, about the 'how' side of right action.

Arguably, the contrast between our expectations of a natural law theory and the Stoic doctrine becomes nowhere so manifest as in Chrysippus' claim that the natural law does not give the same prescriptions to sage and non-sage alike: the law does not contain prescriptions for the non-wise, because they cannot perform the right actions intended by the prescriptions of law.[6] But, as we learn from Plutarch, the law contains 'many prohibitions' directed at the non-wise. The question remains what the Stoics meant by this doctrine. Plutarch claims, when arguing that the Stoic conception of law is implausible, that the Stoics simply overlooked the convertibility of prescriptions into prohibitions (and vice versa). That, however, seems quite unlikely. I want to suggest that the differentiation between appropriate actions (or, more generally, 'proper functions') and right actions stood behind Chrysippus' view. The concept of 'proper functions' or 'appropriate behaviour' (καθήκοντα) has already put in less prominent appearances in the earlier parts of this book. It is now time to place the concept into a broader context. For every living being, certain things agree with its natural constitution.[7] If a living being performs certain proper functions to obtain or preserve the things in agreement with its natural constitution, we can (in principle) understand the point of these proper functions. We understand, for instance, why a vascular plant absorbs water with its roots. Both why the plant takes in water and why it absorbs the water in that way can reasonably be justified.

In human beings reason allows the shaping of impulses, resulting in a wide-ranging control over the form of one's life. Human beings take decisions and make plans to acquire what they consider valuable. Stoic ethics teaches the crucial role of virtue for human life. Happiness, the object of human aspirations, consists in the possession of virtue. From the perspective of the Stoics, things other than virtue or partaking of virtue have a certain relative value if they agree with the human being's natural constitution. Strictly speaking, however, these things are not 'good', because only virtue or things partaking of virtue have that status. Compared with virtue as the true goal of human life, things like wealth, beauty or health are 'indifferent'. Yet, because they agree with the human being's natural constitution, their possession is preferable to not having them. Such indifferents are therefore called 'preferred' (προηγμένα); their contraries are 'dispreferred' (ἀποπροηγμένα).

The acquisition of preferred indifferents is what human beings should try to realize in principle, since it agrees with nature.[8] Therefore, activities directed at the acquisition of preferred indifferents are called *kathēkonta* ('proper functions' or—less odd-sounding when applied to human beings— 'appropriate actions').[9] Any human being can select naturally preferred things and thereby fulfil a proper function; this is in no way restricted to the sage.[10] Specific to the sage are 'right actions' (κατορθώματα), also called 'perfect appropriate actions' or 'perfect proper functions' (καθήκοντα τέλεια).[11] It has become customary to dub the characteristic that distinguishes right action from merely appropriate action as the 'how' (or 'why') an action is performed as opposed to 'what' is actually done.[12]

Proper functions performed by the sage have the additional properties of 'firmness and tenor and their own particular fixity' (τὸ βέβαιον καὶ ἑκτικὸν καὶ ἰδίαν πῆξιν). Although it sounds as if those properties characterize only the action,[13] other texts make it clear that the additional properties of the sage's right actions must be attributed to the special frame of mind with which he performs them. The sage fulfils the appropriate actions on the basis of virtue.[14] I shall return to a more detailed discussion of appropriate and right actions later on in this chapter. For now, I want to argue that the difference between appropriate and right actions stood behind Chrysippus' claim that the law does not prescribe to the sage and to non-sages alike.

Right actions have, as it were, two components: the component of *what* is done (the proper function), and the component of *how* it is done. Whereas the non-wise will fail to perform right actions (for lack of the second component), they can still understand (up to a point) what is preferable, or what is appropriate.[15] Therefore, non-sages can realize that they fail to perform a right action, if the failure is due to missing out on a proper function and if they perceive that this is the reason for their failure. In Chrysippus' view Stoic natural law sets a moral standard; it prescribes right actions. The sage can read in the divinely administered nature what should be done as well as how it should be done. Thus understood, nature teaches virtue. However, non-sages lack this level of insight; therefore, they cannot grasp prescriptions of right actions, since right actions involve virtue; the only thing they can grasp (up to a point) is the 'what' side of right action. For the non-sage the moral law would therefore be manifest in the form of prohibitions, which are crucially about delineating the class of appropriate actions, but the non-sage is not up to the demands of virtue presupposed in prescriptions of right actions.

The difference between the 'what' side and the 'how' side of right action also helps us understand the work Stoic moral law does in providing a basis for more specific types of behaviour and rules. For my argument I shall primarily draw on two texts: Cicero's outline of Stoic natural law theory in his *De legibus* 1 and Seneca's *Letters* 95. My proposal to read Seneca's letter as bearing on the Stoic theory of natural law may come as a surprise to readers who are accustomed to read *Letters* 95 only as a discussion of Stoic rules. However, I shall argue presently that Seneca followed in his letter the same Stoic natural law theory as Cicero in his *De legibus* 1. Cicero's starting point in presenting Stoic natural law theory is a theological premise: the world is divinely ruled (*Leg.* 1.21). After his Epicurean interlocutor Atticus has granted this starting point, Cicero steams ahead at full throttle: He describes the divinely ordained position of man in the world. Since human beings have received the gift of reason, which they share with the gods, there is a clear bond between gods and men. Sharing reason and therefore right reason, they also share law and justice (1.22–3). The Stoic theory of a cosmic city common to gods and men makes its appearance (1.23). The relationship with the gods is further described as a 'family relationship' (1.23–4), substantiated by the equality of human and divine virtue (1.25). The moral demands which result from man's divinely ordained position in the world are nearly lost in Cicero's rhetorical flourish. However, there seem to be two principal demands: first of all to recognize the close relationship with the gods, based on the common possession of reason,[16] and second to perfect reason, manifest in the acquisition of virtue, and summarily referred to as 'justice'.[17]

The concept of justice serves as a stepping stone towards the second main topic in Cicero's presentation: the close bonds among human beings (1.28–34). The similarity of human beings, their common humanity, is more important than apparent dissimilarities. With the sentence 'The similarity of the human race is as remarkable in perversities as it is in proper behaviour' (1.31, trans. Zetzel), Cicero shifts the discussion to the general human tendency to be misled into considering non-moral things like pleasure and glory to be good. Yet the close bonds between human beings are shown in the universal appreciation of 'affability, generosity [and] a grateful mind (. . .) the final result is that the right way of life makes all people better' (1.32, trans. Zetzel). Cicero summarizes the prescriptive content of natural law with respect to fellow human beings in the claim that 'we have been made by nature to receive the knowledge of justice one from another and share it among all people' (1.33, trans. Zetzel).

Let us now turn to Seneca's 95th letter. On the face of it, it is by no means obvious that Seneca's letter is germane to a discussion of Stoic natural law.

Ostensibly the letter is, together with the preceding letter 94, merely a rejection of doubts about the didactic value of teaching philosophical doctrines (*decreta*) in addition to more specific action-guiding rules (*praecepta*).[18] Yet a comparison between Seneca's argument in *Letters* 95.47–57 and Cicero's presentation in *De legibus* 1.21–34 shows that Cicero and Seneca display the same order of topics and draw on the same Stoic doctrines. The best explanation of this is that Cicero and Seneca both follow the same Stoic natural law teaching. The structure of Seneca's argument is as follows: he wants to show that rules are insufficient to guide human practice reliably unless they are grounded in philosophical doctrines. In *Letters* 95.47–57 he illustrates his claim with examples of how *praecepta* must be grounded in philosophical *decreta* to be set in the right perspective and thus to be of use. The examples follow a clear order. Seneca begins with rules guiding behaviour towards the gods (*Letters* 95.47–50). Such rules are insufficient or even misleading unless grounded in accurate theological doctrines. The doctrines that he lists repeat the key points of Stoic theology: the existence of the gods and their benevolent administration of the world and providential care for humankind (95.50).[19] From these doctrines follows a spiritualized and moralized worship: 'You want to render the gods favourable? Be good. Whoever imitates the gods worships them sufficiently' (95.50).

Seneca proceeds to a second question: how to deal with human beings (95.51–3).[20] Here, more specific rules have to be grounded in a correct understanding of nature. The world is a unity which includes gods and men. Equity and justice are called for. Mankind is born for community, and this entails the duty of solidarity (95.53).

Seneca now addresses a third question: how to deal with 'things' (95.54).[21] As examples, Seneca offers the contrasting pairs poverty and riches, glory and ignominy, and fatherland and exile. Instead of offering a detailed theory about such 'things', Seneca presses on his readers to judge them one by one, without paying heed to general opinion. This is a rather contracted reference to the Stoic theory of *oikeiōsis* and its account of the social origin of mistaken evaluations. It is Seneca's shorthand for reminding us of the fact that such non-moral things are in reality indifferent and that we have only been misled by appearances and general opinion into considering them good or bad.[22]

Seneca then embarks on a discussion of virtue (95.55–6). Virtue is not only knowledge about other things but, it presupposes knowledge about the nature of virtue itself (95.56). At 95.57 Seneca returns to the benefits of knowing the principles in which more specific rules are grounded. Knowing those principles produces tranquillity by making the judgement 'unchangeable' and 'certain'. Seneca calls the principles 'the laws of the whole life' (*totius vitae leges*), alluding to the characterization of philosophy as 'the law of life' offered at 94.39.

Seneca thus addresses rules about gods, human beings and non-moral things and then proceeds to a discussion of virtue. At two places (95.51 and 54), his formulations seem to indicate that he follows an established order of topics to be discussed.

When we turn back to Cicero's discussion in *De legibus* 1 we find that he, too, begins with a presentation of the relationship of mankind towards the gods. The recognition of God's existence, prescribed in Seneca's letter as the primary religious obligation, seems presupposed in Cicero's off-hand remark that all human beings, however inchoately, in fact recognize God's existence. As in Seneca, the acquisition of virtue seems to be the worship called for on the basis of an adequate theology. Like Seneca, Cicero proceeds to a discussion of what is due to fellow human beings and sees justice as implied by the close bonds among human beings. The correct estimation of non-moral things, treated by Seneca as a separate item, is run by Cicero into his discussion of the fundamental similarity of human beings; even in their mistaken reaction to appearances, that is, in the wrong estimation of non-moral goods, human beings are strikingly similar. And, finally, with the mention of the universal appreciation of properties as 'affability', 'generosity' and 'a grateful mind' Cicero addresses, as Seneca does, the topic of virtues, only that Cicero once more runs what is a separate item for Seneca into a discussion of the fundamental similarity of human beings.

It seems, therefore, that Cicero and Seneca follow the same Stoic natural law teaching. This natural law teaching must have proceeded from a discussion of obligations towards the gods and fellow human beings to the correct estimation of non-moral things. The arguments would have drawn on Stoic theological premises and doctrines on the unity of the divinely administered world. The conclusion of the discussion would have been a statement of how a careful observation of the reasonable structure in nature leads to a correct appreciation of non-moral things and hence to virtue.[23]

Having argued that Cicero and Seneca used the same Stoic natural law doctrine I want to point out a further similarity, which is crucial for our appreciation of Stoic natural law theory. Cicero and Seneca both present the import of natural law in the same way: Even though to both authors' minds the moral law grounds more specific prescriptions, they write not so much about specific prescriptions that might follow from the moral law but present the natural law as describing *the right attitude* one should have, as demanding that one should take *the right point of view*. Cicero invites his interlocutor primarily to consider the similarity and therefore the close bonds among human beings. The similarity between human beings calls for justice as the only adequate response, but Cicero is far from attempting to determine in what way justice must be understood and put into practice. Seneca attributes to the philosophical *decreta* the force to rid the agent from wrong estimations resulting in fear, avarice and indulgence (95.37) with the stability of the agent's judgement (95.57). Without *decreta* one cannot get the 'how' side of one's actions right (95.40). As in Cicero so in Seneca's presentation, the natural law as expressed in philosophical *decreta* is primarily about the right attitude to take. It is no coincidence that Seneca describes the import of *decreta* with Terentius' verse: 'Homo sum, humani nihil a me alienum puto', which is foremost the evocation of an attitude, and not an attempt to deduce specific rules.

These evocations of the right attitude to take should be read as shorthand references to the sage for whom alone an unfailing deduction of specific rules would be possible. Both Seneca and Cicero convey the conviction that such deductions are possible rather than attempt to provide detailed examples of such deductions. Having said so much, there is nonetheless evidence of an extended reflection on the possibility of giving advice to the non-sage in the form of more or less general rules, and our sources enable us to reconstruct, at least in outline, how the Stoics thought practical reasoning should work.

Rules and *Kathēkonta*

Our most important sources on the Stoic discussion of the role of rules are Seneca's *Letters* 94 and 95.[24] Seneca offers in them his view on Stoic practical ethics, the 'paraenetic' part of philosophy, which consisted in giving concrete practical guidance tailored to the specific situation of the advisee. Aristo had denied the usefulness of this part of philosophical training. The sage does not need detailed precepts, since he has the knowledge necessary to prescribe to himself what should be done in particular circumstances. Cleanthes, by contrast, had offered a qualified defence of the usefulness of such rules: they will be useful if combined with, or grounded in, a knowledge of the doctrines of philosophy.[25] Aristo's critical view had found followers,[26] and Seneca offers in his *Letters* 94 and 95 his own stance on what must have still been a lively debate at his time. Seneca backs the position that more specific rules are useful if supplemented by the doctrines of philosophy. Moreover, he argues that the doctrines of philosophy should be viewed as general rules grounding the more specific ones.[27]

While it seems hardly controversial that Stoic rules prescribe appropriate actions (*kathēkonta*),[28] the role of rules in Stoic ethics has been a matter of intense scholarly controversy. The traditional line of interpretation has viewed the Stoics as originators of the natural law theory.[29] According to this 'natural law' interpretation, the Stoics claimed that there is a 'system of universal, exceptionless and substantive moral commands'. Moral practice has the form of conventional rule-case deduction.[30]

The opposed view ascribes to the Stoics a view similar to a nowadays fashionable interpretation of Aristotle's ethics. As Brad Inwood, the main proponent of this view, has put it, 'law represents the prescriptive force behind the correct moral choice of an ideal moral reasoner, the sage, whatever the content of that choice might be on a given occasion'.[31] Because of the specificity of an individual's circumstances, advice can only be given by fallible 'rules of thumb'.[32] With the limitations of the average agent in view there is still good reason to entrench these 'rules of thumb'.[33] Yet, according to Inwood, what Stoic ethics really is about is to 'prescribe methods of procedure within a framework of sound general principles' rather than to 'dictate determinate actions to moral agents'.[34] I shall call this view 'the rule-of-thumb interpretation'.

In what follows I shall argue that the natural law interpretation is on the whole preferable. However, the potential of the natural law interpretation must not be curtailed as happens in the account given by its opponents. Interpreted as its opponents do, the natural law interpretation is certainly wrong about focusing too much on exceptionless rules. The rule-of-thumb interpretation correctly stresses the responsiveness of Stoic natural law to concrete situations. Stoic natural law should indeed not be likened to a definitive list containing only universal rules. Rather, it embraces general principles as well as the whole train of (intermediate) rules, down to instructions about what the deity would want done in specific circumstances. Moreover, Stoic natural law was not solely concerned with prescribing courses of action; it was crucially about the right attitude to take, giving guidance as to the 'how' side of action.

The rule-of-thumb interpretation errs in claiming that the standard of rightness was *constituted* by the choice of the sage. The evidence points rather to the Stoics' considering the standard as prior to the sage's choice. The sage merely reproduces this anterior, divine standard in his own perfected reason. This is a point the natural law interpretation correctly identifies against the neo-Aristotelian rule-of-thumb interpretation.

Moreover, emphasis on the rule-of-thumb character of rules has led advocates of this interpretation to postulate a wedge between the content of appropriate actions (*kathēkonta*) and of right actions (*katorthōmata*): appropriate actions are generally appropriate, but are not always appropriate in particular circumstances. By contrast, right actions are appropriate in particular circumstances. They are the result of the infallible insight of the sage.[35] I shall show presently that this interpretation is completely unwarranted by our sources.

Because the advocates of the natural law interpretation have generally been too impressed by the demand that rules must be substantive as well as universal and that a class of 'always incumbent proper functions' must be delineable to provide the content of such rules, they have been induced to speculate about 'always incumbent proper functions' for which no evidence can be given (see below).[36] In what follows, I shall substantiate my interpretation by showing in more detail how Seneca describes the deducibility of specific rules from more general ones and by showing that Seneca's account does not rely exclusively on universal exceptionless rules but allows for a whole spectrum of types of rules, from most abstract principles of nature to what we would rather describe as instructions. Finally I shall argue against a wedge between the content of appropriate and right actions, postulated by the advocates of the rule-of-thumb interpretation.

Seneca's *Letters* 94 and 95 show that he intended more specific rules to be deducible from general philosophical doctrines. This is clear with respect to the abstract and general starting points of the deductions, the philosophical doctrines which I identified above as the prescriptions of natural law. In *Letters* 94.31 Seneca characterizes the doctrines of philosophy as 'general precepts'. Seneca thus describes them as most general rules from which more specific rules can be deduced. That Seneca meant specific rules to be deducible from general principles becomes also obvious in a number of other places. Answering the objection that there would have to be infinitely many rules to cover every detail of life, Seneca answers that 'concerning the most important and necessary things, there are not infinitely many; they show minor variations which are made necessary by the times, places and persons concerned, but also for these circumstances general rules can be given' (*Letters* 94.35). Seneca was clearly convinced that the complexities of life do not defy attempts to formulate rules of some generality and to deduce more specific precepts.

Seneca's acknowledgement of the possibility of giving relatively general rules which obtain in the most important circumstances does not entail that he (or, for that matter, any other Stoic) was committed to thinking that rules must prescribe classes of 'always incumbent appropriate actions'. On the contrary, Seneca, who firmly set the topic of rules in the context of giving advice, was convinced that rules have to be geared to the specific circumstances of the advisee.[37] Such circumstances include also the abilities of the advisee. Weaker characters need more specific advice. Seneca's formulation 'avoid this, do this' (*hoc vitabis, hoc facies*) proves that such advice could go so far as to prescribe particular actions.[38] Even if one wonders, as at least one modern commentator has done,[39] whether this is not an instruction rather than a rule, it is telling that for Seneca such very specific advice falls under the concept of rules. We see here that Seneca is not committed to rules as delineating 'always incumbent appropriate actions'. Arguably, rules *can* be absolutely exceptionless. For Seneca, the doctrines of philosophy would probably be the best examples. However, rules need not have such generality. The more specific rules deduced from the doctrines of philosophy should rather be understood as rules that hold more or less generally, but allow of exceptions. Highly specific advice, geared to the specific circumstances a specific advisee is in, would hardly have applicability beyond his current situation.

Of course, in the hand of the non-sage, who does not have knowledge of the principles that ground more specific rules and thus lacks an instruction of how rules have to be understood, the usefulness of rules is limited. The odds are that the non-sage will fail to make sufficient allowance for certain specific but important circumstances. Against the background of the ideal reasoner, the sage, general rules can easily come to resemble mere rules of thumb. It was, however, not Seneca's intention to demote rules in that way. Whether we like it or not, it is precisely the fact that Seneca thought of the most specific advice as an instance of rules which proves that he was convinced that rules can give adequate guidance and can be more than mere rules of thumb.

Both the non-sage's giving advice to others and the non-sage's ability to grasp (up to a point) what the sage would do in comparable circumstances hinge on the fact that appropriate actions (*kathēkonta*) and right actions (*katorthōmata*) are identical as far as their 'what' side is concerned. What makes right actions an exclusive domain of the sage is that they are proper functions *fulfilled on the basis of virtue.*[40] It is the 'how' side or, as Seneca says, the 'why' which serves as differentiating criterion of outwardly identical actions (*Letters* 95.43):

> If someone looks after a friend who is ill, we approve of it. But if he does it for the sake of an inheritance, then he is a vulture, he expects a cadaver.

The same acts can be either shameful (*turpia*) or virtuous (*honesta*). It makes all the difference why and how they are done. Now all our acts will be virtuous, if we attach ourselves to virtue and if we consider virtue and what follows from virtue to be the only good for human beings— other things are short-lived goods.

In their attempt to demote rules, advocates of the rule-of-thumb interpretation have severed the link between appropriate and right actions by allowing for a mismatch between the 'what' side of appropriate actions and right actions. Proper functions, it has been claimed, are generally adequate choices, but they are not always adequate in particular circumstances. In contrast to proper functions, right actions are adequate in particular circumstances.[11] On this interpretation, the fulfilment of a proper function could thus be wrong in certain circumstances, and a right action might be contrary to a proper function.

The serious problems this interpretation would cause for the possibility of a non-sage describing the practice of the sage or giving advice to other non-sages make this a very unlikely option. Moreover, nowhere in our sources do we find the Stoics claiming that some actions remain appropriate, while being wrong in the circumstances. As I shall show presently, the two passages in Diogenes Laertius (7.108–9 and 121) regularly quoted to this effect do not stand up to closer scrutiny.[42]

At Diogenes Laertius 7.108–9 we find a taxonomy of *kathēkonta* (trans. LS 59E, modified):

Of activities in accordance with impulse, some are appropriate actions, others are contrary to appropriate action, and others belong to neither type. Proper actions are ones which reason dictates our doing, such as honouring parents, brothers and country, spending time with friends; contrary to appropriate action are ones which reason does not dictate our doing, such as neglecting parents, not caring about brothers, not treating friends sympathetically, not acting patriotically etc. Activities which are neither proper functions nor contrary to proper function are ones which reason neither dictates our doing nor forbids, such as picking up a twig, holding a pen or a scraper, and such like. Some appropriate actions do not depend on special[43] circumstances, but others do. The following do not depend on special circumstances, looking after one's health, and one's sense organs, and such like. Appropriate actions which do depend on special circumstances are mutilating oneself and disposing of one's property. And so analogously with actions which are contrary to what is appropriate. Furthermore, some appropriate actions are always appropriate while others are not. It is always an appropriate action to live virtuously, but not always an appropriate action to engage in question and answer, to walk about, and such like. The same principle applies to actions which are contrary to what is appropriate.

It is not claimed that an action could be appropriate, but wrong in the circumstances. Rather, the text should be understood as dealing with the obvious point that what *is* appropriate depends in most, if not all, cases on the circumstances, some of them so extraordinary that it will be hard for the non-sage to determine what to do: mutilating oneself and disposing of one's property are offered as examples.[44] Always appropriate actions (or, as others translate, 'always incumbent proper functions') are mentioned in such a way that it is difficult not to feel that they must belong to an exceptional category. It is even hard to think of an example of a specific action type to be thus described. It is no wonder, therefore, that with 'living virtuously' no example is offered of a specific action type but instead there is a characterization of a *form of life*.

In the second Diogenes Laertius passage (7.121) we find the claim that the sage 'will even eat human flesh in certain special circumstances'. However, without further evidence this claim cannot be construed as proof that the sage might decide against the performance of appropriate actions. If the doctrine was in any way meant to clarify the Stoic theory of *kathēkonta* (which must remain conjectural) it would merely show that *kathēkonta* depend on circumstances and that extreme circumstances can make extreme actions appropriate.[45]

To sum up, I have argued that there is no good reason to attribute to Stoic prescriptions the status of mere rules of thumb. Seneca's *Letters* 94 and 95 testify to his belief that rules can be formulated which prescribe correctly even in specific circumstances. Moreover, Seneca held that such rules could be derived from general principles, the doctrines of philosophy. I have shown by comparison to Cicero's presentation of the Stoic theory of natural law in *De legibus* that Seneca's doctrines of philosophy contain what the Stoics considered to be the natural law. Indeed, the natural law interpretation of Seneca's *Letters* 94 and 95 makes best sense of the text, provided it allows for the multiple roles in which the concept of rules is employed and does not attempt to commit this interpretation to an exclusive endorsement of a 'system of universal, exceptionless and substantive moral commands'.

Up to this point the argument of this chapter has been primarily negative and has been more detailed in rejecting the rule-of-thumb interpretation than in offering a vision of how the Stoics conceived of practical reasoning. However, the topic is worth exploring in more detail. In the remainder of this chapter, I shall offer my view of Stoic practical reasoning.

Stoic Practical Reasoning

In rejecting the rule-of-thumb interpretation I have argued that a wedge between the 'what' side of appropriate and right actions is not supported by our sources. The Stoics did not demote the concept of *kathēkonta* by holding that *kathēkonta* describe what is generally appropriate, but can be wrong in the circumstances. Rather, I argued, the Stoics looked for what *is* appropriate in the obtaining circumstances.

Our evidence presents the Stoics as convinced that there is always a single action which is appropriate (and, if performed by the sage, right) in the specific circumstances in question.[46] The sage represents right reason, the divine standard of what is right in the circumstances. Our sources do not perceive as valuable what is central to so many of today's accounts of virtue ethics—individual expression, authenticity and the like—because, fundamentally, the Stoics did not regard individuality as something to be particularly proud of. What counted was to represent reason, the divine right reason, in all circumstances. There is, therefore, good reason to suspect that the Stoic sage is, in the words of David Sedley, 'not an individual at all [but] a (repeatable) *type*'.[47] Even where Stoic sources do recognize differences between agents this does not lead to a sanctioning of some leeway as to what is appropriate in specific circumstances. Epictetus 1.2.5–11 is a text in question (trans. Oldfather):

Now it so happens that the rational and the irrational are different for different persons, precisely as good and evil, and the profitable and the unprofitable, are different for different persons. It is for this reason especially that we need education, so as to learn how, in conformity with nature, to adapt to specific instances our preconceived idea of what is rational and what is irrational. But for determining the rational and irrational, we employ not only our estimates of the value of external things, but also the criterion of that which is in keeping with one's own character (πρόσωπον). For one man it is reasonable to hold a chamber-pot for another, since he considers only that, if he does not hold it, he will get a beating and will not get food, whereas, if he does hold it, nothing harsh or painful will be done to him; but some other man feels that it is not merely unendurable to hold such a pot himself, but even to tolerate another's doing so. If you ask me, then, 'Shall I hold the pot or not?' I will tell you that to get food is of greater value than not to get it, and to be flayed is of greater detriment than not to be; so that if you measure your interests by these standards, go and hold the pot. 'Yes, but it would be unworthy of me.' That is an additional consideration, which you, and not I, must introduce into the question. For you are the one that knows yourself, how much you are worth in your own eyes and at what price you sell yourself. For different men sell themselves at different prices.

In spite of the ostensive difference of appropriate actions for different agents, it is clear that to Epictetus the different agents do not have the same worth. There is a clear preference for one sort of agent, and only one course of action is appropriate for him.

Advocates of the rule-of-thumb interpretation should certainly attempt to stress a model of practical reasoning according to which one weighs a number of *prima facie* appropriate actions, grades them according to what option is more or less appropriate in the circumstances, and considers the most appropriate action one finds as *the* appropriate (or, rather, the *right*) action in the circumstances. Such a model would demote the importance of rules and make right action appear as the result of intuition inexpressible in general rules.

I think, however, that such a model is a far cry from what the Stoics wanted and moreover our Epictetus passage does not point towards it, even if it might appear to do so at first sight. On a straightforward reading our passage makes clear that there is only one appropriate action, placing one's own worth above degrading but punishment-avoiding behaviour. In order to underline his point Epictetus emphasizes (realistically as well as admonishingly) that not every (perhaps hardly any) agent will have the character necessary to realize that and stick to it. Moreover, a model of grading more or less appropriate actions does not square with the Stoic view that all deviances from virtue are equally detrimental, a view which, as I have argued in Chapter 10, can readily be explained by the Stoics' emphasis on the 'how' side of virtue-knowledge and the sage's sharing of the divine perspective. We do, however, find a model of grading more or less appropriate actions in Cicero's *De officiis* 1.10, but it is introduced by Cicero as an improvement on Panaetius, his Stoic source. Had the model been employed within the context of the Stoic *kathēkonta* literature, we could expect Cicero to use that treatise and to mention the author as superseding Panaetius. Since this is nowhere evident, it is far more likely that the model was Cicero's own.[48]

This leaves us with considerable latitude as to how the Stoics conceived of arriving at the appropriate and the right in specific circumstances. An important clarification has been proposed by Tad Brennan, who discusses three possible models of Stoic practical reasoning.[49] He sees the first model represented in Cicero *De officiis* 3.13 (trans. Griffin and Atkins):

> Indeed, when the Stoics say that the greatest good is to live in agreement with nature, this means, in my view, the following: always to concur with virtue and, as for other things that are in accordance with nature, to choose them if they do not conflict with virtue.

Brennan sees in this passage a model of '*Salva Virtute*' deliberation: 'there are two very different kinds of considerations that must go into any decision about action', considerations about what is according to nature and considerations about what is demanded by virtue, 'and it is also clear that one of them, sc. the one concerning virtue, will always trump the other.'[50]

To Brennan's mind, this model is deficient. It cannot account for texts about Stoic practical reasoning in which deliberations about virtue do not seem to play a role. A text Brennan particularly draws our attention to is Cicero's *De finibus* 3.59–61. There, deliberation is said to be about intermediate things, the objects of appropriate actions. Cicero relates at length Stoic discussions about the suicide of the sage. The sage's decision is based on an assessment of the preferred and dispreferred factors that are present in his life at the moment or are inevitable in the future, but, strikingly, considerations about the fact that he is virtuous (and thus happy) do not figure in the balance. Brennan characterizes the picture of practical reasoning evoked by this passage as 'Indifferents-Only' deliberation.[51]

Also the 'Indifferents-Only' model fails to capture all the relevant evidence.[52] Brennan therefore attempts to construe a compromise between the two models, combining what are, to his eyes, the strong points of each. In Brennan's analysis, Cicero's *Salva Virtute* account is correct in presenting a two-tier model of practical reasoning but wrong in identifying virtue as decisive constraining consideration. The Indifferents-Only model correctly discards virtue as consideration entering deliberation, but fails to take account of the complexity of Stoic practical reasoning by limiting reasoning to a mercenary calculation of indifferents.[53] The Stoics should be understood as embracing a two-tier model. The agent is right to strive for preferred indifferents, but within the limits of moral conventions, which make social life possible.[54] Brennan calls this the 'No Shoving' model, in reference to Cicero's *De officiis* 3.42:

> Runners in a race ought to compete and strive to win as hard as they can, but by no means should they trip their competitors or give them a shove. So too in life; it is not wrong for each person to seek after the things useful for life; but to do so by depriving someone else is not just.[55]

In order to argue that the constraining considerations make no reference to virtue, Brennan has to demote the references to justice in the above passage as well as in, for instance, *De officiis* 3.30–1. To Brennan, they are references not to virtue but to 'certain arrangements of indifferents, even when the arrangements arose from accidents of history or convention.'[56] This, however, is unconvincing. The virtues are characteristics of the sage, but they deal with affairs in the world. The virtue of justice is about distributions. There is, therefore, no reason to theorize an incommensurability between a virtue and certain arrangements of indifferents. On a straightforward reading, the abovementioned passages show agents who ask themselves, 'What are the demands of justice in the circumstances?' For an agent asking this question, justice—or any other virtue—enters the deliberation as the *goal* he aspires to. Conversely, the virtues prescribe certain arrangements of indifferents and forbid others. The deliberations of an agent who does not care about virtue are thus decidedly different from someone taking virtue as the goal. The latter's answer to the question, 'Why are you doing this?' will make reference to virtue; the former's answer will not. Even more different from the answer of someone not caring about virtue will be the deliberations of the sage. As we have seen in Chapter 10, the sage shares the divine perspective on the world and thus sees things from the right angle. Stoic accounts stress the concomitant change in the 'how' side of action, but this should not primarily be interpreted in quantitative terms. It is true our sources claim that the sage and the non-sage can perform what appears to be the same action—that is to say, seen by someone else the 'what' sides of their actions are identical—but the account given of the actions would be different.[57] Only secondarily will this qualitative difference also become manifest in quantitative terms; the non-sage will not be able to realize the *kathēkon* as steadily and regularly as the sage. Or rather, as Seneca makes plain, the odds are decidedly against the non-sage's realizing the same *kathēkon* as the sage: if the non-sage did manage to do so at all, it would be a matter of chance, but nothing one could count on.[58]

Stoic practical reasoning aims at dealing virtuously with indifferents. The relationship between the indifferents and virtue is perhaps best described as implying two scales of value. The first scale orders the (relative) values of indifferent things, the second contains virtue, which is the true good, as the standard of value. Seen from the second scale, the first scale is insignificant. The indifferents provide circumstances of action, but they do not excite the sage, whose primary goal is dealing *virtuously* with indifferent things. This is aptly expressed in David Sedley's analogy of a chess-player.[59] The (accomplished) player aims at playing a good game. Compared with this goal, the relative values of the chess pieces are insignificant. This does not mean that the relative values are completely irrelevant; they are important as providing the situation in which the chess-player can exert his skill, but no more than that. The accomplished chess-player understands the rules defining the strengths and weaknesses of different positions, and he also understands that the values of the pieces can vary in different circumstances; he will offer a pawn or even a queen in order to win the game.[60]

The chess-player analogy is particularly well-suited to illustrate the importance of general rules: '[Y]ou will never become a grandmaster if you do not start out by learning the relative values of the pieces on the board.'[61] However, rules have a broader relevance than only at the transient stage of learning to play expertly. Rules (the relative values of the chess pieces) are all-important so long as a situation is unclear and one is uncertain about what the future brings. An expert chess-player is prepared to offer a piece, even early on in the game, as part of a strategy to secure other perhaps decisive advantages, but he would not play a crazy gambit and offer pieces at the beginning of the game without such advantages in view. Just so, the sage will normally stick to established general rules about the *kathēkonta*. Acting without a full knowledge of what the future will bring, the sage will not unnecessarily weaken his position. The case is different if he knows that the situation at hand is calling for a specific offer.[62]

However, unless such certainty can be had (and, arguably, such cases are quite rare) even the sage, who has a limited knowledge of the future, will have to follow general rules. This stance is not—as one might think—inadequate at all; the sage has learnt to allow for the possible inadequacy of following general rules by engaging himself only 'with reservation' (μεθ' ὑπεξαιρέσεως, *cum exceptione*).[63] He thus modifies the way he is engaging himself, so that possible misfits between his designs and the eventual outcomes leave the stability and fixity of his character unchanged.

The chess-player analogy also demonstrates that the Stoics ultimately had two scales of value: the scale of indifferents and the scale of the truly good and bad, virtue and vice. What is valuable on the virtue scale is to deal virtuously with the circumstances evaluated in terms of the indifferents scale. The fact that the Stoics had two scales of value had exercised their ancient critics. Plutarch, for one, claimed that the Stoics had to choose between two horns of a dilemma: either to acknowledge two independent ends or to make their end, virtue, ineffective in matters of action, since actions are about indifferent things.[64]

The apparent oddity of this two-scale theory is understandable against the backdrop of Stoic ethics as an essentially religious theory. Operating with characterizations of the deity from the theistic side of the linguistic spectrum, the Stoics theorized a personal God who benevolently administers the world.[65] From there it is only a small step to the imagery of man's position in the world as a role in a play allotted to him. In this imagery the divine principle is the author or director of the play in which human beings perform. Human beings have the task to fulfil as well as possible the role in which they are cast.[66] The imagery makes understandable why acting well, fulfilling on the basis of virtue whatever role one performs, is of primary importance and integrates as a secondary concern the results one achieves in terms of preferred and dispreferred indifferents.

If considerations of virtue play a pervasive role, as I have argued, it remains for me to explain how the appearance of virtue entering practical reasoning only in the negative form of constraints could have come about. I suggest that the appearance of virtue considerations as a constraining factor can be explained by reference to the specific literary context in which such considerations were formulated. In the context of admonitions directed at non-sages, it would be natural to expect Chrysippus—in line with his conviction that the natural law only contains prohibitions for the non-sage—to dwell on what one should not do. So it is understandable that in his characterization of the goal of life Chrysippus continues, after identifying 'living virtuously' with 'living in accordance with experience of the actual course of nature' and with living 'in accordance with our own nature as well as that of the universe', with the negative formulation 'a life in which we refrain from every action forbidden by the law common to all things'.[67]

That the specific literary context makes the Stoics appear to have defended a two-tier model with virtue as constraining consideration holds also for Cicero's *De officiis* 3.13. I repeat the translation here:

> Indeed, when the Stoics say that the greatest good is to live in agreement with nature, this means in my view, the following: always to concur with virtue and, as for other things that are in accordance with nature, to choose them if they do not conflict with virtue.

Cicero makes it clear that he gives *his own* account of what the Stoic definition of the goal comes down to: he writes 'in my view' (*ut opinor*).[68] And, indeed, we find a theory which is strikingly different from the Stoic model. Characteristically, the possession of virtue does not come down to dealing virtuously with indifferent things. Cicero even severs the link between 'virtue' and 'in accordance with nature'. I suggest that this and the double occurrence of 'virtue', whose awkwardness has led Brennan to postulate a two-tier model, can best be explained as follows: Cicero saw the primary role of virtue in certain top performances, in the realization of certain high-profile actions; sacrificing one's life to honour a promise and risking one's life in order to save one's country would be two examples. Moreover, the performance of certain exceptionally appropriate actions would have been governed by virtue.[69] In any case, one should imagine such actions to be quite rare and the role of virtue thus understood to be quite limited. In addition to such high-profile actions, there is a large class of actions directed at securing preferred indifferents. With respect to such actions, virtue makes a more frequent but very limited appearance; it forbids certain actions as being in conflict with virtue. This should be understood as ruling out 'unfair' behaviour (setting aside the just entitlements of others etc.). In short, in Cicero's model virtue plays a very limited role. Far from informing all the actions of the sage, even minute ones like the bending of a finger, virtue posits a less elusive standard which every honourable Roman citizen could realize—for most of the time, at least.

Cicero's concept of virtue was less demanding than the Stoics', and he must have been convinced that his pragmatic concept of virtue was better suited to his Roman audience in general and to his son Marcus, the dedicatee of the treatise, in particular.[70] The concept of virtue coming to the fore in *De officiis* 3.13 represents Cicero's own view, and was not geared towards offering an accurate account of the Stoic theory.

However, in spite of being informed by Cicero's own philosophical programme, *De officiis* is of considerable value as a witness of Stoic debates about the appropriateness of concrete courses of action. It gives us not only a unique glimpse of how Stoic practical reasoning worked in practice, but it also shows that prominent Stoics could radically disagree on the course of action appropriate in specific circumstances. I shall examine the material in the next chapter.

Chapter 12

The Single *Kathēkon* and the Versatility of Stoic Prescriptions

Stoic practical reasoning looked to the normative content of the reasonable structure of nature. Thus, Chrysippus could describe nature and what is in accordance with nature as the 'material (ὕλη) of virtue'.[1] With the benefit of hindsight we can see perhaps more clearly than the Stoics how they inscribed themselves with their appeal to nature as normative standard into a broader tradition of Greek ethical thought. We can likewise describe how the indeterminacy and contentiousness of normative concepts of nature recurs in Stoic philosophy.

In earlier Greek philosophy, *physis* was frequently contrasted with *logos*. A reference to 'nature' could be used to critique societal norms as mere conventions which are not determined by nature and do not countermand it. Reports by travellers of culturally variable and even radically opposed conventions could furnish this line of argument with numerous empirical data. Wherever radically opposed conventions were observed, the grounding in nature of the norms of one's own culture could be called into question. In this line of reasoning 'nature' is primarily understood negatively, as the absence of societal conventions. As I shall argue presently, this stance recurs in the early Stoa with some 'antinomian' proposals issued by Zeno. On the other hand, a reference to nature could also be used to dignify certain societal norms.[2] The Stoic theory of *oikeiōsis* seems to have played a prominent role in such arguments. As we have seen in Chapter 10, the doctrine of *oikeiōsis* put emphasis on the transforming presence of reason in human beings and could thus serve to undergird an understanding of nature not as a brute absence of conventions but as a reasonable structure, integrating commitments to culturally acknowledged entitlements and conventions. This opened the possibility of integrating a whole array of conventional social values into Stoic ethics.[3]

References to nature could thus be deeply ambivalent, and the fact that the early Stoics' practical philosophy displays a good deal of this ambivalence has produced intense debate among scholars of Stoic political thought. The key issues are doubts about the coherence of early Stoic social and political thought and the apparent discontinuity of the social and political thought in the Stoic school from the early to its later phases. As appears from our scarce sources, Zeno produced a number of recommendations on political matters and on individual conduct which shared the 'antinomian' spirit of similar proposals issued by the Cynics. In his *Republic*, Zeno judged that no temples, law courts or gymnasia should be built in the cities. Wives should be held in common and unisex clothes should be worn.[1] In two parallel reports Sextus Empiricus relates that Zeno advocated considerable sexual liberty and considered the incestuous relationship between Oedipus and Jocasta 'not terrible'.[5] These antinomian proposals, which wielded the axe on some of the foundations of contemporary society, were perceived as scandalous by many and greatly embarrassed later Stoics too. Diogenes records a curious little story about a Stoic librarian at the Pergamene library, Athenodorus, who excised the embarrassing passages from Zeno's work, but was found out.[6] Stoic stratagems for dealing with the troubling doctrines seem to have included declaring the text of Zeno's *Republic* as spurious or as a juvenile indiscretion better quickly forgotten.[7] However, both strategies were doomed to fail. Diogenes Laertius (7.34) invokes the authority of Chrysippus who seems to have acknowledged the authenticity of Zeno's *Republic*. The case for declaring the *Republic* a youthful transient stage in Zeno's development, an explanation also adopted by some modern scholars,[8] rests mainly on a pun in Diogenes Laertius 7.4. Zeno, it is reported, wrote the *Republic* 'on the dog's tail', suggesting that he wrote it as a young student of Cynicism. This, however, will not do, since Diogenes reports (7.34) that the troubling doctrines were also issued in other Zenonian works. There is, therefore, good reason to doubt the historical value of the pun in Diogenes Laertius 7.4.[9] Moreover, Chrysippus is reported to have defended the troubling Zenonian doctrines,[10] which suggests that the problematic antinomian recommendations enjoyed a broader currency and were quite influential among the early Stoics. This, however, seems to contradict reports about a somewhat more conciliatory stance of Zeno as well as Chrysippus towards contemporary societal conventions. Marriage is defended; the sage will take part in politics, in religious rites, and generally in everyday life quite as the non-sage would do.[11] And when reading Cicero or Seneca one cannot help noticing that in later stages of Stoic thought little of Zeno's antinomian zeal survived.[12]

These are complicated issues which merit a more detailed discussion than can be offered here. For our present purposes I want to draw attention to the deeply ambivalent character which references to nature must have had in Stoic thought. Such references enabled the Stoics to employ a whole spectrum of arguments, ranging from attacks on societal conventions to their wholesale endorsement. Nothing precludes the possibility that an attack on some conventions was combined with the endorsement of other societal norms as having a basis in nature.

Seen in this light, it is highly significant that our knowledge of the antinomian proposals derives from Sceptic authors who show no interest in contextualizing them. In contrast to what these sources could make us think, the proposals may have played a more limited role in early Stoic political thought than our sources would have us believe.[13]

I want to suggest, therefore, that the seemingly contradictory endorsement of antinomian proposals as well as of more conciliatory views on societal conventions should be seen as manifestation of the ambivalence in the reference to nature as a normative principle.[14] Later Stoics would have been exposed to the same tensions and could opt either to defend Zeno's antinomian proposals (perhaps only dialectically, but there is no way of knowing that) or to stress the side more hospitable to societal conventions, without experiencing it as a clear rupture with Zeno's tenets.

In any case, if, as Schofield has argued, the more conciliatory proposals had their locus in a discussion of a choice of lives and a recommendation of the political life even in non-utopian circumstances, and if, moreover, such proposals were already issued by Zeno,[15] then a positive engagement with some contemporary conventions was already part and parcel of Zeno's outlook. It would then be probable that Zeno had recognized that human beings find themselves in certain societal roles which make specific and justified demands on their behaviour. This would indicate that the continuity between the practical recommendations in earlier and later stages of Stoicism may have been greater than appears from our sources' (disproportionate) stress on Zeno's antinomian proposals.

This picture receives indirect support by an analysis of the rise of a theory of human roles in Stoicism. The most prominent example of a theory of roles (*personae*, πρόσωπα) is contained in Cicero's *De officiis* 1.107–21. Every human being partakes in four roles (*personae*): (1) every human being has a rational nature which links him to all the other rational beings. Moreover, every human being has (2) specific intellectual talents, (3) a specific social position and (4) can choose an employment, a specific field of action.[16]

Since Cicero follows Panaetius' ethical handbook *Peri tou kathēkontos* in the first two books of his *De officiis*, it has been widely assumed that the four *personae* theory was an innovation of Panaetius, who in devising it might have been guided by his concern for the everyday problems of ordinary, not-yet-wise people.[17] Yet, there is evidence suggesting that a recognition of roles was already part of the early Stoics' ethical theory. Christopher Gill has pointed to the fact that Epictetus' *Discourses* also contain a recognition of roles, albeit less prominently than the theory in Cicero's *De officiis*. Gill argues that Epictetus' interest in roles is different from Cicero's (or rather, his source Panaetius'). According to Gill, Epictetus stresses far more than Cicero 'the idea that the other roles should, in effect, be subordinated to our common human role'.[18] Epictetus allows for this common human role to make more rigorous demands on the agent than Cicero. Moreover, Epictetus is primarily interested in the figure of the philosopher as fulfilling the demands of that common human role, while Cicero sees no difference of value in a wider range of socially acceptable occupations.[19] In short, the role theory in Epictetus demands more of the agent than the role theory in Cicero.[20] Gill argues that this squares better with the early Stoa than with the conciliatory Panaetius. However, even if the interpretation of the role theory in Epictetus as being characteristically different from the one in Cicero is granted, the argument must remain conjectural.[21]

Nevertheless, we have other evidence suggesting that the recognition of roles had played an important part in early Stoic ethics. In the extant work lists of Stoic philosophers we find a number of treatises entitled 'On the *chrēsis* of . . .' (Περὶ . . . χρήσεως, literally: 'On the use of . . .'), which must be understood as examples of an ancient 'How-to' literature, addressing the question how to fulfil the standards of specific relationships.[22] While the vast majority of such titles are attributed to later Stoics, two early Stoics are reported to have contributed to this 'How-to' literature. At Diogenes Laertius 7.167 a treatise on 'How to treat [one's fellow] human beings' is attributed to Dionysius of Heraclea (c. 330–250 BC). If the abstractness of the title is anything to go by, the treatise represented an early, not yet fully developed stage of this Stoic genre. The title of Chrysippus' contribution, 'On how to treat [one's] parents', suggests a specific focus by this stage.[23] Among the later Stoics, Hierocles seems to have been a particularly prolific guidebook writer, having dedicated separate chapters or treatises to discussions of the best way to deal with gods, motherland, parents, brothers, one's wife and other family members.[24]

The titles suggest that the treatises dealt with the roles human beings play, answering questions about good behaviour in relationships felt to be of concern. In addition, we have titles of other works by early Stoics which suggest a similar concern with roles. To Cleanthes, for instance, a treatise on marriage is attributed, in addition to his three books on *kathēkonta*.

Cleanthes is also credited with a work on litigation.[25] It is likely that the treatise dealt with the do's and don'ts of responsible citizens when implicated in legal procedures.

Taken together, the following picture emerges: Zeno's stance concerning societal norms was characterized by a deep ambivalence. On the one hand, he critiqued some societal norms as being unfounded in nature and advanced antinomian proposals which were felt to be shocking. On the other hand, he seems to have proposed more conciliatory views on obligations one has in concrete, non-ideal circumstances. If (some of) these more conciliatory proposals were located in the context of a discussion of the political life, they may have had a more or less optional character. In any case, a degree of tension must have remained between the antinomian and the more conciliatory proposals. Later Stoics could (and did) increasingly continue the more conciliatory strand in Zeno. In so doing, they could (and did) draw on the recognition of role-related obligations already extant in Zeno's description of the political form of life. In fact, we learn from the increasingly specific titles of Stoic How-to treatises that Zeno's followers increasingly focused on more specific roles and role-related obligations.

The extensive discussion of roles suggests the intention on the part of the Stoics to take seriously the conventions and traditional ideas about obligations. However, it is clear that the assessment of roles is an enormously versatile conceptual strategy. The perceptions of what one was obligated to do in a certain role were bound to differ, and of course the same individual could take on different roles at the same time, which made a hierarchy of such roles as necessary as it had to remain controversial. No doubt the versatility of the Stoic concepts would place many a Stoic in the difficult position of attempting to prescribe what he saw as *the* single *kathēkon* in given circumstances while being at the same time confronted with the fact that other high-profile Stoic teachers prescribed a different (and perhaps even a radically opposite) course of action. This difficulty must have added greatly to the excitement of discussing more specific prescriptions and made the *kathēkonta* literature the particularly fertile field that, as we learn from Cicero's *De officiis*, it must have been.[26]

From Cicero's remarks we learn that Panaetius' work *Peri tou kathēkontos* fell into two clearly separated attempts to delineate the *kathēkon*: the first is a discussion of the *kathēkon* structured according to four (areas of) virtues; the second discussed the *kathēkon* with reference to the useful (*utile, sympheron*). This seems to indicate that a discussion of preferred indifferents made part of Panaetius' treatise.[27] We have no direct evidence concerning the organization of earlier Stoic treatises on the *kathēkon*. However, Gomoll's suggestion that the older Stoic treatises (at least from Chrysippus onwards) were organized according to the virtues is one that deserves to be followed, although for reasons different from Gomoll's.[28] An organization according to the numerous preferred or dispreferred indifferents alone would have been hardly feasible and could not at any rate have given the treatises sufficient unity. In Panaetius' treatise, discussions of indifferents can hardly have been more than examples preparing the discussion of the apparent contrast between the virtuous and the useful.[29] Panaetius' combination of a discussion organized according to a schema of virtues and of exemplary discussions of indifferents may thus have been his innovation, stimulated by his interest in the apparent contrast between the virtuous and the useful. It is therefore tempting to assume that the older *kathēkonta* literature followed a schema of virtues.[30]

Perhaps more importantly, the assumption that the older *kathēkonta* literature was structured according to a schema of virtues is also supported by some tensions we find in Cicero's exposition of Panaetius' theory. Although a theory of two kinds of virtue, theoretical and practical virtue, is ascribed to Panaetius at Diogenes Laertius 7.92, Panaetius followed in his treatise on the *kathēkon* a division of four ethical virtues. At first sight, Panaetius' schema of virtues may seem markedly different from Chrysippus', but on closer inspection we find that a number of Panaetian innovations are connected, sometimes awkwardly, to a division of the virtues which thoroughly resembles Chrysippus'. For instance, the sphere of Panaetius' first virtue is truth, not as in Chrysippus the *kathēkonta* (*Off.* 1.15–16; 1.18).[31] This, and the manner in which the first virtue is set against the other three (*Off.* 1.17), squares with Panaetius' differentiation between theoretical and practical virtue. Yet, at the same time, the first virtue, which is called 'wisdom' (*sophia*), is also closely associated with 'practical wisdom' (φρόνησις). The characterization of *phronēsis* at *De officiis* 1.153 is fully consonant with Chrysippean doctrine: *phronēsis* is the 'knowledge of things one should pursue and avoid' and seems to be a part of 'wisdom'. If we do not want to attribute such unnecessary tensions to Cicero—but why should he have wished to complicate things?—there is only one satisfactory explanation of this awkward association of wisdom and practical wisdom: Panaetius followed a Chrysippean schema of the virtues which traditionally structured the *kathēkonta* literature and attempted to integrate his own views into that traditional structure.[32] He thus reformulated the clear-cut Chrysippean schema of primary and subordinate virtues into a less rigid schema of four groups in which different virtues were enjoying more or less prominent places.[33] (We shall see presently that Panaetius did so also in the case of the other virtues.) Panaetius could thus stress the importance of attaining truth (an aspect located by Chrysippus outside the field of ethical virtues), and he could also integrate the Chrysippean emphasis on the first virtue identifying right courses of action. In Chrysippus as well as in Panaetius, a quickness of intellectual perception makes part of the first field of virtues (*Off.* 1.16).

The second virtue is differentiated into justice and liberality (ἐλευθεριότης), probably to bring out more prominently the 'positive', community-binding function of justice (to serve the common advantage) in addition to its 'negative' side of justice (not to harm anyone).[34] The beneficent acts which form the core of liberality make necessary two sorts of considerations. First, whether such activities are sustainable, i.e. whether they affect the financial status of the giver to such an extent that similar acts become unfeasible in the future (*Off.* 1.42 and 44). This gives rise to concerns about the preservation of one's status as financially independent citizens which are very similar to considerations discussed by Aristotle.[35]

A second, complex web of considerations is addressed in a discussion about how beneficence must be regulated by considerations about the weight of claims made on one's resources, considerations which underline the interdependence of justice and liberality. An account of comparative proximity in the bonds between human beings takes an important place among the rules offered for an assessment of the (comparative) weights of such claims (*Off.* 1.53). In descending order parents, children, relatives, acquaintances and so forth have claims of different weight. However, perhaps a little arbitrarily, the citizen's relation to the political community receives precedence even above the relation to one's parents (*Off.* 1.57–8).

An arithmetic of social proximity alone, however, will not do. Cicero allows for circumstances to alter the order imposed by considerations of proximity. In this way, considerations of need enter the calculus of obligations. Thus, neighbours have a greater claim to one's help at the harvest than relatives do (*Off.* 1.58). Obligations of justice may also be altered or made void by very special exceptional circumstances. Normally a promise must be kept, a loan returned and so forth, but in exceptional circumstances the appropriate course of action can turn out to be quite different. Again, the decisions in such exceptional circumstances can be accounted for by the general rules of justice: not to harm anyone and to serve the common advantage (*Off.* 1.31).[36]

The list of claims on beneficence terminates in what is at a minimal level owed to fellow human beings even if they are unconnected to oneself by such bonds of familiarity. What is owed to them is at the same time easy to give and is no great expense to the giver: 'one should not keep others from fresh water, should allow them to take fire from your fire, should give trustworthy counsel to someone who is seeking advice; for they are useful to those who receive them and cause no trouble to the giver' (*Off.* 1.52, trans. Griffin and Atkins). Such services have their foundation in the Stoics' theological concept of nature: 'Moreover, as the Stoics believe, everything produced on the earth is created for the sake of men, so that they may be able to assist one another. Consequently, we ought in this to follow nature as our leader to contribute to the common stock the things that benefit everyone together, and, by the exchange of dutiful services, by giving and receiving expertise and effort and means, to bind fast the fellowship of men with each other.'[37]

The third Panaetian matrix of virtues is characterized as 'magnanimity' (μεγαλοψυχία), which contained also courage.[38] Compared with the Chrysippean virtue table, we see that Panaetius reversed the status of magnanimity and courage, but again this need not betray a far-reaching change of content. As in Chrysippus, the focus of the third matrix of virtues rests on being unsubdued by, and keeping the stability of one's mind in, adverse circumstances.

Panaetius' most distinct development of the Chrysippean model was the fourth matrix of virtues, which he called after its most prominent virtue 'the seeming' (τὸ πρέπον, *decorum*). Like Chrysippean *sōphrosynē*, *to prepon* has the function of keeping the impulses within the limits of reason (*Off.* 1.101–2) and thus leads to, and preserves, agreement with nature (*Off.* 1.100). Two aspects of the Panaetian 'seeming', however, remind us rather of Aristotle than of Chrysippus: (1) the matrix of 'the seeming' prominently contains a 'sense of shame', which could indicate that Panaetius' was familiar with and took seriously Aristotle's ethical theory.[39] (2) *To prepon* has an ambiguous position, which reminds us of Aristotle's characterization of justice. Like that Aristotelian virtue, *to prepon* has a general and a more restricted meaning. In the more general meaning, *to prepon* summarizes the complete range of virtues, while it is also, in a more restricted sense, a specific virtue.

Since *to prepon* relates two terms and describes a fittingness,[40] roles come naturally into play. It seems that Panaetius developed his four-role theory as a part of his discussion of *to prepon*. There is a marked difference between the first, universal human role and the other three roles characterizing the particular talents and social status of a single human being. In effect, the discussion of possible tensions between the demands of the common human role and those of particular roles made it inevitable that the problems addressed under the headings of the other virtues would resurface in the discussion of *to prepon*. Moreover, it seems that Panaetius placed the discussion of the question as to what sort of life one should choose in the context of a discussion of the three particular roles (*Off.* 1.117). It is easy to understand, therefore, that to Panaetius and Cicero the discussion of *to prepon* summarized the enterprise of practical ethics as a whole. Indeed, as with no other virtue, discussions of *to prepon* could help anchor a conventional social code into Stoic virtue ethics (*Off.* 1.127–9). It hardly needs emphasizing that Cicero's and Panaetius' perceptions of *to prepon* must have been deeply affected by their own social positions. When discussing the choice of occupations, Cicero unquestioningly argues what befits a member of the Roman elite. Retailing goods in a small style he considers demeaning (*Off.* 1.150), and trading is only—just—acceptable when undertaken in a grand style.[11] Such economic activities can only be fully redeemed in retrospect if, after having made his fortune, the trader turns ashore and becomes a great land-owner with agricultural concerns (*Off.* 1.151).

To summarize, the framework established in *De officiis* 1 suggests that Panaetius developed a pre-existing core of *kathēkonta* discussions. The short sketch of the discussion of justice given above corroborates the idea that Stoic practical deliberation worked with general rules, which were ultimately grounded in a theological understanding of nature. General rules were even meant to guide deliberations on obligations in exceptional circumstances.

However, the comparative weight and range of such rules was a matter of considerable controversy in the Stoic school. Particularly in book 3 of *De officiis*, Cicero allows us an interesting glimpse of the debates that aided the formulation of general rules and further determined their content and range. Apparently, the Stoics discussed 'hard cases' with the same zeal as contemporary legal experts, to aid the formulation of general rules and the further refinement of their interpretation (*Off.* 3.91). Cicero's main source of such hard cases was Hecato of Rhodes' book *Peri tou kathēkontos*. As Cicero notes, the sixth book of that work 'is full of questions of this kind' (3.89, trans. Griffin and Atkins). Cicero presents at *De officiis* 3.89–92 a number of cases taken from Hecato's book, and it seems likely that also the cases on the limits of keeping promises (*Off.* 3.92–5, see 1.31–2) and the famous cases on business transactions (*Off.* 3.50–7) were taken from the same source.[12]

The discussion of such cases served to clarify the weight and extent of obligations. A good example is the following series of questions and answers (*Off.* 3.90, trans. Griffin and Atkins):

'Suppose that a father despoil a temple, or dig a tunnel to the treasury, will his son denounce him to the magistrates?'

'That would be impious. He should rather defend his father if he is charged.'

'Does one's country not, then, take precedence in all duties?'

'Yes, indeed. But it actually assists one's country to have citizens who revere their parents.'

'And if a father should try to impose a tyranny, or to betray his country, will the son keep silent?'

'He will beseech his father not to do it, and if he has no success, he will rebuke him and threaten him. In the last resort, if the affair would lead to the ruin of his homeland, he will put its safety before that of the father.'

The discussion assumes certain general principles already presented above. Obligations towards a parent have pride of place among the claims graded according to the closeness of bonds between human beings. For the Stoics, therefore, to honour one's parent was a prime obligation.[43] However, Cicero's discussion shows also that the claims of one's parents ranked inferior to the claims of one's country. Undoubtedly, this must have been an important field of discussion. The issue was to delineate the respective claims of parent and country. The solution hinted at in the little dialogue does not allow the country's claim to nullify a parent's claim. The preservation of one's country is the only valid rationale for denouncing one's father, and even then it is only a last resort. However, extreme reluctance is shown to invoke this rationale: ordinary criminal acts, even despoiling a temple or robbing the treasury do not count as acts endangering the country so greatly that the father should be reported. On the contrary, far-reaching solidarity with the father is presented as being in the best interest of the country.

Our little dialogue presents only one solution to the issue at hand, even if it is easy to imagine other solutions that may have found supporters among the Stoics. However, in respect of other hard cases Cicero explicitly points out the diametrically opposed stances that were held. It seems that the distinguished second century BC Stoics Diogenes of Babylon and his pupil Antipater found themselves regularly championing opposed positions concerning such hard cases (*Off.* 3.51). The most prominent case, discussed at length by Cicero, is the following (*Off.* 3.50, trans. Griffin and Atkins):

For example, suppose that a good man had brought a large quantity of corn from Alexandria to Rhodes at a time when corn was extremely expensive among the Rhodians because of shortage and famine. If he also knew that several more merchants had set sail from Alexandria, and had seen their boats en route laden with corn and heading for Rhodes, would he tell the Rhodians? Or would he keep silent and sell his own produce at as high a price as possible? We are imagining that he is a wise and good man; our question is about the deliberations and considerations of a man who would not conceal the facts from the Rhodians if he judged it dishonourable, but is uncertain as to whether it is dishonourable.[44]

In such cases as this, Antipater defended the view 'that everything should be disclosed, so that there was nothing at all the seller knew and the buyer did not know' (*Off.* 3.51, trans. Griffin and Atkins). Diogenes, by contrast, defended the view (*Off.* 3.51, trans. Griffin and Atkins):

> that the seller ought to mention such faults as the civil law requires, and to do everything else without trickery; but since he is selling, he ought to want to sell at the best price: 'I have transported this here, I have offered it for sale, and I sell it for no more than others do, perhaps even for less, when the supply is more plentiful. Who is treated unjustly?'

Cicero now goes on to elaborate the clash between the two positions in the form of a dialogue. Undoubtedly this exchange was Cicero's literary invention. However, Cicero would have made use of Hecato's presentation of Diogenes' and Antipater's views. There is no need to suppose that Cicero must have misunderstood or misrepresented the nature of the contrast between the two positions.[45]

In the ensuing fictitious exchange Antipater argues from natural law: the fact that private and public benefits are identical can be derived from the principles of nature (*Off.* 3.52). The fellowship among human beings is such that full disclosure is called for (*Off.* 3.53). Antipater appeals to Diogenes to recognize these principles as presuppositions they both share, which is explicitly granted by Diogenes. He recognizes the same principles, but denies that they entail the course of action advocated by Antipater. His stance is that *celare*, 'wilful concealment' (not telling what someone else ought to know at a given moment) is reprehensible, but that non-disclosure in the case at hand is of a different nature: it is merely a non-reprehensive *tacere*, 'keeping silent'. Against Antipater, who argues against this distinction as being inconsistent with the shared principles, Diogenes presses its pivotal importance for the institution of private property (*Off.* 3.53, trans. Griffin and Atkins):

> But is that fellowship of a kind that nothing belongs to any one person? If that is so, then nothing can be sold at all, but must be given.

The assumption undergirding Diogenes' remark must have been that an asymmetry of knowledge between contractors is a factor legitimately influencing the price, as long as the stipulations of the law are observed. Trade gains stemming from such asymmetries are irreproachable and the rightful property of the selling party. Denying such profits by pressing for full disclosure would thus undermine private property. And, after all, the activity of trading was undertaken for the sake of profit: 'since he is selling, he ought to want to sell at the best price' (*Off.* 3.51).

Cicero's sympathies, however, lie with Antipater's cause. Perhaps not entirely fairly, he transfers the discussion to another case, the sale of an objectively unhealthy house, to discredit Diogenes' defence of non-disclosure (*Off.* 3.54–6), and reaches the conclusion 'that the corn dealer ought not to have concealed anything from the Rhodians' (*Off.* 3.57). Yet, Cicero is not satisfied to let the case rest there. In a lengthy discussion of Roman legal practice, he shows that on the venerable Quintus Scaevola's interpretation the Roman legal stipulations actually pull in the same direction as Antipater's philosophical argument (*Off.* 3.70) and concludes that in truth what is virtuous and what is beneficial are one and the same (*Off.* 3.74).

Interesting as the arguments voiced in this fictitious encounter may be in their own right, for our present purposes it is even more instructive to look at the way the clash of positions is presented. It is striking that Cicero, though he strongly favours Antipater's position, introduces both philosophers in the same positive light: 'In cases of this type', we read at *De officiis* 3.51 (trans. Griffin and Atkins), 'Diogenes of Babylon, a great and respected Stoic, tended to have one view, his pupil Antipater, an extremely intelligent man, another.' Nowhere do we find a hint that one of the opinions voiced would have been attacked as falling outside the doctrinal range of the Stoic school. In other words, the difference of opinion is presented as an entirely *legitimate* one. Diogenes' and Antipater's different views indicate the leeway that existed in interpreting the practical bearing of shared principles. In the corn merchant case, the issue was how practically demanding the principle of human fellowship is. While the principle was accepted by both philosophers, Diogenes considered its practical import to be far more restricted than Antipater. According to Diogenes, the principle of human

fellowship should not restrain the making of profit as long as business transactions are conducted within the limits of the law. According to Antipater,
however, the principle had a more extended application: the principle
made forfeiture of certain entirely legal sorts of profit unavoidable.

However, what strikes us most about Cicero's presentation is not the
practical versatility of Stoic ethics regularly commented on by scholars,[16]
it is *the limited nature of the conflict* between Diogenes and Antipater. Above
all, the two philosophers are presented as sharing the same theologically
underpinned principles. The disagreement is presented as if the two philosophers were consciously engaged in a common enterprise of clarifying
the practical import of shared principles.

It is perhaps not over-bold to suggest that this view of the conflict
might have had some historical foundation. Antipater's outright rejection
of Diogenes' position must have placed him in a difficult position. He could
hardly have failed to realize that his teacher drew on shared Stoic principles. His own argument for a radically different course of action must
have been imbued with the awareness that, passionately as he believed that
a more demanding interpretation of the principle of human fellowship
was the right one, his teacher drew likewise upon shared Stoic principles.
He must have realized that his own interpretation, as fervently as he believed
in it, was only one of the options available for a Stoic, and so perhaps it
was Antipater who suggested that they were both engaged in a process of
clarifying the practical import of these shared principles, without of course
repudiating his claim to offer the right interpretation.

Epilogue

The discussions in Chapters 11 and 12 have shown something of the long way that Stoic practical prescriptions travelled from Zeno's (as I have argued, ambivalent) antinomian prescriptions to a philosophy that went down well with the conservative land-owning elite of the late Roman Republic. Chapter 12 has shown, furthermore, the far-reaching synchronic versatility of practical prescriptions as witnessed by the positions advocated by Diogenes and Antipater. If stances on practical matters were not felt to define what it was to be a Stoic, what then ensured the identity and cohesion of the Stoic school?

The question of school cohesion is, of course, of broader interest in respect of the Hellenistic period, where school allegiances played an important role. David Sedley has argued that the identity and cohesion of Greco-Roman philosophical schools generally depended on the members' commitment to the school founder's writings. Certainly this must have been an important factor, and the material presented by him points to its particular salience for the Epicurean school.[1] However, our analysis in Chapters 11 and 12 has suggested that for the Stoic school other factors were more important. Cicero's presentation of Stoic practical deliberation in his *De officiis* is particularly interesting for its silence on the continuing influence of Zeno's writings. Apart from one passing mention of the 'Zenonians' (meaning the Stoics) at 3.35, we find no mention of the school's founder. If we can attach any significance to this silence, as I suggest we should, it seems that by the time of Panaetius, Diogenes and Antipater, Zeno's writings had ceased to be a profitable reference point for practical ethical debate. We can only speculate why that was the case. It is possible that Zeno's memory was so much associated with the antinomian strand in Stoic thinking as to make it embarrassing to quote him.[2] But perhaps it is safe to assume that, given the flight that Stoic literature on role-related obligations had taken subsequently, Zeno's writings were felt to be just not sophisticated enough to continue to serve as a guideline.

It is tempting to assume that Chrysippus' writings supplanted Zeno's and played the integrative role that could explain the identity and cohesion of the Stoic school. And indeed, up to a point this seems to be right. Panaetius' acknowledgement of the interrelatedness yet separateness of the virtues and his constructive engagement with the four-virtues schema suggest that Chrysippus' virtue theory remained a pivotal point of reference. However, in Cicero's text no effort on Panaetius' part is evident to attribute these doctrines to Chrysippus (or, for that matter to any other individual Stoic). This suggests that the cohesion of the Stoic school was safeguarded by agreement on certain general principles which were accepted on their own merits, not because they were issued by this or that famous school head.

What could these common fundamental principles have been? In my analysis I have pointed to shared theological principles and to a shared religious outlook that must have formed the common denominator. The theologically underpinned principle of human fellowship is a striking example of a principle that served as a basis for disagreement on practical stances, while at the same time limiting the scale of such disagreement.

If this is true, it all points to a rather distant attitude of later Stoics towards their founder figure and to a pivotal role for shared theologically underpinned ethical principles. The surprising career of Zenonism, from its inconspicuous beginnings in 300 BC Athens to its being a leading philosophical movement in Imperial Rome and a pivotal point of reference in the Christian era, may have depended on these characteristics.

Appendix 1

Table 1 A Stoic virtue table

	Ethical virtue				Physical virtue	Logical virtue	
Spheres	appropriate actions τὰ καθήκοντα	impulses αἱ ὁρμαί	cases of endurance αἱ ὑπομοναί	distributions ἀπονεμήσεις			
Primary virtues	Practical Wisdom φρόνησις	Temperance σωφροσύνη	Courage ἀνδρεία	Justice δικαιοσύνη	Physics φυσική	Dialectic διαλεκτική	Rhetoric ῥητορική
Subordinated virtues	good judgement εὐβουλία	good ordering εὐταξία	perseverance καρτερία	piety εὐσέβεια	(e.g.) meteorology μετεωρολογική	non-precipitancy ἀπροπτωσία	
	good practical overview εὐλογιστία	propriety κοσμιότης	confidence θαρραλεότης	kindness χρηστότης		uncarelessness ἀνεικαιότης	
	quick moral sense ἀγχίνοια	sense of honour αἰδημοσύνη	magnanimity μεγαλοψυχία	sociability εὐκοινωνησία		irrefutability ἀνελεγξία	

	discretion νουνέχεια	self-control ἐγϰράτεια	mental stoutness εὐψυχία	blameless companionship εὐσυναλλαξία	non-randomness ἀματαιότης
	shrewdness εὐστοχία		industry φιλοπονία		
	resourcefulness εὐμηχανία				
Other subordinated virtues[a]	understanding σύνεσις		constancy ἀπαραλλαξία	equality ἰσότης	
			vigour εὐτονία	fairmindedness εὐγνωμοσύνη	
Other virtues[b]	e.g. conviviality (συμποτική), erotic virtue (ἐρωτιϰή)				
Traits whose role is unclear[c]	e.g. prophetic virtue (μαντιϰή), economics (οἰϰονομιϰή)				

[a] Probably not Chrysippean.
[b] Not clearly subordinated to a specific generic virtue; not certain if Chrysippean.
[c] These traits could be either virtues or pursuits.

Chrysippus' and Aristotle's Lists of Virtues—a Comparison

Students of Stoic ethics have often contrasted Aristotle with the Stoics. Regularly, this has been done with the intention of showing that Stoic ethics manifests some sort of moral progress towards ideals held dear nowadays. Julia Annas (1993), for instance, has claimed that the Stoics argue for a progression to the 'completely impartial concern for all humans', which contrasts most favourably with Aristotle's communitarian virtue of friendship, carefully limited to a few people near and dear.

Such claims suggest that the Stoics must have advocated a practice which was wholly distinct from that of Aristotle. Underlying this book is a quite different assumption. In my view, what unified Stoic ethics as well as set it apart from other ancient ethical theories was the extent to which it was religiously imbued and the way it drew on theological concepts. I am quite hesitant to attribute novelty and distinctness to the practice envisaged by the Stoics. In fact, where we do have additional material, in the form of prescriptions of specific courses of action, our—admittedly often rather late—material points to a great versatility in Stoic practice and does not suggest that Stoic practice was distinct.[1]

In support of this assumption, I compare in this appendix Chrysippus' catalogue of ethical virtues to Aristotle's virtue table.[2] By comparing Aristotle's and Chrysippus' lists of virtues, I do not want to suggest that Chrysippus actually read or knew Aristotle's work on ethics. Sandbach's (1975) sceptical stance has rightly made scholars rethink bold assumptions about what Chrysippus or other early Stoics 'must' have read and known. In fact, I believe that the material presented in this appendix does not imply that Chrysippus must have known, and reacted to, Aristotle's definitions or theories.

Speculative as such a comparison must be, it seems to me that it can serve a negative purpose: to make us think twice before issuing grand claims about the distinctness of Stoic practice. A comparison between the two virtue tables will reveal clear differences, but these differences need not point to completely different practical concerns or to markedly different practices.

The Aristotelian virtue table analysed here is described in the *Nicomachean Ethics*. At 2.7 Aristotle lists, and gives short characteristics of, the virtues he is going to discuss in greater detail. The text indicates that Aristotle thought of the virtues as arranged in a proper table (διαγραφή).[3] The table itself is not extant in the manuscripts of the *Nicomachean Ethics*, but it can safely be reconstructed from Aristotle's comments and from a similar table offered in the *Eudemian Ethics*. The virtues are human excellences in specific spheres of action or spheres of feeling; they are means between two extremes, constituted by the respective excesses and deficiencies, which are each to be considered vicious. For instance, concerning the sphere of experiencing fear and confidence, the right mean is the virtue of courage (ἀνδρεία). Lack of fear (or excess of confidence) is rashness (θρασύτης); the corresponding contrary vice is cowardice (δειλία), i.e. excessive fear (or lack of confidence).[4]

In the same way, short descriptions of the following virtues are given: courage (ἀνδρεία), temperance (σωφροσύνη), liberality (ἐλευθεριότης), magnificence (μεγαλοπρέπεια), magnanimity (μεγαλοψυχία), an unnamed middle that denotes proper ambition, patience (πραότης), truthfulness (ἀλήθεια), wittiness (εὐτραπελία), friendliness (φιλία), and righteous indignation (νέμεσις).[5] Another quality, which is praised as a mean between extremes, but which is not considered a virtue by Aristotle, is shame (αἰδώς).[6] So far, these qualities can be described within the schema of the right mean between deficiency and excess regarding actions and emotions. For the pivotal virtue of justice, this schema could not be applied straightforwardly. Aristotle will say later on in the *Nicomachean Ethics* that justice is a mean in a different way from the other virtues.[7] In consequence, Aristotle mentions justice in book 2 only in passing and promises a detailed treatment at a later stage (in book 5).

Up to this point, the virtues mentioned are 'ethical' virtues, virtues of character. Apart from these ethical virtues, Aristotle discusses (in book 6) some 'intellectual' virtues as well. One of them, 'practical wisdom' (φρόνησις), is indispensable for planning one's conduct. In total, we get a list of fourteen virtues or virtue-like qualities (including shame and righteous indignation), which can be ordered as follows:

Table 2   Aristotelian virtues (EN 2.7)

Sphere of action or feeling	Excess	Mean/Virtue	Deficiency
Fear and confidence	rashness (θρασύτης)	courage (ἀνδρεία)	cowardice (δειλία)
Pleasure and pain	licentiousness (ἀκολασία)	temperance (σωφροσύνη)	insensibility (ἀναισθησία)
Getting and spending (minor)	prodigality (ἀσωτία)	liberality (ἐλευθεριότης)	illiberality (ἀνελευθερία)
Getting and spending (major)	vulgarity (ἀπειροκαλία, βαναυσία)	magnificence (μεγαλοπρέπεια)	pettiness (μικροπρέπεια)
Honour and dishonour (major)	vanity (χαυνότης)	magnanimity (μεγαλοψυχία)	pusillanimity (μικροψυχία)
Honour and dishonour (minor)	ambition (φιλοτιμία)	an unnamed middle that denotes proper ambition	unambitiousness (ἀφιλοτιμία)
Anger	irascibility (ὀργιλότης)	patience (πραότης)	lack of spirit (ἀοργησία)
Self-expression	boastfulness (ἀλαζονεία)	truthfulness (ἀλήθεια)	understatement (εἰρωνεία)
Conversation	buffoonery (βωμολοχία)	wittiness (εὐτραπελία)	boorishness (ἀγροικία)
Social conduct	obsequiousness (ἀρέσκεια); flattery (κολακεία)	an unnamed kind of friendliness which is close to friendship (φιλία)	cantankerousness (δυσκολία, δύσερις)
Shame	shyness (κατάπληξις)	shame (αἰδώς)	shamelessness (ἀναισχυντία)
Indignation	envy (φθόνος)	righteous indignation (νέμεσις)	malicious enjoyment (ἐπιχαιρεκακία)
		justice (δικαιοσύνη)	
		practical wisdom (φρόνησις)	

Let us compare this table with the list of Chrysippean 'ethical' virtues and their definitions as presented by Stobaeus and Pseudo-Andronicus of Rhodes.[8] In a tabular arrangement it looks as follows:

Table 3   Chrysippean ethical virtues (Stobaeus/Ps.-Andronicus of Rhodes)

Spheres	Proper actions τὰ καθήκοντα	Impulses αἱ ὁρμαί	Cases of endurance αἱ ὑπομοναί	Distributions ἀπονεμήσεις
Primary virtues	Practical Wisdom φρόνησις =df. ἐπιστήμη ὧν ποιητέον καὶ οὐ ποιητέον καὶ οὐδετέρων / ἐπιστήμη ἀγαθῶν καὶ κακῶν καὶ οὐδετέρων φύσει πολιτικοῦ ζῷου	Temperance σώφροσύνη =df. ἐπιστήμη αἱρετῶν καὶ φευκτῶν καὶ οὐδετέρων	Courage ἀνδρεία =df. ἐπιστήμη δεινῶν καὶ οὐ δεινῶν καὶ οὐδετέρων	Justice δικαιοσύνη =df. ἐπιστήμη ἀπονεμητικὴ τῆς ἀξίας ἑκάστῳ
Subordinated virtues	good judgement εὐβουλία =df. ἐπιστήμη τοῦ ποῖα καὶ πῶς πράττοντες πράξομεν συμφερόντως	good ordering εὐταξία =df. ἐπιστήμη τοῦ πότε πρακτέον καὶ τί μετὰ τί καὶ καθόλου τῆς τάξεως τῶν πράξεων	perseverance καρτερία =df. ἐπιστήμη ἐμμενητικὴ τοῖς ὀρθοῖς κριθεῖσι	piety εὐσέβεια =df. ἐπιστήμη θεῶν θεραπείας
	good practical overview εὐλογιστία =df. ἐπιστήμη ἀνταναιρετικὴ καὶ συγκεφαλαιωτικὴ τῶν γινομένων καὶ ἀποτελουμένων	propriety κοσμιότης =df. ἐπιστήμη πρεπουσῶν καὶ ἀπρεπῶν κινήσεων	confidence θαρραλεότης =df. ἐπιστήμη καθ' ἣν οἴδαμεν ὅτι οὐδενὶ δεινῷ μὴ περι-πέσωμεν	kindness χρηστότης =df. ἐπιστήμη εὐποιητική
	quick moral sense ἀγχίνοια =df. ἐπιστήμη εὑρετικὴ τοῦ καθήκοντος ἐκ τοῦ παράχρημα	sense of honour αἰδημοσύνη =df. ἐπιστήμη εὐλαβητικὴ ὀρθοῦ ψόγου	magnanimity μεγαλοψυχία =df. ἐπιστήμη ὑπεράνω ποιοῦσα τῶν πεφυκότων ἐν σπουδαίοις τε γίνεσθαι καὶ φαύλοις	sociability εὐκοινωνησία =df. ἐπιστήμη ἰσότητος ἐν κοινωνίᾳ

(*Continued*)

Table 3 (Continued)

Spheres	Proper actions τὰ καθήκοντα	Impulses αἱ ὁρμαί	Cases of endurance αἱ ὑπομοναί	Distributions ἀπονεμήσεις
	discretion νουνέχεια =df. ἐπιστήμη τῶν χειρόνων καὶ βελτιόνων	self-control ἐγκράτεια =df. ἐπιστήμη ἀνυπέρβατος τῶν κατὰ τὸν ὀρθὸν λόγον φανέντων	mental stoutness εὐψυχία =df. ἐπιστήμη ψυχῆς παρεχομένης ἑαυτὴν ἀήττητον	blameless companionship εὐσυναλλαξία =df. ἐπιστήμη τοῦ συναλλάττειν ἀμέμπτως τοῖς πλησίον
	shrewdness εὐστοχία =df. ἐπιστήμη ἐπιτευκτικὴ τοῦ ἐν ἑκάστῳ σκόπου		industry φιλοπονία =df. ἐπιστήμη ἐξεργαστικὴ τοῦ προκειμένου οὐ κωλυομένη διὰ πόνον	
	resourcefulness εὐμηχανία =df. ἐπιστήμη εὑρετικὴ διεξόδου πραγμάτων			

I begin the comparison with the four 'cardinal' Stoic virtues.

Practical wisdom (φρόνησις). Two definitions of practical wisdom are offered in Stobaeus. They are roughly equivalent, with the first stressing the practical import of the knowledge of things good and bad, and the second emphasizing the fundamentally social nature of human beings.

Aristotle defines practical wisdom as 'a correct disposition related to reason, which is concerned with doing the human good'.[9] In a less formal manner, Aristotle describes the practically wise person as being able to reason well about what is good and advantageous for himself concerning the good life in general.[10] The consideration of advantageousness, which is central to Aristotle's description, is arguably less prominent in Chrysippus; nonetheless it is present: it is borne out by a virtue subordinated to practical wisdom, good judgement (εὐβουλία).

Apart from this difference of emphasis, both concepts of practical wisdom are similarly broad—indeed, so broad that one cannot help wondering if practical wisdom on its own does not exhaust the field of the virtues. In fact, Aristotle theorizes an interentailment of the virtues on the basis of practical wisdom as the unifying base of the other virtues.[11] In spite of his similarly broad concept of practical wisdom, Chrysippus does not attribute such a unifying role to practical wisdom. Possibly Chrysippus was wary of such a theory, because it made it more difficult to account for a plurality of different virtues.[12]

Temperance (σώφροσύνη). The scope of temperance is much narrower in Aristotle's than in Chrysippus' account: Aristotle holds that temperance deals with the pleasures of touch and taste.[13] Aristotle is prepared to limit the scope of temperance even further: in his view, temperance is *not* concerned with, for instance, warm baths.[14] Chrysippean temperance, by contrast, has a far broader scope. It is concerned with human impulses (ὁρμαί) in general. It would therefore have been possible for Chrysippus to criticize, for example, the excessive enjoyment of warm baths as a form of licentiousness.

Courage (ἀνδρεία). Any account of courage must depend on what is or is not considered bad and thus objectively fearful. For the Stoics, the possession or lack of virtue exhausts the range of the things good and bad; nothing is objectively fearful.[15] Moreover, the virtues are manifest in all actions, even apparently trifling ones. The Stoics, therefore, could hardly be interested in narrowing the scope of courage to peak-performance situations such as war. The absence of any limiting conditions in Chrysippus' definition of courage could reflect these assumptions.[16] Aristotle's account of courage, by contrast, shows his intention to address peak-performances of courage specifically. Courage is primarily displayed in facing (objectively fearful) death in battle. However, like the Stoics, Aristotle offers a revisionary account of courage: it prioritizes the avoidance of vices rather than the fear of things not in one's control (*EN* 1115a17–19).

Justice (δικαιοσύνη). Temperance and courage are Chrysippean virtues that have a broader scope than their Aristotelian counterparts. The reverse, however, can also be found, namely that an Aristotelian virtue has a broader scope than a Stoic virtue. Justice is a case in point. Aristotle distinguishes (1) general and (2) specific justice. General justice is the other-related use of the virtues;[17] from this it follows that, in a broad sense, general justice is complete virtue with special reference to other people.[18] While we find a similarly broad conception of a virtue in a later Stoic,[19] there is no inkling of such a broad scope in Chrysippus' definition of justice.

As far as specific justice, one among the specific virtues, is concerned, Aristotle differentiates and discusses it in so much detail as to underline the special status it has in the Aristotelian virtue table. He differentiates between (2a) distributive justice, the branch of specific justice which is concerned with the distribution of goods, and (2b) corrective justice, which is the part of specific justice concerned with compensations in trade or court decisions. Aristotle remarks that it is a universally acknowledged fact that distributive justice consists in distribution according to some sort of value (κατ' ἀξίαν τινά).[20] Chrysippus' definition of justice similarly evokes distributions according to value. Erskine has argued that *axia* refers to reason as a general human characteristic and that the definition of justice should therefore be understood as having far-reaching democratic and egalitarian implications (possibly a deliberate attack on Aristotle).[21] However, this seems off the mark: the fact that Chrysippus used the formula 'according to value' or 'what is due' (κατ' ἀξίαν) to describe justice in punishments, shows that he held value to be a differential property.[22]

Good judgement (εὐβουλία). That the wise man is able to find an advantageous course of action is a common characteristic in both Stoic and Aristotelian accounts. Although εὐβουλία is not itself contained in Aristotle's virtue table, it is an aspect of practical wisdom: 'to have judged well is characteristic of the practically wise'.[23] Practical wisdom has to do with 'what is advantageous with respect to the end'.[24]

The main difference between the two accounts lies in the notion of *epistēmē* employed by Chrysippus. For Aristotle, good judgement is not an *epistēmē*, on the grounds that *epistēmē* is about things one knows, whereas one exerts εὐβουλία concerning things one does not yet know.[25] It is possible that the different terminological choices are indicative of a larger difference in theorizing the role of practical deliberation: Aristotle's terminological choice might reflect the belief that there cannot be an application of general rules to individual cases. Rather, he stresses the role of 'seeing' what is right in a given situation.[26] Chrysippus' terminological choice, by contrast, could indicate that practical deliberation is rule-based and directed at putting into practice what is demanded by the normative structure of the world.[27]

Good practical overview (εὐλογιστία). This virtue is a kind of 'weighing knowledge', taking stock of the situation one has to act in. It ensures that the Stoic sage has a clear perception of the circumstances in which he has to act. Again, Aristotle does not recognize this as a particular virtue, but we may assume that he would grant the intellectual capacity of good practical overview to the good agent. This is evidenced by Aristotle's emphasis on practical experience, which provides the good agent with an 'eye' for the situation, a clear perception of the relevant circumstances.[28]

Quick moral sense (ἀγχίνοια). Of course, the agent cannot deliberate endlessly, but should be able to reach a decision quickly. This is recognized by Aristotle as well, even though ἀγχίνοια does not appear on the 'official' list of virtues. For him, ἀγχίνοια is not restricted to ethics, but is an excellence to do with syllogistic reasoning in general. Therefore, ἀγχίνοια is treated in the *EN* only in passing (at 1142b5–6) and gets a broader treatment in the 'epistemological' treatise *Analytica posteriora* (89b10–20). There it is described as 'the ability to find the middle term in an unnoticeably short time'.[29]

Discretion (νουνέχεια). Why does the Stoic sage need an '*epistēmē* of what is worse and better' in addition to the other aforementioned virtues related to practical wisdom? The most probable guess is that discretion is the knowledge involved in balancing possible courses of action, whereas good practical overview is about reviewing the external circumstances in which an action has to take place. In Aristotle, discretion does not occur as a virtue term at all, but again it is reasonable to assume that for him a quality like discretion was entailed by practical wisdom.

Shrewdness (εὐστοχία). Shrewdness is the knowledge of how to achieve one's aim in every individual case. Again, it is hard to see why one would need shrewdness in addition to good practical overview, quick moral sense and discretion. Perhaps the specific characteristic of shrewdness is a more detailed knowledge than that of the other three virtues, i.e. knowledge of the *specific* means one has to employ in a *specific* situation. Aristotle talks about εὐστοχία as well, but only as an explanans of other (in his view apparently more important) qualities, not as a virtue in its own right. Crucially, εὐστοχία is for Aristotle a non-rational quality.[30]

Resourcefulness (εὐμηχανία). In Aristotle's biological writings, birds are called 'resourceful' with reference to their being able to find a way of living in unfavourable circumstances.[31] The Stoic term 'resourcefulness' has a similar meaning. Resourcefulness is the *epistēmē* of finding a way out of difficulties. Again, it is hard to tell why Chrysippus thought it was necessary to list a separate virtue of resourcefulness in addition to shrewdness. It is possible that by making resourcefulness a separate virtue Chrysippus wanted to emphasize that in any situation, even in the most difficult one, there is a rational strategy for coping.

Good ordering (εὐταξία). At first sight it seems strange that a virtue concerned with the appropriate ordering of things to be done should not belong to the group of virtues subordinated to practical wisdom, since they are primarily concerned with finding appropriate actions. An explanation for the surprising locus of good ordering[32] could be that Chrysippus wanted to highlight the derailing influence of emotions. He held that emotions are caused by impulses not fully controlled by reason. Since temperance deals with impulses, the subordination of good ordering to temperance would convey the message that it is the emotions which are responsible for the agent's missing the right moment for action and his failing to realize the appropriate order of actions. Like resourcefulness, good ordering is not contained in Aristotle's virtue table. While the broader theoretical assumptions probably standing behind the Stoic virtue of good ordering are incompatible with Aristotle's framework, there is no reason to assume that Aristotle would have denied that the actions of his *spoudaios* are well-ordered, fitting and, if needs be, resourceful.

Propriety (κοσμιότης). I suggest translating the definition of propriety as 'knowledge of seemly and unseemly behaviour'. If Panaetius' development of Stoic virtue theory is anything to go by, then propriety should be construed as being about the fulfilment of (reasonable) role expectations in the widest sense. Panaetius must have promoted this aspect of Chrysippean temperance to a central role (and demoted temperance to the status of a subordinate virtue) in order to give his theory of roles a proper systematic locus in the discussion of *kathēkonta* which was—as I argued in Ch. 12—traditionally systematized according to a schema of four primary virtues.

Such role expectations may have changed during the history of the Stoic school. A point in question relates to early Stoic 'antinomian' recommendations such as promiscuous sexual relationships and unisex clothing, which later Stoics were probably not too keen on maintaining.[33] The Stoics' claim that the virtues are the same for men and women may have originally supported such antinomian recommendations, but it did probably little by way of preventing more traditional delineations of gender roles.[34] In any case, the gravitas which characterizes the virtuous citizen in the account of Cicero/Panaetius stands in clear continuity to earlier Stoic accounts of the sage and bears at the same time much resemblance to Aristotle's description of the *spoudaios*.[35] Presumably, Aristotle, whose table does not contain propriety as a separate virtue, would have taken it to be included in practical wisdom.

Sense of honour (αἰδημοσύνη). Aristotle uses a similar concept with his 'sense of shame' (αἰδώς). For Aristotle, sense of shame is not a virtue proper, but rather a passion (πάθος). He argues that sense of shame is a kind of preventive, 'hypothetical' feeling of remorse.[36] It is a feeling that only people who are prone to deficiencies in their behaviour can have. Accordingly, it is appropriate for the young, who are prevented by shame from misbehaving, but it should not be felt by older citizens.[37] If a mature citizen is morally good, he does what is good and will therefore not feel shame. If he is bad, however, he acts badly—but then his feeling shame is not laudable, because it evidences his defective character.[38] Like Aristotle, Chrysippus judges the actual *feeling* of shame undesirable. It seems, therefore, that *aidēmosynē* has a similarly preventive role.

Self-control (ἐγκράτεια) *and perseverance* (καρτερία). Aristotle's discussion of self-control and perseverance starts from the received opinion (ἔνδοξον) that both qualities are closely linked and that both belong to the temperate (σώφρων).[39] However, in his own assessment Aristotle clearly differentiates between self-control and perseverance. He does so by assuming a difference in value: perseverance (successful resistance) is inferior in value to self-control (complete mastery), in the same way as 'not losing' is to 'victory'.[40] Aristotelian self-control is therefore not a proper virtue. Like shame, self-control is a quality which exists only as a counterweight to certain defective character traits, but it is not a quality of the fully virtuous, since they have no conflicting desires. Yet, since the virtuous agent's good actions look as if he had successfully subdued his desires, the virtuous agent can be talked of as self-controlled by analogy.[41] Chrysippus also distinguishes between self-control and perseverance, but on completely different grounds. He attaches them to different spheres. Self-control, by being subordinated to temperance, is concerned with the sphere of impulses, whereas perseverance is subordinated to courage and thus deals with cases of endurance.

Confidence (θαρραλεότης). For Aristotle, confidence is not a virtue in its own right. Rather, it is an aspect of courage: showing confidence is a sign of being courageous.[42] Chrysippus' definition of confidence reflects a reasoning which is incompatible with Aristotle's. Aristotelian courage presupposes that there are objectively fearful things; and with respect to them, the passion of fear seems to be justifiable, even necessary.[43] Aristotelian courage is about facing these justifiable and necessary fears, especially in war, when the agent is confronted by death or by the imminent danger of death.[44] Chrysippean confidence, by contrast, consists in the knowledge that *nothing* really terrible can happen to the sage. In consequence, Chrysippus maintains that the feeling of a passion like fear is never justifiable or necessary. Accordingly, he does not restrict the range of situations in which courage can primarily be displayed to situations in war. His broader notion of courage matches our contemporary common usage better than Aristotle's account does; a woman facing a difficult childbirth, or people facing a terminal illness can be said to be 'courageous' in the same central sense as a warrior.

Magnanimity (μεγαλοψυχία). Chrysippus' definition of magnanimity reads 'the *epistēmē* which makes one be above those things whose nature it is to happen to good and bad persons alike'. It reflects fundamental Stoic doctrines: one should be above things that are independent of the virtue of the person concerned. Such non-virtue factors—discussed as 'preferred indifferent things' (προηγμένα) and 'dispreferred indifferent things' (ἀποπροηγμένα)—are in themselves indifferent to the central, virtue-related self-concept of the agent. Interestingly, Aristotle's discussion of courage betrays a similar tendency to prioritize the virtue-related self-concept of the agent (see above), which sits uneasily with his recognition of objectively fearful things.

Aristotelian magnanimity is about finding a balance between the agent's justified self-esteem and his share of external goods.[45] Aristotle claims that magnanimity is primarily concerned with the greatest of external goods, namely honour.[46] His depiction of the magnanimous person is somewhat undecided: on the one hand the magnanimous person should attach paramount importance to his justified claim to honour, but on the other hand he should not value honour much, and *a fortiori* he should value the minor external goods even less.[47] As in the case of courage, we find here a tendency to (partly) devalue external goods which sits uneasily with his recognition of their objective importance. The importance that Aristotle attaches to honour is confirmed by the fact that he recognizes, in addition to magnanimity (which is about honour on a large scale), a special virtue concerned with honour on a small scale (an unnamed middle denoting proper ambition) and another virtue concerning the justified claim to honour in conversation (truthfulness). From Aristotle's description of truthfulness, it is clear that the agent's claim to honour is important enough to make understatement a serious moral defect.

Chrysippus' understanding of magnanimity betrays no such hesitancy. Seen from the viewpoint of virtue, external goods have no relevant value. In consequence, Chrysippus does not express any interest in singling out honour as being of central importance to the concept of magnanimity.

Mental stoutness (εὐψυχία). The virtue of mental stoutness supports the inner strength of the virtuous person's soul. Lack of evidence makes it impossible for us to understand what mental stoutness adds to confidence. In any case, Aristotle would certainly have considered qualities as mental stoutness contained in his notion of courage.

Industry (φιλοπονία). Chrysippus' description of industry is close to Aristotle's description of a quality that the *spoudaios* has: he cannot be deterred by trouble or pain from doing in a concrete situation what he knows ought to be done. Industry is very similar to perseverance.[48]

Piety (εὐσέβεια). Chrysippus subordinates piety to justice. Piety is thus a special case of giving everybody what is due to them. With his subordination of piety to justice, Chrysippus may have followed Socrates' lead.[49] The fact that Chrysippus makes piety part of his list of virtues reflects the fundamentally religious character of his philosophy.

While this explicit recognition of piety is in clear contrast to Aristotle's virtue catalogue, which does not contain piety,[50] it seems unlikely that the envisaged practices of the Aristotelian and Chrysippean virtuous men were markedly different. Both philosophers stand in the broader Greek tradition of a spiritualizing philosophical theology which combines a somewhat revisionary account of the divine with a strong presumption in favour of participation in traditional religious cults.[51]

Kindness (χρηστότης). Kindness is defined as 'the *epistēmē* of doing good'. While kindness is not discussed in the *Nicomachean Ethics* and none of the Aristotelian virtues does exactly the same job as Chrysippean kindness, the practical concerns of the two accounts are by no means dissimilar. This becomes clear once we examine the Aristotelian candidates for the role played by kindness in Chrysippus' virtue catalogue:

(1) Aristotelian patience (πραότης) is a virtue in the non-excessive feeling of anger; it ensures that no excessive retaliation takes place after suffering a slight. Thereby Aristotelian patience is concerned with preventing harmful actions to others. It plays a role very similar to justice as interpreted by Cicero/Panaetius, who attribute to justice a 'negative', harm-preventing role.[52] In order to complement this negative harm-preventing role with a positive, community-binding one, Cicero/Panaetius differentiate between justice and liberality and promote the latter virtue from a virtue subordinated to justice to a virtue on a par with justice. It seems that this positive, community-binding function is realized by Chrysippean kindness.

(2) The Aristotelian virtues concerning getting and spending do not have the same scope as Chrysippean kindness: Aristotelian liberality and magnificence are about spending money, not about doing good in general. Moreover, these Aristotelian virtues ensure that income and expenditure are in a balance. They ensure that the agent does not waste his property, thereby securing the social status of the agent in the long run.[53] It is perhaps not unfair to say that the Stoic axiology, which classes property and civic status among the indifferents, inevitably demotes them in comparison to Aristotle's account. Nonetheless, the practical concerns standing behind Aristotle's virtues of liberality and magnificence would have been recognizable to Chrysippus. Property was a Stoic *preferred* indifferent after all and concern about its conservation was thus considered reasonable. The extensive discussion in Cicero/Panaetius on the balance between income and expenditure is no more than a reflection of this.[54]

(3) Aristotelian friendship (full φιλία, not the unnamed kind of friendliness which is close to friendship) does not have the same scope as Chrysippean kindness either: Aristotelian friendship is highly selective in that (among other characteristics) it presupposes affection and goodwill to people who know that they are the object of those attitudes.[55] Chrysippus' definition of kindness as the *epistēmē* of doing good evidences no restriction on the basis of bonds of affection. On the strength of that definition, it seems perfectly conceivable that kindness is directed at someone who is not aware of it, or to somebody one does not know personally.

(4) In addition to friendship proper, Aristotle describes a less restricted feeling of goodwill (εὔνοια), which can be felt towards strangers and can be unknown to its object.[56] But goodwill does not include active assistance to the person to whom one entertains goodwill, and Aristotle therefore suggests the label 'inoperative friendship'.[57] Chrysippus' catalogue of virtues does not evidence such a gradation of the obligation of assistance according to the closeness of bonds with other people. Could we therefore suppose that the Stoic sage would have scored higher on other-regard than the Aristotelian *spoudaios*? This has sometimes been claimed, with reference to the Stoic theory of *oikeiōsis*.[58] Julia Annas, for instance, has argued that the Stoics insist on a 'progression to completely impartial concern for all humans just as such, instead of stopping with a form of *philia* or commitment to particular other people' as Aristotle did.[59] I doubt that the emphasis on completely impartial concern would have resulted in a markedly different practice. Our evidence from the Stoic literature on role-related obligations shows that the Stoics recognized, as Aristotle did, that human beings occupy different roles and stand at different distances from one another. Ignoring such differences would precisely result in the annihilation of social roles and their normative, behaviour-regulating function. Completely impartial concern for others, therefore, need not and cannot entail that such differences should be disregarded. Already the considerable energy devoted by Cicero/Panaetius to delineating and weighing role-related obligations (e.g. to a neighbour as opposed to a relative) tells us as much.[60]

Sociability (εὐκοινωνησία) *and blameless companionship* (εὐσυναλλαξία). Erskine attempted to support his egalitarian and democratic interpretation of Stoic justice with a reference to the virtue of sociability.[61] However, I doubt that sociability has specific political overtones. We should perhaps translate the definition as 'the *epistēmē* of equality in social intercourse'. It seems more to the point to see in sociability and blameless companionship two virtues that regulate social intercourse. They would thus betray a similar concern as the virtue of conviviality.[62] Sociability would ensure that the Stoic sage strikes the right tone, or chooses the right register in social intercourse. The virtue of blameless companionship would have a more limited focus by highlighting the negative, blame-avoiding aspect of good social intercourse and by concentrating on specific obligations to neighbours. Again, no great practical difference between Aristotle's and Chrysippus' accounts must be suspected. The Aristotelian *spoudaios* would be as keen as the Chrysippean sage to socialize in an adequate way, which inevitably entails some reference to accepted societal standards of right behaviour.[63]

Notes

Introduction

[1] This is not, of course, to deny the importance of the shorter discussions by Long (1991) and Gass (2000).

[2] Passions: for example, Inwood (1985: ch. 5); Nussbaum (1994: esp. chs. 9–12); Sorabji (2000); Tielemann (2003); Graver (2007). Appropriation: for example, Pohlenz (1940); Pembroke (1971); Striker (1983); Engberg-Pedersen (1986 and 1990a); Long (1993); Lukoschus (1999: 91–143); Radice 2000); Lee (2002); Reydams-Schils (2002); Algra (2003a); Bees (2004); Brennan (2005: 154–68); Laurand (2005, esp. 9–58); Zagdoun (2005); Roskam (2005: chs. 1–2).

[3] At least in the now fashionable readings of Aristotle, stressing contextualistic and particularistic aspects of Aristotle's theory and advocating forms of virtue ethics independent of general rules (a trend stemming from Anscombe's 1958 revival of ancient virtue ethics).

[4] See Appendix 2.

[5] See Sedley (1989), stressing the spirit of reverence for the school founder. That choice of school membership was the choice of a form of life that has been detailed in numerous studies: for example, Rabbow (1954); I. Hadot (1969); Voelke (1993); Decleva Caizzi (1993); Nussbaum (1994) and P. Hadot (1995 and 2002).

[6] This is the upshot of Diogenes Laertius 7.179, where Chrysippus is reported to have said to Cleanthes 'that all he wanted was to be told what the doctrines were; he would find out the proofs for himself' (trans. Hicks). The claim immediately before, that Chrysippus 'differed on most points from Zeno, and from Cleanthes as well' is, as it stands, an overstatement, presumably inspired by Chrysippus' central position in the establishment of Stoic doctrine.

[7] Babut (1974: 172).

[8] Previous treatments which stimulated my own efforts include: Long (1983, 1989 and 2003); Menn (1995); Forschner (1995a, 1995b, 1999); Sedley (1999a) and Gass (2000).

[9] See, for example, Inwood (1985 and 1999); Engberg-Pedersen (1990a and 2000) and Annas (1993).

[10] Plutarch *Stoic. rep.* 1035B–C, quotation at 1035C.

[11] I am particularly indebted to Algra (2003b).

[12] For my own reconciliatory attempts, see Jedan (2001); Jedan and Strobach (2002) and Jedan (2004).

[13] For instance by suggesting, as Susanne Bobzien (1998) has done, that Chrysippus, in contrast to his predecessors, did not endorse a 'personal fate'.

Chapter 1

[1] See, for example, Babut (1974: 172): 'Il est banal de constater le charactère profondément religieux de la philosophie stoïcienne. Aucune de celles qui l'ont précédée n'est aussi intimement liée avec la religion'.

[2] It should be noted that Zeno's Cynicizing 'antinomian' stance (resulting in quite controversial ethical recommendations, see Ch. 12) did not include irreverence concerning traditional religion. On the contrary, to all appearances, Zeno seems to have argued from the reverence unquestionably due to the gods to the inadequacy of temples to fully express it. Zeno's stance is thus rather an example of the broader trend in Greek philosophy of an interiorizing or spiritualizing interpretation of religious duties, but it is by no means dismissive of traditional religion. Zeno's successors seem to have followed his lead. See Plutarch *Stoic. rep.* 1034B–C, trans. Cherniss: 'Moreover, it is a doctrine of Zeno's not to build temples of the gods, because a temple not worth much is also not sacred and no work of builders of mechanics is worth much. The Stoics, while applauding this as correct, attend the mysteries in temples, go up to the Acropolis, do reverence to statues, and place wreaths upon the shrines, though these are works of builders and mechanics'.

[3] See, for example, Babut (1974); Gerson (1990); Mansfeld (1999); Algra (2003b); Sedley (2007).

[4] See Babut (1974: 199).

[5] Given this trait of Greek religion, one can describe the Stoic remarks on traditional religion 'conciliatory pronouncements', as Frede (2002: 95) does, provided this is understood to mean that the Stoics were sincere in issuing them. The Stoics were representatives of an 'overall tendency [i.e. among ancient philosophers] towards conservatism' concerning traditional religion (Algra 2007: 9). It seems unwarranted to attribute a primary 'strategic' purpose to the Stoics' support for traditional polytheism (*pace* Meijer 2007). On the absence of specific doctrines of faith, see Burkert (1987: 71); Bremmer (1999: 6).

[6] Even if atheism must be considered practically non-existent in ancient times (see Bremmer 2007), new religious practices, the rise of a new argumentative philosophical culture (see Muir 1985), and behaviour dismissive of traditional piety, could lead to the perception that traditional religion was threatened. Instances of the last factor are two events as early as 415 BC: the mutilation of the herms and the profanation of the mysteries by Alcibiades. For the first deed, a certain Andocides was banned from the Athenian Agora and sanctuaries. Accused of the second offence, Alcibiades was recalled for trial from Sicily. Prosecutions of intellectuals (Anaxagoras, Protagoras, Prodicus, Socrates, Euripides) for impiety could have resulted from the same feelings (see Price 1999: ch. 4), but there are doubts on the accuracy of some of the reports and on the impact of those trials that took place (see Dover 1988 and Meijer 1981: 220).

[7] See Burkert (1985: 321, 326, 331, 334, 337). Of course, the philosophers' defence of traditional religion was quite different from the colourful richness of traditional polytheism. Unwittingly they put additional pressure on the very institution they were set to defend; but then the history of philosophy is full of well-meant cures worsening the disease.

8 See White (2003: 133).

9 Sedley (1999a: 384).

10 See, for example, Hahm (1977); Sedley (1999a); White (2003) and Wildberger (2006: 6).

11 See LS § 27.

12 See Sextus Empiricus *M* 1.21; 9.226, Plutarch *Col.* 1116D; see also Hahm (1977: 10f.).

13 See Plutarch *Comm. not.* 1073E (= *SVF* 2.525). Other texts include *SVF* 2.319, 320 and 329. See Hahm (1977: 3).

14 See, for example, Hahm (1977: 12); Sedley (1999a: 383).

15 According to the Stoics, qualities are 'matter in a certain state' (ὕλη πως ἔχουσα). See *SVF* 2.376, 380. On Stoic ontology, see LS §§ 28–29; Sedley (1999a) and Brunschwig (2003).

16 See LS § 27; Sedley (1999a); Brunschwig (2003) and Wildberger (2006: 83–201).

17 There has been some speculation on the predecessors of the Stoic conception of the two principles. Whereas Hahm gives Aristotle a prominent place, Sedley argues, to my mind convincingly, that Theophrastus' reading of Plato's *Timaeus* stands in the immediate background of the Stoic conception of the two principles (Sedley 1999a: 385). Sedley (2002) has suggested that the Academy under Polemo deviated from the incorporealism defended earlier in the Academy, and thereby prepared the Stoic corporealism.

18 For the debate on Posidonius' theory of the ontological status of matter, see Steinmetz (1994: 686) (with literature).

19 See, for example, White (2003).

20 As we shall see in more detail later (Part Three), virtue consists in taking the viewpoint of the Stoic God.

21 Todd, for instance, has claimed that the interdependence of the principles requires their incorporeality (1978: 140). For a full historiography, see Wildberger (2006: 459n.40).

22 See, for instance, the report of Aristocles (*ap.* Eusebius *Praeparatio evangelica* 15.14.1, trans. LS 45G): 'He [Zeno] says that fire is the element of what exists, like Heraclitus, and that fire has as its principles god and matter, like Plato. But Zeno says they are both bodies, both that which acts and that which is acted upon, whereas Plato says that the first active cause is incorporeal'. See also Forschner (1995a: 3).

23 See also LS 1.273.

24 See also, for instance, LS 1.274.

25 See Ch. 2.

26 See above, Diogenes Laertius 7.136, trans. Hicks.

27 On conflagration, see White (2003: 137f.); Wildberger (2006: 49–59).

28 The biological cosmogony of the Stoics lends itself to comparisons with genetics. Hunt (1976: 38), for instance, claims that 'we have here an hypothesis not unlike that of the modern geneticists who hold that in one tiny cell are contained all the instructions necessary for the development of the animal destined to be formed from it. The diversity of things and creatures is explained, in the Stoic theory, by the multiplicity of the *spermatikoi logoi*'.

29 This differentiation may have been a Peripatetic innovation, but we have no evidence that the Stoics took it over directly from a Peripatetic source (*pace* Hahm 1977: 93).

30 See, for example, Stobaeus 1.213.17–24.

31 See, for example, Gould (1970: 99f.); Hahm (1977: 159); Lapidge (1978: 168ff.); Todd (1978: 149); Sedley (1999a: 388f.); Wildberger (2006: 75–78).

32 Some sources even give the impression that Zeno restricted his analysis of soul as warm *pneuma* to the human soul (see *SVF* 1.128 and 135), but this is certainly a distortion (see *SVF* 1.138).

33 See Sedley (1999a: 389). For a more detailed analysis of the Chrysippean concept of *pneuma*, see Sambursky (1959: ch. 2).

34 See, for example, Alexander of Aphrodisias *De anima libri Mantissa* 26.13–8 Bruns (= *SVF* 2.786) and *De mixtione* 224.14–17 (= *SVF* 2.442 part).

35 Alexander *De mixtione* 224.25.

36 Nemesius *De natura hominis* 2.44 (see LS 47J).

37 See Alexander *De mixtione* 223.34; Nemesius *De natura hominis* 2.42.

38 See Nemesius *De natura hominis* 2.42.

39 This is shown by the definition of *physis* (the second level of the *hexeis* to be mentioned below) in Philo, *Legum allegoriae* 2.22: *physis* is a *hexis* which already has the capability to move. Although Chrysippus is not mentioned by Philo, it is clear that Philo is reporting his doctrine (cf. Plutarch's polemic in *De virtute morali* 451B, as usual directed against Chrysippean doctrines).

40 See Simplicius *In Aristotelis Physica commentaria* 671.4. For a detailed study, see Algra (1988).

41 Stobaeus 1.79.1–2.

42 To our intuitions, shaped by conceptions of matter as compound of atoms, the Stoic notion of body is quite alien. For attempts to understand the Stoic notion of body, see LS § 48; White (2003: 146–51); Wildberger (2006: 11–13).

43 The following rephrases Alexander *De mixtione* 216.14–217.13, a passage which is unfortunately too long to print here in full (see *SVF* 2.473 part). For a detailed commentary on the text and Chrysippus' doctrine reported there, see Todd (1976).

44 Alexander *De mixtione* 216.25–217.2, trans. LS 48C.

45 See Alexander *De mixtione* 217.31–2.

46 See Plutarch *Comm. not.* 1078E (= LS 48B).

47 See Stobaeus 1.155.5–11 (= LS 48D).

48 See above and Plutarch *Comm. not.* 1084A–B. I shall discuss the deterministic consequences of this view in Ch. 3.

49 Galen *PHP* 3.1.9, trans. Hahm (1977: 159).

50 Nemesius *De natura hominis* 2.46 (= *SVF* 2.790), trans. Hahm (1977: 15). For a detailed discussion of the passage, see there.

51 See the texts collected in *SVF* 2.596–632 and LS § 46. The literature includes Hahm (1977: 185–99); Mansfeld (1979); Long (1985); Salles (2003 and 2005b); Wildberger (2006: 49–59). Even the gods of the traditional religion, identified by the Stoics as mere aspects of the divine principles (see Ch. 2), were held to perish during conflagration (see Plutarch *Stoic. rep.* 1051F–1052B).

52 See Diogenes Laertius 7.157.

[53] It is possible that Chrysippus' characterizations of conflagration were intended to offer a less gloomy perspective on the soul's perishing during conflagration. In any case, Chrysippus seems to describe conflagration as a positive, welcome event in which the divine element (Zeus) is finally by itself, which is the only completely virtuous state (on the evidence, in part. Seneca *Letters* 9.16 and Plutarch *Comm. not.* 1067A, see Mansfeld (1979), but cf. also the critique of Long (1985) and the more guarded reformulation in Mansfeld 1999). Of course, the efficacy of such consolations is dependent on one's identification with the permanent divine principle. Chrysippus' perspective appears decidedly more positive than Cleanthes' (see Salles 2005b).

[54] See Part Three.

[55] See, for example, Calcidius *In Tim.* 232.12–234.4.

[56] See, for example, Aetius *Placita* 4.21.1–4 (= LS 53H).

[57] One could ask why such a deficiency of rationality should occur, given the providence of the completely rational divine principle. Here, the Stoics are confronted with the problem of theodicy in very much the same way as other theological systems are. Ultimately, it seems, the Stoics would have been at a loss for a satisfactory answer. For the problem of theodicy in Stoic philosophy, see Long (1968); Kerferd (1978a) and Frede (2002).

[58] See Galen *PHP* 4.2.1–6, 10–18 (= LS 65D and J). On the Stoic theory of emotions, see, for example, Inwood (1985: 127–81); Brennan (1998 and 2005); Gill (1998); Price (2005) and Graver (2007). On Stoic therapy to extirpate the passions, see Nussbaum (1994: esp. ch. 10) and Sorabji (2000).

[59] The difference between Chrysippus and Zeno seems to be a merely verbal one: Chrysippus identifies affections with 'judgements of a kind', whereas Zeno regards them as psychic motions 'following on judgements' (see Galen *PHP* 4.3.1–2 = LS 65K). See also Price (1995: 19). Sorabji has recently (2000) reiterated Galen's view that there indeed were major differences between Chrysippus and Zeno, but this seems (as Tieleman's discussion shows [2003: ch. 5]) hardly tenable (see also Gill 2005 and Price 2005). On the concept of assent (συγκατάθεσις), see Ch. 3.

[60] See Plato *Protagoras* 352C.

[61] See *Republic* 435A–441C.

[62] In *Timaeus* 69C, Plato talks about the rational soul as the 'immortal principle of the soul' (ἀρχὴ ψυχῆς ἀθάνατος) and contrasts it with the other two parts which he refers to as 'another kind of soul' (ἄλλο εἶδος ψυχῆς).

[63] See Plutarch *De virtute morali* 440E–441D, 446F–447A (= LS 61B, 65G). See also Price (1995); Long (1999) and Sorabji (2000).

[64] See also Price (1995: 161).

[65] See esp. Chs. 5 and 11.

[66] See Part Three, esp. Ch. 11.

[67] See Seneca *Letters* 106.3–10.

[68] This evokes the third of the four Stoic categories or genera (1. 'substrate', 2. 'qualified', 3. 'disposed in a certain way', 4. 'disposed in a certain way in relation to something else'). On the Stoic categories, see LS §§ 28–9; Brunschwig (2003); Wildberger (2006: 86–91). For the use of categories in Chrysippus' rejection of Aristo's virtue theory, see Ch. 6.

[69] See Seneca *Letters* 113, esp. 7 and 11, and Stobaeus 2.64.18–65.6. The Stobaeus reference is to a passage of the *Anthologium* which makes part of a lengthy report (stretching from p. 57 to p. 116 in Wachsmuth's edition) entitled 'The doctrines of Zeno and the other Stoics concerning the ethical part of philosophy'. The *communis opinio* (*pace* Göransson 1995) is that this report was originally authored by a philosopher named Arius (who was also the author of a summary of Peripatetic ethics included in the *Anthologium*). Scholars argue that this Arius was Arius Didymus, a late first century BC Stoic philosopher and associate of the emperor Augustus. The sources quoted in the epitome of Stoic ethics are consonant with this identification. For discussions of Arius Didymus' work, see Fortenbaugh (1983) and Hahm (1990). For the purposes of this book, the authorship of Arius Didymus, however likely, is not relevant. I continue, therefore, to speak about Stobaeus as our source when referring to the *Anthologium's* report on Stoic ethics.

[70] Soul is the factor through which an animal is alive, and thus the characteristics of the animal's being alive—'life' and 'awareness'—are attributed to the soul (see Seneca *Letters* 113.2).

[71] See Seneca *Letters* 113.2–3.

[72] See Seneca *Letters* 113.4.

[73] This problem is also discussed in Stoic ontology. The Stoic theory that common qualities can coexist in the same portion of matter (the same is possible for peculiar qualities) stirred considerable interest in competing philosophical schools. For a concise presentation, see Sedley (1999a: 405f.).

[74] See Ch. 6.

Chapter 2

[1] See Auvray-Assayas (2005: 244).

[2] See Mansfeld (1999: 453–4). This is unwittingly confirmed by Gelinas (2006), who attempts to reinterpret a Stoic argument for the existence of God as an argument concerning the nature of God.

[3] I leave aside arguments listed summarily by Dragona-Monachou as 'other probable arguments of Chrysippus'. By reproducing the above list I want to convey an idea of how the Stoics argued for the existence of (the) god(s). Nothing in this chapter depends on the view that these arguments *originated* with Chrysippus (in fact, it is quite clear that he reformulated earlier Stoic arguments, see below) or that all of them were intended as separate arguments (which is doubtful, see Cicero *ND* 2.16–19, for an example). For an extended examination of the evidence, see Meijer (2007).

[4] Dragona-Monachou (1976: 112).

[5] Dragona-Monachou (1976: 115).

[6] Dragona-Monachou (1976: 117).

[7] Dragona-Monachou (1976: 119).

[8] Dragona-Monachou (1976: 120).

[9] See Dragona-Monachou (1976: 120).

[10] Dragona-Monachou (1976: 122).

[11] See Dragona-Monachou (1976: 124).

[12] Dragona-Monachou (1976: 125), where a variant of this argument is also quoted (Sextus Empiricus, *M* 9.129).

[13] Dragona-Monachou (1976: 126).

[14] Sextus Empiricus claims that the Stoic arguments for the existence of the gods fall into four classes: from the agreement among all men, from the orderly arrangement of the universe, from the absurd consequences of rejecting the existence of the gods, and from refutation of the opposing arguments. It is possible that this is an interpretative device of Sextus' own and not a schema 'officially' advocated in the Stoic school. However this may be, the above argument figures as a member of the third class.

[15] See Schofield (1980: 300).

[16] It has been observed that the Stoic attempt to give their arguments a conclusive, syllogistic appearance did not necessarily help their case (see Schofield 1983: 38f.; Brunschwig 1994: 175f.; Algra 2003b: 163). In casting these arguments in syllogistic form the Stoics may have been overrating their strength. Nevertheless, the formal presentation may at least in part also serve a dialectical purpose, as Cicero, *ND* 2.20 reports (see below). In any case it is better to see the arguments as 'inductive inferences to the best explanatory hypothesis' rather than as proofs (see Barnes 1980 and Schofield 1980: 306).

[17] It is tempting to interpret this in the light of the all-pervasiveness of Greek religion in society—there was practically 'no sphere of life [that] lacked a religious aspect' (Bremmer 1999: 2; see also Burkert 1985: 246–58; Bruit Zaidman and Schmitt Pantel 1992: 92–101). A good example is the institution of oaths (see Burkert 1985: 250–4).

[18] As has often been remarked in the literature. See, for example, Pohlenz (1959: 1.96–8); Algra (2003b: 165f.); Frede (2005: 214). It seems hardly feasible to distinguish between arguments concerning the nature of a single divine principle and arguments for the existence of traditional deities (*pace* Meijer 2007).

[19] See, for example, Diogenes Laertius 7.147.

[20] For characteristic traits of ancient philosophical allegory, see Goulet (2005: 101–4).

[21] A sceptical view on Stoic allegorical interpretations of Homer takes Long (1992), but see the critique of Goulet (2005: 112–18).

[22] See Algra (2003b: 169).

[23] Goulet (2005: 112).

[24] See Ch. 1.

[25] As Plutarch was quick to point out (*Stoic. rep.* 1051E–1052B).

[26] Algra (2003b: 169).

[27] See Algra (2003b: 167f.).

[28] See Cicero *ND* 2.20: 'Haec enim, quae dilantur a nobis, Zeno sic premebat'.

[29] See *ND* 2.37: 'Scite enim Chrysippus'. One could perhaps argue that Cicero used Chrysippus for the compilation of *ND* 2.20–36 and thus viewed the doctrinal core of Stoic theology through Chrysippus' eyes. If the language of *ND* 2.19 really suggests Chrysippus as the source, as Lapidge has suggested (1989: 1388), then *ND* 2.29–30 might also recapitulate an account by Chrysippus.

[30] *ND* 2.37: 'perfectum expletumque sit omnibus suis numeris et partibus'. For parallels to the imagery of numbers, see Pease (1958). As Long and Sedley observe, it is a 'standard Stoic image for the completeness or perfect harmony of virtue and virtuous actions' (LS 2.361). See also Long's detailed treatment of the topic (1991).

[31] See *ND* 2.30: 'in partibus mundi', 'pars universi'; *ND* 2.32: 'Ut enim nulla pars est corporis nostri, quae non minoris sit, quam nosmet ipsi sumus, sic mundum universum pluris esse necesse quam partem aliquam universi'; *ND* 2.36: 'Quid autem est inscitius quam eam naturam, quae omis res sit conplexa, non optumam dici'.

[32] *ND* 2.37: 'Scite enim Chrysippus'.

[33] *ND* 2.38: 'perfectus undique est'.

[34] This step of the argument is not formulated carefully. The 'in omni mundo' (*ND* 2.38) is confusing, since it unnecessarily repeats the problematic shift from parts of the world to the world itself.

[35] *ND* 2.36: 'Homo enim sapiens fieri potest, mundus autem, si in aeterno praeteriti temporis spatio fuit insipiens, numquam profecto sapientiam consequetur; ita erit homine deterior'.

[36] *ND* 2.39: 'Sapiens est igitur'.

[37] See the seminal Schofield (1980) and Algra (2003b: 157f.).

[38] See also Epicurus' *Letter to Herodotus* (D.L. 10.37–8)

[39] See Schofield (1980: 293). Of course there was some disagreement between Stoics and Epicureans as to what exactly had to be considered as preconception of God. Upholding against the Epicureans the existence of divine providence, the Stoics characterized qualities such as beneficence and care for mankind as ingredients of the preconception of God. See Plutarch *Stoic. rep.* 1051 D–E and Algra (2003b: 157f.).

[40] Cf. Sextus' claim that the first of the four classes into which Stoic arguments for the existence of God fall, is the class of arguments 'from the agreement of all men' (see above).

[41] Cicero *De div.* 2.130.

[42] See Cicero *De div.* 1.82–3 (= LS 42D).

[43] Cicero *De div.* 1.118 (trans. LS 42E). Another field of tension between the meaning of the traditional practice of divination and the Stoic philosophical reconstruction must have been that traditional divination practices would have presupposed that foreknowledge of the future could enable human beings to influence (at least in part) the course of events—by, for instance, taking care. The Stoics, however, interpreted divination as mechanism working *within* a deterministic framework, playing the part of a 'cofated' event (see Gourinat 2005: 265–73; on cofated events, see Ch. 3). A similar tension is observable in the Stoic attitude towards prayer. Cleanthes' *Hymn to Zeus* qualifies clearly as such. Yet, the Stoics could have hardly expected prayers to be causally effective in any other way than by being cofated events. We see here again a tension between the implicit trust placed by the Stoics on traditional religious practices and the systematic constraints imposed by their philosophical system. Algra's suggestion (2003b: 173–6) to interpret Stoic prayers as 'a form of self-address' cannot do away with the tension.

Chapter 3

1 LS 1.342f., 392; and Sedley (1993).
2 This is Bobzien's (1998) coinage. Already at this point I want to draw attention to the fact that I will continue to use the word 'picture' to characterize the two Stoic strands of thinking about fate. The words 'concept' or 'conception' might suggest that the Stoics reached a high degree of conceptual clarity about the two strands of thought they harboured, whereas I shall argue that the crucial differences between the two ways of depicting fate must have (at least to a large extent) escaped their notice.
3 LS 1.342.
4 There is a degree of (for our present purposes negligible) inaccuracy involved in speaking of a succession of world states. In Stoic causal analysis, it is ultimately the material things in the world, not world states, which are so connected.
5 See, for example Salles (2001); Jedan (2001); Salles (2005a).
6 LS 1.342.
7 LS 1.392.
8 LS 1.343.
9 Lactantius *Divinae institutiones* 4.9; Tertullian *Apologeticus* 21 (both texts in *SVF* 1.160); see also Bobzien (1998: 56).
10 Bobzien (1998: 55).
11 See Bobzien (1998: 351ff.). (For a discussion of the dog-and-cart simile, see below.)
12 See Sedley (1993: 316–20).
13 Sedley (1993: 316).
14 Bobzien (1998: 218f.).
15 See Epictetus 2.6.9 (trans. LS 58J): 'Therefore Chrysippus was right to say: 'As long as the future is uncertain to me I always hold to those things which are better adapted to obtaining the things in accordance with nature; for God himself made me disposed to select these. But if I actually knew that I was fated now to be ill, I would even have an impulse to be ill. For my foot too, if it had intelligence, would have an impulse to get muddy'. On the Stoic theory of proper functions (καθήκοντα) underlying this text, see Chapter 11.
16 Bobzien (1998: 55f., 217ff., and 351ff.) argues that the dog-and-cart simile does not represent Chrysippus' opinion. This is, however, not plausible. Even if we discount the analysis given above, is it impossible to explain away the pointed reference to both Zeno and Chrysippus as a sort of general reference to an opinion held by some other member of the Stoic school.
17 I return to this point below.
18 See Bobzien (1998: 354–7).
19 Bobzien (1998: 354).
20 See Epictetus 2.6.9 quoted above.
21 Bobzien (1998: 355) points to the word αὐτεξούσιον ('spontaneous act'), which may be a post-Chrysippean terminological innovation.
22 See, for example, Stobaeus 2.99.19–100.6.
23 See, for example, Forschner (1995a: 96f.): I can only note in passing that the concept of assent is crucial for the Stoic psychological monism (see Ch. 2; see also Long 1999: 572ff.).

[24] We know from two other sources that this indeed was a Stoic view, Pseudo-Plutarch *De fato* 574D and Cicero *Topica* 59, and we have no reason to doubt that it originated from Chrysippus (for the opposite view, see Bobzien 1998: ch. 4). For a discussion of the concept of preliminary causes, see LS 1.343 and Hankinson (1998: 24f.).

[25] Chrysippus' writings must have abounded with literary quotations. In fact, the peculiarity of Chrysippus' literary style was so marked that Diogenes Laertius found it worthwhile recording the following ironic statement (D.L. 7.180, trans. Hicks): 'in one of his treatises he copied out nearly the whole of Euripides' *Medea*, and some one who had taken up the volume, being asked what he was reading, replied, "The *Medea* of Chrysippus".' See also Galen *PHP* 3.2.10–3.3.2 (= *SVF* 2.907) and Steinmetz (1994: 592).

[26] Moreover, even if Chrysippus had been fully aware of the fact that he employed two different pictures of fate, he could have easily come to the conviction that the two pictures were compatible after all. According to the picture of all-embracing fate, all events are necessitated by the preceding states of affairs. The picture of personal fate might be understood as focusing on a small subclass of events, certain pre-ordained landmark events that are necessitated by the divine resolution to bring them about, being silent about the ways other events come about. (These events are, on closer analysis—according to the picture of all-embracing fate—necessary too, but it could seem legitimate to stress in all cases the indispensable role of human agency by using the vocabulary of choice prompted by the picture of personal fate.)

[27] For the difference between two concepts of necessity, see Bobzien (1998: 136–43).

[28] Sextus Empiricus *M* 9.211. For discussions of the Stoic theory of causation, see Frede (1980); LS 1.340–3; Duhot (1989); Bobzien (1999); Hankinson (1999: 481–98) and Frede (2003: 186–200).

[29] See Alexander of Aphrodisias *De fato* 192.18.

[30] With this, Chrysippus did not want to say that human character develops in an indeterministic way as if it were separable from an outer world, not governed by the causal nexus governing the latter. On the contrary, human beings, their mind and characters are part of the world and stand in ordinary causal relationships with other material items in the world. The Stoics' emphasis on the pivotal role of climatic influences on character development is a forceful corroboration of this point. See Cicero *De fato* 7–9 and its interpretation by Sedley (1993). Chrysippus' differentiation between causal factors internal and external to the agent has received a thorough analysis by Salles (2005a: esp. ch. 3).

[31] Even though Chrysippus is not mentioned as the author of these definitions, it is certain that they are his (see Bobzien 1998: 119ff.). For a discussion of the textual evidence on Chrysippus' definitions, see Frede (1974: 107ff.) and Bobzien (1986: 40ff.)

[32] See Bobzien (1998: 131ff.); Hankinson (1999: 528) and Salles (2005a: esp. ch. 5). A Stoic author later than Chrysippus may have defended the Stoic theory of the modalities with an epistemic interpretation. A reflection of this may be Alexander of Aphrodisias *De fato* 176.14–24.

[33] For an analysis of the Stoic theory of an interentailment of the virtues, see Ch. 6.

34 See also Frede (2002: 106), who points to the Stoic metaphor of the world as a house.
35 I follow Malcolm Schofield in his reconstruction of the imagery of the cosmic city and in particular his emphasis on the imagery's locus in the Stoic theory of providence (1999: 64f.).
36 Schofield (1999: 70).
37 I follow again Schofield's interpretation, who convincingly points to Dio Chrysostomus *Orationes* 36.23. The text reads, in Schofield's translation (1999: 78): 'This is the only constitution or indeed city one should call purely happy: the community of gods with one another—even if you include also everything that is capable of reason, counting in men with gods, as children are said to partake in the city along with men, being naturally citizens, not because they understand and perform the duties of citizens nor because they share in the law, being without comprehension of it'.

Chapter 4

1 Ar. *Met.* 1021b20–1.
2 The assumption that there is one unitary virtuous state, virtue *tout court*, which connects different interrelated virtues seems deeply ingrained in Greek culture, as was argued by John Cooper (1998a). Cooper points to Plato's dialogues as evidence for the naturalness of the idea that there must be one unitary virtue (1998a: 235ff.). Cooper—following Julia Annas (1993)—suggests that it was the philosophers' preoccupation with the improvement of one's personal life which made the assumption attractive to them that particular virtues form a coherent set and ultimately form one unitary virtue. However, this is misleading if understood as implying that the Stoics argued in an inductive way for the existence of a unitary virtue. We do not have any evidence to that effect, and this is not surprising, since the interconnectedness of specific virtues would not have been sufficient to show that there is indeed a single unified state of human excellence. On the contrary, the occurrence of arguments for the interconnectedness of the particular virtues is plausible only if the Stoics *began* with the assumption that there is one unitary virtue *tout court*.
3 That this must have become the standard view is corroborated by the diversity of sources which refer to it. Cf. for example the Stoicizing definition in the *Scholia on Lucan's Bellum Civile* 75.3–8 = *SVF* 3.199) and the reflection of Panaetius' virtue theory in Cicero's *De officiis* (see Ch. 12).
4 Step (?) in Galen's argument really consists of two clauses: (2a) the perfect state of each thing that exists is single (μία γὰρ ἑκάστου τῶν ὄντων ἡ τελειότης); (2b) virtue is the perfect state of the nature of each [sc. thing that exists] (ἡ δ' ἀρετὴ τελειότης ἐστὶ τῆς ἑκάστου φύσεως).
5 Compare also the Stoic definition of the human good in Diogenes Laertius 7.94 (trans. Hicks): 'Another particular definition of good which they give is "the natural perfection of a rational being qua rational (τὸ τέλειον κατὰ φύσιν λογικοῦ ὡς λογικοῦ)." To this answers virtue and, as being partakers in virtue, virtuous

acts and good men.' Rationality is also characteristic of the deities. The common possession of rationality ensures that human beings and the deities can share the same virtues (see below).

[6] In Chrysippus' psychology, the claim that rationality is the unitary characteristic of human beings is expressed in the conception of the soul as rational through and through. To Galen, this deviation from the psychology of Plato, who theorized separate rational and non-rational parts of the soul, was the pivotal mistake of the Stoic school. He applauds Posidonius for his return to Plato's psychology (see Ch. 1).

[7] See also Galen *Hipp. Hum.* 303.11–17 = *SVF* 3.260: 'Nonetheless some say that the substance of the soul is single, but they claim that virtue is the perfect state of the nature of each (τὴν δ' ἀρετὴν εἶναι βούλονται τελειότητα τῆς ἑκάστου φύσεως). If now virtue is some such thing, then it will be single, if also the perfect state is single. And so it is necessary that the virtue which applies to the reasoning part of the soul is knowledge. And if this is the only part in the souls, the reasoning, then one should not look for several virtues'.

[8] Von Arnim (1905: xxxix). The words inserted above to fill the lacuna have been suggested to me by David Sedley. I think it is the best conjecture imaginable to fill the gap, already for paleographical reasons. The omission of the phase ἡ δὲ ἰδίως οἷον τεχνήματος [or: σκευαστοῦ] τελείωσις is rendered likely by homoioteleuton. The ἡ μέν-phrase must be counterbalanced by a ἡ δὲ-phrase, and it is most likely that the definition of virtue in the broadest sense (τις . . . τελείωσις) was not felt to need further explication. By contrast, giving an example like the perfection of a statue is already so specific that it can best be understood as example of a specific sort of perfection, the perfection of an artefact.

[9] The definition need not be dependent on a reading of Aristotle's works.

[10] The transition is rather clumsy; the καὶ should be taken to mean 'and then we have also'.

[11] A first century BC Stoic, who was a pupil of Panaetius' and himself one of the leading philosophers of the 'Middle' Stoa.

[12] Which is precisely what previous conjectures attempted to do.

[13] My interpretation thus avoids two implausibly extreme positions: (a) Philippson's (1930: esp. 358–78), who argued (drawing on observations made by Hirzel 1877–83) that the *whole* passage, including the first general definition of virtue, derives from Hecato; (b) Wildberger's (2006: 339), who sees no difficulty in ascribing to orthodox Stoicism the recognition of physical virtues.

[14] Pseudo-Andronicus of Rhodes *De passionibus* 259.73–261.97, paralleled by Stobaeus 2.59.4–62.6 (for a detailed discussion, see Ch. 7).

[15] Galen *PHP* 5.5.38–40.

[16] See Ch. 5. This is of course not to deny that the tonic strength of the soul's *pneuma* was an adequate analysis of virtue in physical terms (see Voelke 1973: 91–5; cf. also Mansfeld 1991: 115–8 with the qualification made by Sedley 1991); Cleanthes had even defined (in his *Physical Treatises*) the Zenonian virtues in terms of a certain 'strength and might' applied to different fields of action (see Plutarch *Stoic. rep.* 1034C–E and the discussion in Ch. 6).

[17] In Pseudo-Andronicus of Rhodes and in Stobaeus (see the discussion in Ch. 7).

[18] Chrysippus as well as other Stoics came up with different definitions which must have been considered as equally good and compatible with one another (compare the definitions by Sphaerus of Borysthenes, a third century BC Stoic, pupil of Zeno and Cleanthes, quoted immediately before Chrysippus in Cicero *TD* 4.53).

[19] See Stobaeus 2.60.7–8. I discuss the definition below.

[20] See the texts collected at *SVF* 3.245–52.

[21] See for example, Sedley (2003b: 21f.).

[22] See Pohlenz (1959: 1.241).

[23] A. A. Long's (1991) interpretation of the standard of rightness as a form of harmony (against the background of musical theory) is an example of the first alternative. Menn (1995) has also offered an interpretation in line with the first alternative. Opting for the second alternative, Brennan has recently claimed that the translation 'consistent character' is simply mistaken. The translations 'agreeing character' or 'disposition to agree', so Brennan claims, must be preferred (Brennan 2005: 140f.).

[24] See Ch. 1.

[25] I cannot address the import of having a 'technique' (*technē*) here. However, for a short discussion of how the word *technē* is used in definitions of the virtues, see Ch. 5. For attempts at reconstructing on the basis of in particular later Stoic authors the outlines of Stoic practical 'exercises', see for example, Hadot (1995 and 2002), both with detailed bibliographies. For discussions of Stoic philosophy as a *technē*, see also Sellars (2003 and 2007).

[26] See Simpl. *In Arist. Cat.* 237.25–238.2 = LS 47S part.

[27] I owe this interpretation to David Sedley. It is important to bear in mind that Simplicius claims that stability was not at issue *in the Stoic differentiation between tenors and characters.* We shall see below that the Stoic concept of virtue combines the non-graduality of virtue with its stability, but this is not settled by the terminological choice of 'character' as opposed to 'tenor'.

[28] I follow Schofield's (2003: 237) suggestion that the words καὶ τῶν πράξεων have become misplaced and should be placed at the end of the list to specify an eighth item.

[29] This has been suggested by Schofield (2003: 238f.).

[30] Special attention is given to the *scala naturae*, which determines for a particular entity what is in accordance with nature. Nature regulates the vegetative life of plants without impulse and sensation. Animals have (sensation and) impulse. It is therefore in accordance with nature (κατὰ φύσιν) that they pursue the things appropriate to their condition on the basis of their impulse (ὁρμή). Since rational beings have been given a more perfect guiding principle, 'for them life according to nature rightly becomes life according to reason' (τὸ κατὰ λόγον ζῆν ὀρθῶς γίνεσθαι <τού>τοις <τὸ> κατὰ φύσιν – D.L. 7.86). In the present context, I cannot discuss in detail the wide-ranging Stoic theory of appropriation (οἰκείωσις). For a short discussion, see Ch. 8.

[31] A slightly different version is offered at Stobaeus 2.75.11–76.15: Zeno described the end as 'living consistently' (ὁμολογουμένως ζῆν) and explained this as 'living according to one consonant reason, for those who live in conflict [sc. with themselves] are unhappy'. Zeno's successors, 'assuming that it was an incomplete

predicate', extended the formula to 'living in agreement with nature', and then came up with a number of formulations to further explain the meaning of this extended formula. I would argue that the difference between Stobaeus' and Diogenes' versions should not be overrated. Stobaeus does not suggest that the extended formula contradicted the purport of Zeno's formula in any way. Moreover, the very fact that Zeno was also credited (at D.L. 7.87) with having himself formulated the end as 'living in agreement with nature' shows that Zeno was either using different formulae (and his successors merely attempted to unify the usage) or that the extended formula was in line with his teaching. Presumably the difference between the shorter and the extended formula was perceived as purely verbal and Zeno's successors were convinced (and, I should argue, right in assuming) that Zeno would have shared their view.

[32] However, Diogenes indicates in no way that Chrysippus' formula formed a breach with the basic tenets of the Stoic theory of the end. Chrysippus' formula should, therefore, be considered an especially fortuitous (and therefore noteworthy) account of the general Stoic position.

[33] Significant are occurrences of musicological terminology, see Long (1991).

[34] Stobaeus 2.60.7–8.

[35] Plutarch *De virtute morali* 441C: λόγον . . . ὁμολογούμενον καὶ βέβαιον καὶ ἀμετάπτωτον.

[36] This will be discussed in Ch. 5.

[37] As Chrysippus stated (see above, D.L. 7.87).

[38] Cf. the texts collected in *SVF* 3.557–66.

[39] See the evidence discussed by Bénatouïl (2006: 169–74).

[40] See Plutarch *Comm. not.* 1068F–1069A. The Stoic doctrine under attack in this passage is the claim that every sage will benefit from the virtuous movements of another sage even if they do not know each other. It is a consequence of the 'holistic' Stoic view of the cosmos as formed and held together by the divine *pneuma* (see also Plutarch *Stoic. rep.* 1054E–F; cf. Brunschwig 2003: 231 and Schofield 1999: 97–101).

[41] I have adopted this label from Halper's (1999) differentiation between peak-performances and lesser realizations of the virtues in Aristotle's *Nicomachean Ethics*.

[42] This is borne out by Plutarch's poking fun at Chrysippus for making his sage virtuously abstain 'from an old crone with one foot in the grave' and virtuously endure the bite of a fly (*Stoic. rep.* 1039A). It seems that Chrysippus acknowledged different levels of demand upon virtue by saying that whereas all the sage's actions are virtuous, they are not all (to the same degree) praiseworthy (see also Algra 1990). See also Ch. 6.

[43] In my view Bénatouïl (2006: 163–74), for his otherwise perceptive remarks, makes too much of what I interpret as different emphases.

[44] More precisely, the Simplicius passage seems to discuss two different but reconcilable theories on the question of whether virtue can be lost. In the first part the view presented is that a change from virtue to vice is impossible. In the second part, something different is discussed, namely the question of whether or not virtue is a stable condition in all circumstances. The answer to this question is that virtue is not stable in all circumstances. In extreme cases (illnesses or the taking of drugs) the rationality of the agent can (temporarily) be inhibited to

such an extent that he falls into a sub-rational state. Since virtues are bound to the rationality of an agent (see above), the agent is in such extreme cases is not vicious, but incapable of being virtuous. This state is described as 'a state which the old [philosophers] called a medium state'.

Simplicius does not distinguish between temporary and permanent losses of the use of reason. The examples given are such that one is led to think of both types, temporary and permanent losses. Since the text does not present details of the Stoics' argument on this point, it also fails to provide us with an answer to the question how the Stoics thought about regaining virtue after a temporary loss of it. However, it is most likely that the Stoics would have allowed the sage, in regaining proper use of his reason, to regain his virtue immediately. The idea of a 'fallen sage' re-approaching the state of virtue would be an absurd construction, and of course no Stoic source mentions this as a possibility.

[45] If Philo *De plantatione* 142 does indeed portray Cleanthes' and Chrysippus' views, as Bénatouïl argues (2006: 287–92), following von Arnim's lead. Chrysippus' view was probably that the sage would not drink much in the first place.

[46] A reflection of this view can be found at Diogenes Laertius 7.118.

[47] See Chs. 1 and 3.

[48] See Ch. 7.

[49] Plutarch *Comm. not.* 1062A.

Chapter 5

[1] For a discussion of Chrysippus' catalogue of virtues, see Ch. 7.

[2] For the introduction of the labels 'what' and 'how' into Stoic scholarship, see Kerferd (1978b) and Kidd (1978).

[3] For a more detailed discussion, see Ch. 7.

[4] See Cicero *Academica* 1.41.

[5] Sextus Empiricus *M* 7.248, trans. LS 40E.

[6] LS 1.250.

[7] The context of the description of knowledge suggests that it was intended to be analogous to the description of opinion. Thus, what defines knowledge is the certainty, firmness and unchangeability of *assent* to the cognitive impression— Sextus uses the concept of *katalēpsis* in a loose way to refer to assent as such, since *katalēpsis* is defined in terms of assent to cognitive impressions. A similar looseness can be perceived in Sextus' claim that cognition (κατάληψις) is the 'criterion of truth', even though, strictly speaking, it is not the epistemically neutral cognition which plays the role of a criterion but only a component of cognition, cognitive impression (καταληπτικὴ φαντασία).

[8] See Sextus Empiricus *M* 11.207.

[9] See Stobaeus 2.66.20–67.1.

[10] Stobaeus 2.63.6–7: πάσας δὲ τὰς ἀρετάς, ὅσαι ἐπιστῆμαί εἰσι καὶ τέχναι κτλ.

[11] See Hülser's comments on frag. 414 and 415–415a *FDS*.

[12] See Ch. 4.

[13] Stobaeus 2.66.20–67.1.

[14] See Simplicius *In Arist. Cat.* 284.33–4 (= *SVF* 2.393).

[15] Sextus Empiricus *M* 7.372: σύστημα . . . καὶ ἄθροισμα καταλήψεων.

[16] This was put forward by Zeno (see *SVF* 1.73) and became the orthodox view (see *SVF* 2.94–5).

[17] See *SVF* 1.73.

[18] Compare Cleanthes' remark that technical knowledge achieves *everything* (it should, of course, be understood: everything the technical knowledge in question sets out to achieve) methodically (*SVF* 1.490).

[19] This is the upshot of Chrysippus' rejection of Herillus' 'heretical' position. The latter radicalized the standard Stoic view which saw in knowledge an 'unmixed' good (Stobaeus 2.74.15–16) and a good in the strict sense (D.L. 7.98). He claimed that knowledge—or living according to knowledge—was the end (τέλος), see Diogenes Laertius 7.165. Chrysippus argued against Herillus that knowledge was only instrumental to the end (living in accordance with nature) and hence inferior to it (see, for example, Plutarch *Comm. not.* 1070D).

[20] The first sentence reproduces the translation in LS 61J.

[21] The precise extent of the difference between the Stoic sage's practice of (non-) assenting and the sceptic's depends of course on the number of cognitive impressions available to the sage. The sceptical stance in the famous exchange on cognitive impressions between the Academy and the Stoa was that since there were no cognitive impressions, the Stoics would be obliged by their own premises to embrace the sceptical position (see Sextus Empricus *M* 7.151 = LS 41C). A useful survey of the issues involved is LS 1.256–9.

[22] This is apparent from *P. Herc.* 1020, frag. IIIn (= frag. 88 *FDS* part). As far as we can tell from the remains of the text, the author admits that the sage may not know, and may be in need of an introduction to, some techniques. However, this is not to be regarded as a cognitive error or as incompetence. We then have a stretch which is not legible. The text continues with a description of *doxa*. Presumably, the author explained in the missing lines that characterizations like 'cognitive error' or 'incompetence' are only justified when assent is given on an insufficient basis. The sage, however, who does not give assent beyond his knowledge, is not guilty of such reprovable acts and, therefore, the sage's lack of knowledge cannot be characterized as 'cognitive error' or 'incompetence'.

Chapter 6

[1] Our principal sources are two passages by Plutarch, *Stoic. rep.* 1034C–E (= LS 61C) and *De virtute morali* 440E–441B (= LS 61B).

[2] In Cleanthes' analysis this was a high level of the soul-*pneuma*, which he called 'strength and might' (ἰσχὺς καὶ κράτος).

[3] See the entry in Diogenes' catalogue of Chrysippus' works (D.L. 7.202) and Galen's report in *PHP* 7.1.

[4] For this reason, we should be wary of attributing the introduction of the fourth category to Aristo (*pace* Menn 1999: esp. 234–6). While earlier commentators have doubted whether a schema of four categories can be attributed to Chrysippus

(see Gould 1970: 107), Long and Sedley observe that the very fact that Chrysippus employed the first, second and fourth genera makes it 'unreasonable to doubt that the full scheme was operative in his day' (LS 1.178; see also Menn 1999). Moreover, the concise formulation of the title of Chrysippus' polemic treatise against Ariston suggests that an established terminology was being used. It seems therefore most likely to assume that Chrysippus relied on the schema of four categories (genera) to interpret the clash between Aristo's position and his own.

5   See Simplicius *In Arist. Cat.* 166.15–29 (= LS 29C) and the comments in LS 1.177f.

6   Plutarch *De virtute morali* 440F, trans. LS 61B.

7   See Schofield (1984); Long (1988); Schofield (2003: 246–49); Sedley (2003b: 14); Bénatouïl (2006: 183–202). The best general survey of Aristo's theories is still Ioppolo (1980); but cf. Schofield (1984).

8   Plutarch *De virtute morali* 440F, trans. LS 61B.

9   See Ch. 1. See also LS 28K–L and their explanation at LS 1.172. On the Stoic schema of genera, see also Wildberger (2006: 86–91), with an extensive survey of the literature.

10 Other texts discussed below are Plutarch *Stoic. rep.* 1046E–1047A; Diogenes Laertius 7.125–6 and Seneca *Letters* 67.10. For additional texts see *SVF* 3.295–304.

11 Although the view of the interconnectedness of the virtues reported in the passage stems from Chrysippus, the phrasing may (deliberately) have been made to fit later developments, such as Hecato's theories, as well (see Ch. 4). The passage does not pronounce on the existence of non-intellectual virtues in human beings and certainly does not rule out the existence of non-intellectual virtues in non-rational beings. The mention of both *epistēmai* and *technai* could indicate a broadening of the range of virtues, but would equally fit Chrysippus' view. *Technai* would have to be understood in a generic sense (see Ch. 5).

12 Other translations have been suggested: 'perspectives' (LS), 'topics' (IG²), 'main points' (Annas 2002), 'main concerns' (Cooper 1998a) and 'main functions' (Pomeroy 1999).

13 The Stobaeus passage echoes Chrysippus' description of the spheres of action in his virtue catalogue. See the discussion in Ch. 7.

14 It is significant that the interentailment thesis is only formulated in respect of the four Zenonian virtues, which are generic virtues with a number of subordinated virtues in Chrysippus' virtue catalogue (for a detailed discussion, see Ch. 7). This suggests that Chrysippus' interentailment theses were designed as a defence of Zeno's double claim of the difference and inseparability of the four virtues.

15 See LS 1.384.

16 In my view, Cooper has been right to ask for a more positive role of the secondary considerations of the virtues when suggesting that all the virtues actually cooperate in producing the virtuous action (Cooper 1998a: 256ff.). Cooper, however, is mistaken in denying that each virtue has a separate special area of conduct. Evidence to the contrary is provided by Plutarch *Stoic. rep.* 1046E–1047A. According to Plutarch, Chrysippus denied that the sage is always 'being courageous' (ἀνδρίζεσθαι) because the activation of a virtue is dependent on stimuli specific to a virtue. Chrysippus must have assumed separate special areas of conduct corresponding to the different virtues.

[17] Let me repeat that it is remarkable that interentailment is only presented on the level of cardinal virtues. This suggests that Chrysippus invoked the interentailment of the virtues in order to strengthen his interpretation of Zeno's virtue theory. Would Chrysippus have considered the interentailment theses also to apply to relations between the subordinate virtues? Although we have no direct material to answer the question and have to speculate, I want to suggest that the answer should be affirmative. The subordinate virtues are specialized 'elements' of the virtuous state described by the four generic virtues. It seems natural to assume that one cannot have a specialized subordinate virtue without having the other specialized subordinate virtues falling under the same generic virtue. The interentailment between the subordinate virtues could then work via the generic virtues.

[18] The same point is made in Plutarch *Stoic. rep.* 1046E–1047A. A pivotal issue in the interentailment theory under attack is perfection: perfection of the agent and perfection of the action (expressed by the repeated use of the adjective *teleios*).

Chapter 7

[1] In one instance (2.61.4–5), we can even fill a lacuna in the text of Stobaeus with the parallel account in Pseudo-Andronicus.

[2] Pseudo-Andronicus of Rhodes *De passionibus* 259.73–261.97.

[3] Here, it is not possible to keep the translation close to the Greek, which uses the same verb, πράττειν, twice.

[4] 'trouble or pain': this is to render the Greek πόνος, for which no single equivalent is available in English.

[5] See Ch. 6.

[6] See Vlastos (1991: 210). In addition to the four virtues which also appear at centre stage in Plato's *Republic*, piety (εὐσέβεια or ὁσιότης) seems to have been frequently discussed by Socrates (see, for instance, *Gorgias* 507B–C and *Protagoras* 349B).

[7] See Ch. 6.

[8] See Stobaeus 2.60.9–10.

[9] The topic of virtue as knowledge is pursued further in Chs. 10 and 11.

[10] Here we encounter problems of translation again: the Stoics use the names of the philosophical disciplines physics, logic (or dialectic) and ethics as the names of (generic) virtues and speak of physical, logical and ethical virtues. This sounds a little odd to modern ears and it is important to bear in mind that in speaking of physical virtue, it is not a virtue of the (human) body that is meant but a virtue that relates to (the knowledge of) physics. This, however, is a minor awkwardness compared to the constructions which would be consequent upon translating *physikē* as 'understanding of nature' etc. (as has been suggested by Martha Nussbaum 1995 against Menn's pathbreaking 1995 article on 'Physics as a Virtue').

[11] Diogenes Laertius 7.92 does not allow us to settle the point; the text credits unnamed Stoics with a tripartition of logical, physical and ethical virtue and goes on saying that Cleanthes, Chrysippus and Antipater recognized 'more than four virtues'. It seems clear that the tripartition mentioned in the text is not

a tripartition of three *generic* virtues, but the recognition of only three virtues, whereas Chrysippus, among others, recognized more than four (specific) virtues.

¹² Milton Valente has argued that Cicero probably drew upon a fairly conservative Stoic handbook which was written by (or in the circle around) Antipater. It attempted to present a Stoic orthodoxy, sometimes trying to integrate later specifications. (An example is the attempt to fuse Chrysippus' and Antipater's *telos*-formulae: see Valente 1956: 13ff.). We can expect that major controversies or innovations would have been mentioned. Since we do not find more detailed interpretations of the status of dialectic and physics as virtues, we can expect that their status as virtues was either seen as being very much in line with the Chrysippean Stoa, or indeed as originating with Chrysippus himself (and perhaps even with his predecessors).

¹³ See Diogenes Laertius 7.62.

¹⁴ This has been conclusively argued by Long (1978).

¹⁵ Cf. the Roman numerals inserted in the translation.

¹⁶ For instance, at Diogenes Laertius 7.126 understanding (σύνεσις) is said to be a specific virtue belonging to practical wisdom (φρόνησις), which is not the case in Chrysippus' catalogue of ethical virtues in Stobaeus and Pseudo-Andronicus. In total, five specific virtues are mentioned at Diogenes Laertius 7.126 which are not listed in Chrysippus' catalogue (understanding, equality, fairmindedness, constancy, vigour—σύνεσις, ἰσότης, εὐγνωμοσύνη, ἀπαραλλαξία, εὐτονία). They cannot be attributed to Chrysippus with any certainty and it is probable that they were added by a later Stoic to the schema of primary and subordinate virtues. Hecato, whose name is mentioned immediately before (at 7.125), is a likely candidate.

¹⁷ With this I oppose Long's (1978) ascription of the schema of dialectical virtues to Chrysippus. Long argues that (1) all four terms for the specific virtues 'are neologisms of the kind that he [sc. Chrysippus] liked to make' and that (2) two of these virtues—freedom from precipitancy and wariness—recur in the Herculanean papyrus mentioned above (*P. Herc.* 1020), whose attribution to Chrysippus Long considers 'highly probable' (Long 1978: 108 and 123n.20), basing his interpretation on von Arnim's preliminary judgement (1890). It should be noted, however, that Chrysippus is not mentioned in the legible parts of the papyrus at all. (This still holds after Capasso's work on the papyrus, see Hülser's comments on frag. 88 *FDS*.)

¹⁸ See Quintilian *Inst. orat.* 2.15.34.

¹⁹ See *ibid.*

²⁰ The topic will be dealt with in more detail in Ch. 12.

²¹ For a detailed treatment of the theological aspects of physics as a virtue, see Menn (1995). For the role of religion in the acquisition of virtue, see Chs. 9 and 10.

²² The text is included in *SVF* 3.301; on its import, see Bénatouïl (2006: 181–3).

²³ We find the same contextualization in Diogenes Laertius 7.125–6. At the end of the discussion on unity and difference of the virtues, the doctrine of primary and subordinated virtues is introduced by adducing two exemplary subordinated virtues for each of the four cardinal virtues. Interestingly, five of the eight subordinated virtues mentioned are not contained in Chrysippus' table (see above).

²⁴ See Ch. 6.

²⁵ See Long (1991: 110–11).

²⁶ To practical wisdom, temperance, courage and justice, six, four, five and four virtues are subordinated respectively.

²⁷ See Ch. 5. The pursuits can play their double role because they are defined as tenors (ἕξεις), which means that they admit of different degrees. For instance, one can be more or less fond of books and one can be so in wrong and right ways. Whereas becoming fond of books is an important step towards the acquisition of virtue, only the sage is truly fond of books. He is fond of books in the right way, because in his life, this fondness is regulated by the right principles and seen in proper perspective.

²⁸ Discretion and dialectic are not defined and discussed in detail in the passage; perhaps it was felt that their status was uncontroversial.

²⁹ Trans. IG² II 95.

³⁰ Philo *De ebrietate* 88–92 (see above). Conviviality is mentioned immediately after economics, which probably was not considered a virtue (see Stobaeus 2.95.9–24).

³¹ Or: 'for a life in agreement with virtue'; for different understandings of, and improvements to, the Greek text, see Wachsmuth's apparatus.

³² See Schofield (1999: ch. 2. Schofield also shows that there is good reason to understand Zeno's conception of erotic love not as exclusively male, but as allowing the inclusion of women (see 1999: esp. 43–6). Attempts have been made to interpret erotic love in a 'desexualised' way (against Schofield), because erotic love seems to contradict the sage's freedom from the passions (most recently Vogt 2008, drawing on Stephens 1996). Given the sexually charged Stoic rhetoric describing erotic love, that seems hardly feasible. It was most likely Chrysippus who proposed a 'spiritualized' definition of erotic love, which made erotic love practically identical with friendship (see next note).

³³ At the end of the passage the discussion turns (rather abruptly) to a discussion of erotic love, defined (in abbreviated form—the full definition is offered much later, at 2.115.1–2) as an 'attempt' (ἐπιβολή)—this is the translation suggested by Schofield (1999: 29)—to befriend beautiful young men. The context of Stobaeus 2.115.1–2 shows that being 'erotic' was considered a characteristic which, in its best sense, is exclusive to the sage, but betrays no commitment to there being an erotic virtue. That the behavioural 'attempt' definition of erotic love was held broadly within the Stoic school is an impression we get from Diogenes Laertius 7.130. Chrysippus' is identified in this passage as the author of a treatise on erotic love; his contribution seems primarily notable for a spiritualized interpretation of Stoic erotic love—erotic love is about friendship (see previous note). Chrysippus is not identified as the author of the definition.

The evidence on the Stoic concept of *philia* has been examined by Anne Banateanu (2001). The fact that there are degrees of *philia* allows *philia* to play a role in preparing for virtue as well as to have (in its highest form) the status of a trait exclusive to the sage. *Philia* in the latter sense perhaps played the role of a virtue, and seems to have been related to justice, but again there is no certainty as to Chrysippus' stance.

³⁴ For a tabular overview of the virtues discussed here, see Appendix 1. For Panaetius' reformulation of the Chrysippean nuclear schema of virtues, see Ch. 12.

Chapter 8

1 'Like the Phoenix', we read in Seneca, the sage 'will perhaps be born only once in five hundred years' (*Letters* 42.1).
2 See Brouwer's discussion of the evidence (2002).
3 See, for instance, Stobaeus 2.65.7. The case of pre-rational human beings is discussed below.
4 See, for example, Plutarch *Stoic. rep.* 1042A.
5 Plutarch *Stoic. rep.* 1048C–E. The characterization of the vicious as 'impious' is particularly telling. It should be understood as implying more than the fact that bad agents do not have the specific virtue of piety (for this, see Stobaeus 2.68.8). The Stoics also wanted to emphasize that every wrong action has to be understood as a breach of the duties owed to the deity (see Stobaeus 2.105.24). This squares with the general religious character of Stoic ethics, which I analyse in more detail in the remainder of this book.
6 Galen *PHP* 7.2; see also Sextus Emp. *M* 7.432.
7 Cic. *TD* 4.29, trans. LS 61O.
8 See, for example, Diogenes Laertius 7.93. For Chrysippus, see Galen *PHP* 7.1.8–16 and Stobaeus 2.58.14–59.3 (it is probable that the latter account combined Chrysippus' and Posidonius' views).
9 See, for example, Plutarch *Stoic. rep.* 1038C.
10 See Sen. *De beneficiis* 4.27; Stobaeus 2.67.2–4.
11 See, for example, Sextus Empiricus *M* 7.432; Plutarch *Stoic. rep.* 1048E.
12 As has been done, for instance, by Inwood and Donini, who suggest that the contrast 'did not have the status of an objective description of the human condition' but rather 'a pedagogical and protreptic meaning' (1999: 726). While the stark contrast between virtue and vice could also be seen as pedagogically necessary to the formulation of the elated goal of virtue, we have no evidence that the Stoics wished to restrict its role to pedagogy and did not see it as a truth about the human condition.
13 Long (1968: 343).
14 See Ch. 5.
15 See Stobaeus 5.906.18–907.5 = LS 59I; for a more detailed discussion, see Ch. 11.
16 See Alexander *Quaestiones* 4.3 = *SVF* 3.537. See also Pembroke (1971: 121).
17 See Seneca *Letters* 49.11. See also Cic. *Fin.* 5.41–43.
18 Galen reports that according to the Stoics 'all vice afflicts our souls from the outside (ἔξωθεν ἐπέρχεται ταῖς ψυχαῖς ἡμῶν τὸ σύμπαν τῆς κακίας)' (Galen *Quod animi mores corporis temperamenta sequantur* 820.13–15 Kühn; I follow the improved text in *SVF* 3.235, which reads ἐπέρχεται instead of Kühn's ἐπεὶ ἄρχεται). See also Long (1968: 336). Kerferd (1978a: 492) confounds this theory of the inducement to vice during early childhood with adults' responsibility for their actions.
19 See Diogenes Laertius 7.89.
20 See Diogenes Laertius 7.89.
21 Calcidius *In Tim.* 196.22–4.
22 Calcidius offers the example that we all have an inclination towards honour and deserved recognition, because their possession is a sign of virtue. Yet, we

choose fame instead of honour, being corrupted by the two influences (*In Tim.* 197.9–198.3).

23 The invocation of corrupting influences during early childhood made it necessary to offer an account of how truth still remained accessible to human beings. The line taken by the Stoics was that human rationality is never so fundamentally corrupted as to exclude its attaining truth. The Stoics allowed for the spontaneous formation of 'preconceptions' (προλήψεις) in the first seven years of life (see Aetius *Placita* 4.11 = *SVF* 2.83 and Schofield 1980: 293–8). The preconceptions form the material stock of rationality and thus yardsticks of truth. Thus, nature herself provides human beings with the material to reach true judgments (see Galen *PHP* 5.3 = *SVF* 2.841). (With this interpretation I attribute to the preconceptions a strong role in the process of reaching truth, following, for instance, Long 1974: 127f.)

24 Again a term which is notoriously difficult to translate. Other suggestions in the literature include 'affiliation', and 'orientation'.

25 The most important ancient reports on *oikeiōsis* include Diogenes Laertius 7.85–9; Sen. *Letters* 121; Cic. *Fin.* 3.16–25, 3.62–8; Plutarch *Stoic. rep.* 1038A–C; Epict. 1.6 and (parts of) Hierocles' *Elementa Ethica* (ed. Bastianini and Long 1992; but cf. the older edition of von Arnim 1906 for the passages included in Stobaeus). The literature on *oikeiōsis* is vast. It includes Pohlenz (1940; Pembroke (1971); Striker (1983); Inwood (1984 and 1996); Brunschwig (1986); Engberg-Pedersen (1986 and 1990a); Long (1993); Lukoschus (1999: 91–143); Radice (2000); Lee (2002; Reydams-Schils (2002); Algra (2003a); Bees (2004); Brennan (2005: 154–68); Laurand (2005, esp. 9–58); Zagdoun (2005); Roskam (2005: ch. 1–2). Of particular interest are the questions (1) if *oikeiōsis* is the foundation of Stoic ethics or plays a more limited role, (2) how continuity of the developmental process can be maintained in the face of the changing constitution which is the object of appropriation and (3) continuity or discontinuity between *oikeiōsis* at work in individual development and *oikeiōsis* as a development of sociality.

26 Diogenes Laertius 7.85–6, trans. LS 57A.

27 For the transformative role of reason, see also Epict. 1.6.12–22; Cic. *Fin.* 3.21. It is possible that the expressions 'first impulse' (πρώτη ὁρμή) and 'first thing appropriate' (πρῶτον οἰκεῖον) used at Diogenes Laertius 7.85 have in addition to the obvious temporal meaning also the meaning of 'systematic priority': first impulse and first appropriate would thus continue to be relevant factors for human behaviour after acquiring the use of reason (see Inwood 1985: 187–8).

28 Hierocles *ap.* Stobaeus 4.671.7–673.11 = LS 57G.

29 See Ch. 5.

30 Diogenes Laertius 7.91, trans. Hicks. See also Clem. *Strom.* 1.336.

31 See above. The possibility of unearthing by careful education the uncorrupted roots of human ambitions was of course pivotal for the Stoic appeal to follow nature.

32 Stobaeus 2.107.21–108.4, trans. IG² II 95. Cf. Cicero, who maintains unequivocally that virtue is accessible in principle, but it is not certain how broadly shared this position was in the Stoic school: 'There is no person of any nation who cannot reach virtue with the aid of a guide' (*Leg.* 1.30, trans. Zetzel).

Chapter 9

[1] Galen *PHP* 5.5.30–1 = Posidonius frag. 31A EK, piece quoted from Kidd's translation.

[2] Chapter 11 analyses the differentiation between precepts and doctrines of philosophy. In advance of a more detailed examination I want to suggest that the difference between precepts and doctrines of philosophy can perhaps also contribute to an explanation of Chrysippus' pedagogical conception: if a proper defence of ethical precepts depended on theological doctrines, the exposition of ethics had to stay on a preliminary level until the last part of philosophy was taught and the preliminary teaching of precepts was deepened and grounded by (theological) doctrines. Yet, some anticipation of doctrines later to be taught systematically and in greater detail must have been desirable in order to lend some support to the advocated precepts.

[3] See also *TD* 5.68–72, discussed in Ch. 10.

[4] See *KP*, *s.v.* τελετή.

[5] *OCD*, *s.v.* τελετή.

[6] See *KP*, *s.v.* τελετή.

[7] The text (*s.v.* τελετή) is accessible at *SVF* 2.1008. (For a short general characterization of the *Etymologicum magnum*, see *OCD*, *s.v.* 'etymologica' and *LAW*, *s.v.* 'Etymologika'.)

[8] See, for example, Babut (1974: 172); Mansfeld (1979: 134–6; 1999: 469); Algra (2003b: 154). Chrysippus was not the only Greek philosopher who used mystery cult terminology. The pervasive use of mystery cult terminology in Plato has been studied (see Des Places 1981 and Riedweg 1987).

[9] Of course, I cannot claim to do justice to the complex topic of ancient mystery cults, and I have to restrict myself to the aspects pertinent to our immediate concerns. From the rich literature on ancient mystery cults and their position within ancient polytheism, I found the following extremely useful: Burkert's overview on Greek religion (1985, the first German edition had appeared in 1977), the critical survey of more recent developments in the field by Bremmer (1999), Burkert (1987) and Price (1999).

[10] Burkert (1987: 12).

[11] Burkert (1987: 10). See also Price (1999: 108).

[12] It flourished from the sixth century BC, see Burkert (1987: 2).

[13] See Burkert (1985: 285).

[14] Bremmer (1999: 84), notes and cross-references left out.

[15] See Burkert (1985: 286).

[16] Burkert (1987: 69); in the case of the Samothracian mysteries, the knowledge transferred included cosmological revelation (see Price 1999: 120). See, however, below on the importance of experience in contrast to learning.

[17] See also Seneca *Letters* 95.64.

[18] See Burkert (1987: 71, 78).

[19] See above and see Price (1999: 113).

[20] See Burkert (1985: 277, 289, 293f.; 1987: 23ff.).

[21] See Burkert (1987: 92ff.).

22 Price (1999: 116).
23 For a discussion of the role of precepts and doctrines, see Ch. 11.
24 See Burkert (1985: 295; 1987: 12). On the question of Orphic and even Eleusinian influences on the text of the 'Thurii gold leaves', see Bremmer (1999: 86–9).
25 See Burkert (1987: 43–8, 89f.).
26 See Ch. 10.
27 See Burkert (1987: 45). As Burkert has observed, the obligation of secrecy can be understood in the light of group-forming processes.
28 See Chs. 3 and 10.
29 In effect, I shall suggest (*pace* Annas 1993: ch. 5) that taking the divine perspective was a constitutive feature of Stoic virtue ethics in general, not a late innovation.

Chapter 10

1 On Plato, see Annas (1999: ch. 3) and Sedley (2003a). However, one had better not lump the quite different metaphors together into the single motif 'becoming like God' (ὁμοίωσις θεῷ), as is customarily done. The metaphors represent clearly different degrees of a similarity or closeness to the divine, which gets lost if the focus lies on its highest realization, the *homoiōsis*. On *homoiōsis* see Merki (1952); Roloff (1970); Wilken (2003: ch. 11); van Kooten (2008: ch. 2).
2 *Phaedrus* 247B–C, trans. Nehamas and Woodruff.
3 *Phaedrus* 248A, trans. Nehamas and Woodruff.
4 *Theaetetus* 176A–B, trans. Levett. The Greek reads: διὸ καὶ πειρᾶσθαι χρὴ ἐνθένδε ἐκεῖσε φεύγειν ὅτι τάχιστα. φυγὴ δὲ ὁμοίωσις θεῷ κατὰ τὸ δυνατόν· ὁμοίωσις δὲ δίκαιον καὶ ὅσιον μετὰ φρονήσεως γενέσθαι.
5 Cicero *ND* 2.37.
6 See Epict. 2.6.9; for a more detailed discussion, see Ch. 11.
7 See Ch. 3.
8 See, for example, Origines *Contra Celsum* 4.29 and 48 (= SVF 3.248–9).
9 On the problem of the temporal limitation of human happiness, see below.
10 Plutarch *Comm. not.* 1076A, trans. Cherniss. Plutarch's polemic corroborates the claim put forward made in passing in Ch. 1: the support of Hellenistic philosophers for traditional religion could also endanger the very institution they wanted to protect. Plutarch does not deny the good intentions of the Stoics, however misguided he finds their philosophical theories. The fact that Stoic doctrines are attacked with reference to time-honoured traditions shows again the doctrinal underdetermination of ancient religion and the lack of effective societal pressure against innovation. It might be expected that the radicalism of the Stoic imitation of the divine formed a barrier against the adoption of Stoic motifs in early Christian thought. This was, however, not the case: Clement's remark (*Strom.* 7.14) that the Stoic view is 'atheistic' seems exceptional. Perhaps the Stoic acknowledgement that the sage is an (unrealized) ideal helped to soften the offensiveness of the doctrine. In general, the early Christian authors seem to have appreciated the similarities between Stoic and Christian thought

more than they felt inclined to focus on such doctrinal differences. (Tertullian's remark 'Sicut et Seneca saepe noster' [*De anima* 20.1] characterizes that spirit well. See also Waszink's comment on *De anima* 20.1 and on 2.1 [1947].)

[11] Cf. the somewhat deprecating remark about Zeno at *TD* 5.34.

[12] As mentioned above, Cicero would have been prepared to argue that the Stoic position was merely an elaboration of what had been formulated in previous Greek philosophy. The most noticeable occurrences of Stoic concepts and doctrines are the following:

(1) Moral development begins with a naturally gifted man, since 'virtue is not easily found to go with sluggish minds' (*TD* 5.68). Virtue relies on natural talents, even if some compensation is possible (acquiring as it were a second nature).

(2) At *TD* 5.68, Cicero alludes to the Stoic curriculum of three disciplines and the corresponding highest generic virtues (physical, ethical and logical).

(3) The investigation into 'the seeds from which all things got their origin' (*TD* 5.69) recalls the Stoic theory of seminal reasons.

(4) The soul seeing 'that the causes of things are linked one to another in an inevitable chain, and nevertheless their succession from eternity to eternity is governed by reason and intelligence' (*TD* 5.70) alludes to the divinity's providential determination of the world process.

(5) The mention of 'knowledge of virtue' (*TD* 5.71) recalls the Stoic conception of virtue as knowledge.

(6) The 'kinds and species of the virtues' allude to the Stoic schema of primary and subordinated virtues (*TD* 5.71).

(7) Cicero's mention of 'duties' (*officia*, in the context of Cicero's adaption of Stoic terminology indeed best translated as 'duties') renders the Stoic concept of *kathēkonta* (*TD* 5.71).

(8) The phrase 'virtue is self-sufficient for leading a happy life' (*TD* 5.71).

[13] For a long time it has been fashionable to point towards Posidonius (see for example, Merki 1952: 9f.), but such interpretations seem to have little more to go by than Cicero's use of Platonic rhetoric. Forschner (1999) seems to assume that Zeno was the ultimate source. Both attempts are unconvincing. The allusion to a Stoic schema of subordinate virtues points rather to Chrysippus (and the post-Chrysippean Stoa) than to Zeno. The invocation of three highest generic virtues seems at odds with the Posidonian doctrine (see D.L. 7.92) and squares rather with Chrysippus' theory of virtue.

[14] As has been done by Forschner (1999: 180–84), to whose otherwise excellent interpretation I am much indebted.

[15] Cicero would then describe the same order of subjects in the Stoic curriculum as Diogenes Laertius 7.40, a testimony of dubious value (see Ch. 9).

[16] See Ch. 1 on postmortal existence and cyclical conflagration.

[17] As if to explain 'immortality', Cicero continues by invoking the appreciation of the divine governance by fate (*TD* 5.70).

[18] Motifs such as 'physics as spiritual exercise' and 'viewing human affairs from above' date back to Plato at the very least, making it possible that he stood behind Cicero's account. (For a short presentation of these and similar motifs in the context of ancient philosophical spiritual exercises, see P. Hadot 1995: esp.

309–22.) However, the fact that we find some of the motifs in Cicero's account also in later Stoic authors such as Seneca (for example, *Letters* 102.21–30) can lend some probability to Cicero's dependence on a Stoic source.

[19] Plutarch *Comm. not.* 1063A–B, trans. LS 61T.

[20] Plutarch *De profectibus in virtute* 75C, trans. LS 61S.

[21] Plutarch *Comm. not.* 1062B, trans. LS 61U.

[22] The prevalence of the 'how' side can also help to defend the Stoics against another charge: if, as Brouwer (2002) has shown, the Stoics did not claim that any of them was a sage, how could they claim to know what virtue is about? The Stoics could have replied that they offer a glimpse at the content of the sage's knowledge (the 'what' side), but that they do not themselves have the sage's way of looking at the world (the 'how' side).

[23] Menn (1995) employs the term 'cool' motivation, which perfectly renders the spirit of the Stoic theory.

[24] I note in passing that the devaluation of such ordinary goods is found more broadly in theological systems of thought, to do with the (arguably sometimes less radical) partaking in the divine perspective. Examples include *Ps.* 73.25–6 for the Judaeo-Christian, *Rom.* 8.31–9 for the Christian, and *Koran* 2.271–2 and 33.71 for the Islamic tradition.

Chapter 11

[1] Diogenes Laertius 7.87–8, trans. Hicks (modified). We find a (rather contracted) reflection of this view, for example, in Philodemus' hostile report in his *De pietate*. On the basis of the reading of *P. Herc.* 1428 offered in *SVF* 2.1076—the more recent edition in Henrichs (1974) reconstructs here the same text—Philodemus claims that Chrysippus believed that the sun, the moon, the other stars and the law are gods (col. VI).

[2] See Cicero *Leg.* 1.18 and 2.11.

[3] See Watson (1971); Inwood (2005: ch. 7).

[4] See also Cicero *Leg.* 1.18 ('law is the highest reason [or: principle] implanted in nature, prescribing what has to be done, prohibiting the contrary') and the Stoic definition quoted in Philo *De Iosepho* 29 ('law is 'the *logos* of nature which pre-scribes what has to be done and prohibits what must not be done'). Seneca's *Letters* 94 and 95 also rest on the assumption that very specific rules or instructions can be deduced from the moral law (see for example, *Letters* 94.31 and 50). I shall argue below that the highest philosophical principles (the *decreta*), from which more specific rules (the *praecepta*) are deduced, describe the content of the natural law.

[5] I shall suggest that the embracing of general rules in practical reasoning can help us understand accounts of the sage's acting 'with reservation'.

[6] At *Stoic. rep.* 1037C–D, Plutarch attributes to Chrysippus the view that 'Right action [. . .] is what law prescribes and wrong what it prohibits; that is why the law has many prohibitions for the base but no prescriptions, for they are incapable of right action' (trans. Cherniss). It is unlikely that Plutarch wilfully misrepresented the starting-point for his polemic, and I take his account, as far as it goes, to be accurate (*pace* Pohlenz 1959: 2.75 and Kidd 1971: 172n.139).

7 For the Stoic theory of *oikeiōsis*, see Ch. 8.

8 On exceptions to this rule and the consequent refinement of the concept of *kathēkonta*, see below.

9 See, for example, Diogenes Laertius 7.107. For a detailed account of 'proper functions', see LS § 59.

10 However, the corruption of the non-sages' reason will make their actions highly fallible. They will often fail to recognize what is in agreement with nature and therefore fail to fulfil proper functions. Nevertheless, it is possible in principle that inferior agents fulfil their proper functions, even all of them (see Stobaeus 5.906.18–907.5 and my comments below).

11 See Stobaeus 2.85.18–86.1.

12 See, for example, Pohlenz (1959: 1.131); Kidd (1978: 248) and, of course, Kerferd (1978b).

13 Cf. also the report (Stobaeus 2.93.14–5) that the sage's action has 'all the measures' and Long's comments (1991).

14 See, for example, Stobaeus 2.113.18–23.

15 Of course the Stoics had reservations when it came to complicated issues arising from exceptional and difficult cases (see below).

16 Cicero argues that all human beings, however inchoately, recognize the existence of God (*Leg.* 1.25).

17 Cicero says that nothing is 'more worthwhile than clearly to understand that we are born for justice and that justice is established not by opinion but by nature' (*Leg.* 1.28, trans. Zetzel).

18 For more on Seneca's *Letters* 94 and 95, see the next subchapter.

19 See Ch. 2

20 The way Seneca introduces this question (*Ecce altera quaestio: Letters* 95.51) suggests that he follows an established order. I shall comment on this aspect below.

21 Again Seneca's formulation could indicate that he follows an established order (*Post deos hominesque dispiciamus quomodo rebus sit utendum*).

22 References such as this one show that to the Stoics' mind 'downward' natural law arguments and 'upward' empirical *oikeiōsis*-arguments must have been inextricably intertwined (*pace* Schofield 1995).

23 We cannot be more definite as to the precise sources of Cicero and Seneca. In the literary context of his *Letters*, Seneca does not lay open his sources, and Cicero's silence on his sources in *Leg.* 1 has exerted an amount of (unsuccessful) speculation (paraded by Dyck 2004: 49–52).

24 It has been claimed that Seneca is an unreliable witness for a Stoic 'orthodoxy' (see for example, Rist 1989). Leaving aside for the moment the problematic claim of the existence of a Stoic 'orthodoxy', there is a clear tendency in recent scholarship to stress the extent of Seneca's engagement with early Stoic doctrine (see for example, Wildberger 2006).

25 See Seneca *Letters* 94.2–4.

26 See Seneca *Letters* 94.5.

27 For my interpretation of the principles of philosophy as natural law, see above.

28 See for example, Sedley (1999b: 129). A notable exception is Vogt, who claims that 'the Stoic examples do not seem to prescribe or forbid types of action (. . .)

they are best understood as saying that, for example, health and our sense organs have *value*, and should be taken into consideration accordingly when we decide what to do' (2008: 191). This, however, seems to contradict our evidence. Seneca *Letters* 95.43 ('looking after a friend who is ill') and Diogenes Laertius 7.108 (for example, 'spending time with friends') are best understood as prescribing or forbidding types of action (on the two passages, see below).

29 See Striker (1987).

30 The characterization is Inwood's (1999: 96). In recent scholarship the natural law interpretation of Stoic ethics has been defended by (among others) Watson (1971); Mitsis (1986); Striker (1987); Striker (1991); Mitsis (1993); Annas (1993); Mitsis (1994); DeFilippo and Mitsis (1994).

31 Inwood (1999: 96f.).

32 Inwood (1999: 108).

33 Ibid.

34 Inwood (1999: 124). This view, the 'rule-of-thumb interpretation', is implicit in Inwood (1985). It has been elaborated and defended by Inwood (1986); Inwood (1987); Vander Waerdt (1994a) and Inwood (1999). Their emphasis on the concreteness and situational responsiveness of natural law has been supported by Brennan (2005) and Wildberger (2006). Vogt (2008) has reissued a largely Inwoodian interpretation while allowing for the fact that Stoic law is 'substantive': 'the theory of appropriate action makes claims about what considerations should count as relevant in action, and in this way provides a *substantive* guide to life' (2008: 163). While Vogt (to my mind rightly) attacks the rule-of-thumb interpretation's neglect of the substantiveness of Stoic law, I remain unconvinced that a meaningful defence of the law's substantiveness can be achieved, as she believes, independently of the framework of a natural law interpretation.

35 See Inwood (1999: 109f., 125).

36 For example, 'honouring one's parents, brothers and country and living in the society of friends', see Mitsis (1994: 4837); DeFilippo and Mitsis (1994: 267). That such always incumbent proper functions lack textual support was correctly pointed out by Vander Waerdt (1994a: 274) and Inwood (1999: 103).

37 See *Letters* 71.1.

38 *Letters* 94.50. See also Kidd (1978: 252). On problems concerning Stoic uses of the concepts 'law' and 'rules', see below.

39 Kidd (1978: 252).

40 See Sextus Emp. *M* 11.200–1 = LS 59G.

41 See Inwood (1999: 109f., 125).

42 See, for example, Inwood (1999: 102).

43 In adding 'special' to Long and Sedley's translation I follow White's interpretation (1978).

44 Nonetheless, we should think of such exceptionally appropriate actions as determined by general rules. Cic. *Off.* 1.31–2 discusses a number of such exceptionally appropriate actions, for example, not carrying out a promise, and names two general rules belonging to the virtue of justice: 'first that one should harm no one; and secondly that one serve the common advantage'.

45 At Diogenes Laertius 7.121 the cannibalism claim is intended to underline a convergence of Cynic and Stoic ethics, a goal also evident in other Diogenes

passages. (For a detailed examination of the evidence, see Mansfeld 1986: esp. 317–51 and Schofield 1999: esp. 1–21.) It is tempting but perhaps unwise to connect the cannibalism claim in Diogenes Laertius 7.121 with other, more elaborate recommendations to eat human flesh (recorded by Sextus Empiricus *M* 9.194 and *PH* 3.247–8). It is by no means certain that the claim recorded in Diogenes Laertius 7.121 was taken from the same context. For more on the 'antinomian' proposals of Zeno and Chrysippus, see Ch. 12.

[46] Seneca's mention of instruction as 'do this, avoid that' illustrate this (*Letters* 94.50), see above.

[47] Sedley (1999b: 150).

[48] The same conclusion is reached by Barney (2003: 335). Cf. also Dyck (1996: 82).

[49] See Brennan (2005: esp. chs. 12 and 13), improving on Brennan (2003) and superseding Barney (2003), who draws on Brennan's earlier interpretation.

[50] Brennan (2005: 183). Barney discusses it as the 'Dualist Model' (2003: 330–32).

[51] Brennan (2005: 182f.). In her discussion, Barney (2003: 314ff.) calls it the 'principle of deliberative sufficiency' (of indifferents). She claims that on this principle Stoic practical reasoning has to be 'non-revisionist', i.e. the possession of virtue does not change, but merely reinforces, decisions about indifferents made without virtue. If true, this would indeed make it difficult to understand how a particularly self-denying line of conduct, like that of Atilius Regulus, could ever be chosen (Barney 2003: 320). Barney overlooks, however, two things: first, she allows insufficiently for the transformative presence of reason and of virtue as its highest manifestation, which makes a considerable change to the sage's evaluations of indifferents. Second, considerations of virtue need not enter Stoic deliberations in an indirect way only (as the 'Salva Virtute' or 'Dualist' Model represents it).

[52] For instance Cic. *Fin.* 3.70, with a reference to 'justice'.

[53] Brennan (2005: 203–5).

[54] Brennan (2005: 206–11).

[55] Trans. Brennan (2005: 206).

[56] Brennan (2005: 210).

[57] See Sen. *Letters* 95.39 and 43.

[58] See Sen. *Letters* 95.39.

[59] See Sedley (1999b: 131).

[60] Epictetus (2.5.15–17) offers the analogy of a ball game. The players are not interested in the ball for its own sake, but in playing expertly with it. But cf. Long (2002: 201f.) who (in my eyes mistakenly) interprets Epictetus' stance as an echo of Aristo rather than as an argument against Aristo.

[61] Sedley (1999b: 131).

[62] This is the meaning of the well-known Chrysippus quotation at Epictetus 2.6.9 (trans. LS 58J): 'Therefore Chrysippus was right to say: 'As long as the future is uncertain to me I always hold to those things which are better adapted to obtaining the things in accordance with nature; for God himself made me disposed to select these. But if I actually knew that I was fated now to be ill, I would even have an impulse to be ill. For my foot too, if it had intelligence, would have an impulse to get muddy.' (See also Ch. 3.)

[63] See, for example, Sen. *De beneficiis* 4.34. The most recent examinations of Stoic reservation are provided by Brennan (2000) and Brunschwig (2005).

[64] See Plutarch *Comm. not.* 1071A–B.

[65] See Ch. 2.

[66] The imagery of the theatre play occurs in later Stoic texts, particularly often in Epictetus 1.25; 4.7 and *Ench.* 17, but the same teaching was perhaps meant to be expressed by the early Stoic imagery of the sage as an expert flute or cithara player, doing well everything he does (see Stobaeus 2.66.14–67.2): a musician can (and probably often has to) perform pieces he has not selected himself.

[67] Diogenes Laertius 7.87–8, trans. Hicks.

[68] Strangely this is not discussed by Dyck (2004). That Cicero meant to cut across entrenched positions and give his own opinion is also evident in his critique of Panaetius' treatment of *officia* (see above).

[69] See above.

[70] This interpretation is in line with Cicero's own acknowledgement that he sometimes uses virtue terms less rigorously than in standard Stoic doctrine and his pointing to Panaetius as a precedent (*Off.* 2.35).

Chapter 12

[1] Plutarch *Comm. not.* 1069E.

[2] See for example, Cic. *Off.* 1.126–9.

[3] As we shall see presently in more detail, Stoic thought on *oikeiōsis* and social obligation could draw on extensive speculation on social roles, which contradicts Bryant's negative assessment of the Stoics as lacking a 'coherent theory of social obligation that could countenance their anticonsequentialist individualism' (1996: 448).

[4] See Diogenes Laertius 7.33.

[5] Sextus Emp. *M* 9.189–94 and *PH* 3.245–8.

[6] Schofield (1999: 8f.) argues that the story should be taken seriously and places Athenodorus' attempt in the early years of the first century BC.

[7] See Diogenes Laertius 7.4, Philodemus *On the Stoics* 9.1–6 and Diogenes Laertius 7.34.

[8] See for example, Sandbach (1975: 20).

[9] Argued forcefully by Erskine (1990: 9–15) and reiterated by Schofield (1999: 25).

[10] See for example, Diogenes Laertius 7.122 and 187–9; Sextus Empiricus *PH* 3.146. It is tempting to understand Chrysippus' defence of Zeno's doctrines as one instance of the commitment to the founder's writings which provided (at least in part) the cohesion and identity of Hellenistic philosophical schools (see Sedley 1989).

[11] Marriage: for example, Diogenes Laertius 7.121; politics: for example, Plutarch *Stoic. rep.* 1034B; religion: Plutarch *Stoic. rep.* 1034B–C; everyday life: for example, Diogenes Laertius 7.120 and Sextus *PH* 3.243. Schofield has shown that some of these more conciliatory recommendations had their locus in Stoic discussions of the political form of life (see his 1999: in part. 119–27), but this does not help to solve the problem at hand.

[12] In a sweeping reconstruction of this development, Erskine (1990) has suggested that the Stoics from Diogenes of Babylon and Panaetius onwards traded off the democratic and egalitarian radicalism of the early Stoics against support for the

Roman empire. However, the democratic credentials of the early Stoics should be viewed with some reservation (see Schofield 2000: 447) Schofield's reconstruction (1999) puts emphasis on the transition from a republican paradigm extant in Zeno's *Republic* to a natural law paradigm.

[13] See Vogt (2005 and 2008: ch. 1).

[14] The report at Diogenes Laertius 7.3 that Zeno, due to his sense of shame, had reservations against bringing Cynic antinomianism into practice could be the reflection of such an ambivalence. For evidence to consider the attack on conventions as limited and not affecting a sincere support for traditional polytheism, see Ch. 1.

[15] See Schofield (1999: 119–27).

[16] See Cic. *Off.* 1.107 and 115. It is widely acknowledged that the 'Four *personae* theory' (as it is often called) is not designed to bring out something irreducibly individual in every human being. Rather, the theory attempts to describe human beings as inhabitants of social positions, roles, from which specific proper actions follow. See Kerferd (1972); Fuhrmann (1979); Gill (1988) and Forschner (1993: ch. 3). *Contra:* De Lacy (1977); Engberg-Pedersen (1990b).

[17] Panaetius' conciliatory character appears in the story reported by Seneca (*Letters* 116.5, trans. LS 66C): 'I think Panaetius gave a charming answer to the youth who asked whether the wise man would fall in love: "As to the wise man, we shall see. What concerns you and me, who are still a great distance from the wise man, is to ensure that we do not fall into a state of affairs which is disturbed, powerless, subservient to another and worthless to oneself."' For an account of Panaetius' philosophy, see Steinmetz (1994: 646–69).

[18] Gill (1988: 189).

[19] See Gill (1988: 189f.).

[20] See Epictetus 1.2, already referred to in Ch. 11.

[21] There are reasons to doubt that Epictetus displays an emphasis on the common human role much at the expense of other roles and thus markedly different from Panaetius. Epict. 2.10 (repeating the whole-part motif of 2.6) explains that a vast array of roles create their own proper actions, but there is no sign that such specific roles are perceived as contradicting the demands of our common human role. See also 3.7, where the fulfilment of specific roles is considered obligatory by Zeus' providential organization of the world. Just as in Panaetius-Cicero (see for example, *Off.* 3.69), so in Epictetus considerations of what is due to the common human role sets limits to the fulfilment of the more specific roles.

[22] My attention was drawn to the '*On the chrēsis of* . . .' literature by Bénatouïl (2006: 271f.).

[23] In Diogenes Laertius the list of Chrysippus' work on ethics breaks off very early on. The title is ascribed to Chrysippus in a papyrus (see for details Bénatouïl 2006: 271n.2).

[24] See Bénatouïl (2006: 272), with detailed references to von Arnim's edition of Hierocles (1906).

[25] See Diogenes Laertius 7.175.

[26] See Cic. *Off.* 3.91. In *Off.* 3, Cicero offers us a unique glimpse of such scholarly controversies within the Stoic school and furthermore attempts to offer his own stance, drawing for his arguments on the resources of Panaetius' *kathēkonta* theory.

[27] A third question, how an apparent conflict between the virtuous and the useful could be resolved, was left off by Panaetius and is addressed by Cicero on his own account in the third book of *De officiis*, yet clearly operating within the Panaetian conceptual framework (see below).

[28] For a critique of Gomoll's suggestion (1933: 27–34), see Dyck (1996: 58f.).

[29] Otherwise, it would be hard to imagine that Panaetius could have failed to discuss with the appropriate care for health and money two pivotal Stoic examples of preferred indifferents (see Cic. *Off.* 2.86).

[30] It is easy to see how discussions of more specific obligations we hear about in our sources could have been integrated in the framework of a discussion organized along the four virtues. The burial of one's parents, for instance, could be discussed in the context of justice: 'what is owed to parents?'

[31] For Chrysippus, cf. Appendix 1.

[32] Also the view that the virtues are separate, yet interrelated (*Off.* 1.15) suggests that a Chrysippean discussion of *kathēkonta* stood behind Panaetius' treatise.

[33] The clearest example is the matrix of the fourth virtue (see below). Panaetius called it after its most prominent virtue 'seemliness' or 'the seeming' (*to prepon*). However, there is no commitment to the view that the other virtues are strictly speaking subordinate to seemliness. He names 'a sense of shame and what one might call the ordered beauty of a life, restraint and modesty, a calming of all the agitations of the spirit, and due measure in all things' (*Off.* 1.93).

[34] See *Off.* 1.20, to be compared with *Off.* 1.31. See also Dyck (1996: 106). At *Off.* 1.153, the second virtue is simply called 'community'. The positive function of justice was probably also present in Chrysippus' conception. The virtue of kindness (χρηστότης), 'the *epistēmē* of doing good' is subordinated to justice (see Appendix 2).

[35] See Appendix 2. While the preservation of civic status receives a far more direct treatment here than is obvious in Chrysippus' table of virtues, no difference in practice need be supposed: Also the early Stoics saw in the preservation of one's fortune a preferred indifferent and would have given up their fortune only in exceptional circumstances (see D.L. 7.107 and 109).

[36] For further discussion, see below.

[37] Cic. *Off.* 1.22. However, how far this obligation will stretch must have been a matter of debate. Cicero stressed, perhaps more than his source Panaetius, that such minimal obligations are easily fulfilled, possibly with a view to defending the sanctity of private property, which he has very much at heart.

[38] See Dyck (1996: 183f.).

[39] However, it is equally possible that it was an addition of Cicero's, owing to the Peripatetic leanings of his son, the addressee of *De officiis*.

[40] See Dyck (1996: 240).

[41] 'If, however, men trade on a large and expansive scale, importing many things from all over, and distributing them to many people without misrepresentation, that is not entirely to be criticized' (*Off.* 1.151, trans. Griffin and Atkins).

[42] See Gomoll (1933); Dyck (1996: *ad loc*).

[43] See Diogenes Laertius 7.108.

[44] For detailed discussions, see Annas (1989); Dyck (1996: 556–64) and Schofield (1999: 160–77).

[45] Annas' (1989) suggestion that Diogenes' endorsed the legality of the corn merchant's not sharing his knowledge, while Antipater was concerned with the doubtful morality of the line of conduct has been cogently refuted by Schofield (1999). What is undoubtedly Cicero's own contribution is the argumentative function to which the exchange is put in *De officiis* 3: to dissolve the apparent contrast between the virtuous and the useful.

[46] See for example, Erskine (1990), who attempts to reconstruct a development of Stoic political thought, and Bénatouïl (2006: 219–320).

Epilogue

[1] See Sedley (1989).
[2] For an outright rejection of Cynicizing strands in Stoicism, see Cicero *Off.* 1.128.

Appendix 2

[1] The argument in Ch. 12 indicates that considerable discretion in the prescription of courses of action was admitted within the Stoic school. Even if the material discussed there originated in Stoic controversies during the second century BC, it seems unlikely that the early Stoics reached a greater unity in issuing precepts.

[2] I focus on the table as reproduced in Pseudo-Andronicus and Stobaeus, but, wherever necessary, additional Chrysippean virtues (as discussed in Ch. 7) will be included.

[3] See Aristotle's *EN* 1107a33.

[4] See *EN* 1107b1–4.

[5] The translation of the virtue terms follows Thomson (1976). It is not stated explicitly in the text but it is quite likely that Aristotle would not grant the status of a virtue proper to righteous indignation—rather, it seems to be similar to a quality like shame (αἰδώς).

[6] See *EN* 1108a4–9.

[7] See *EN* 1133b33–4.

[8] For the extended table, cf. Appendix 1.

[9] See *EN* 1140b20–1: ἕξις μετὰ λόγου ἀληθής, περὶ τὰ ἀνθρώπινα ἀγαθὰ πρακτική.

[10] *EN* 1140a25–8.

[11] See *EN* 1145a1–2.

[12] See Ch. 6.

[13] See *EN* 1118a26.

[14] See *EN* 1118b4–8.

[15] See below, on confidence.

[16] This is, of course, not to deny that Stoic philosophy can be an illuminating point of reference in the discussion of a military ethic (see Sherman 2005).

[17] See *EN* 1130b19–20.

[18] See *EN* 1130a8–10.

[19] The virtue of 'seemliness' (*to prepon*) in Panaetius, see Ch. 12.

[20] See *EN* 1131a26.

[21] See Erskine (1990: 114–22). Erskine supports his reading *inter alia* by reference to the virtue of sociability (εὐκοινωνησία), which in his view has a strong egalitarian meaning. I disagree (see below on sociability).

[22] See Stobaeus 2.96.5.

[23] See *EN* 1142b31–2.

[24] *EN* 1142b32–3: ὀρθότης ἡ κατὰ τὸ σύμφερον πρὸς το τέλος.

[25] See *EN* 1142a34–b2.

[26] See below, on good practical overview.

[27] See Chs. 11 and 12 and cf. below, on good practical overview.

[28] See *EN* 1143b13–4, see also 1144a29–31.

[29] Aristoteles *Anal. post.* 89b10–11.

[30] See *EN* 1142b2–3.

[31] See Aristoteles *HA* 614b34.

[32] Also allotted to it by Panaetius, see Cicero *Off.* 1.142.

[33] See Ch. 12.

[34] Pomeroy (1999: 107n.20) may be right in suggesting that 'correct deportment and appropriately masculine gesture for males (females also being expected to conduct themselves as appropriate to their sex)' were the focus of propriety, but we cannot be certain to what extent the *early* Stoics would have recognized gender-specific roles.

[35] Cf. the well-known description of the virtuous citizen's unhurried movements, deep voice and calm enunciation at *EN* 1125a12–15.

[36] See *EN* 1128b29–31.

[37] See *EN* 1128b18.

[38] See *EN* 1128b21–2.

[39] See *EN* 1145b14–15.

[40] See *EN* 1150a33–b1.

[41] See *EN* 1151b32–1152a3.

[42] See *EN* 1115b17–10, 1117a12–14.

[43] See *EN* 1115a7–9 and 1115b17–20. Cf. the above remarks on courage.

[44] See *EN* 1115a32–5.

[45] See, for instance, *EN* 1124a4–5.

[46] See *EN* 1123b15–20.

[47] See *EN* 1124a12–19. At one point, Aristotle claims emphatically that to the magnanimous person nothing is great (*EN* 1123b32).

[48] For comments on this and the Aristotelian counterparts, see the section on self-control and perseverance.

[49] In the *Euthyphro* Plato has Socrates suggest that piety is a part of justice, the part concerned with worshipping the gods (12E9–10: τὸ μέρος τοῦ δικαίου εἶναι εὐσεβές τε καὶ ὅσιον, τὸ περὶ τὴν τῶν θεῶν θεραπείαν).

[50] In a recent article, Sarah Broadie (2003) has suggested that piety is present in book 10 of the *Nicomachean Ethics*, albeit in a 'veiled' way. She explains the lack of explicit recognition of piety as a virtue by a far-reaching circumspection on Aristotle's part: in view of his Macedonian affiliations he thought it extremely unwise to draw attention to his revisionary account of piety. Furthermore, Broadie

suggests, he may have wanted to protect his view from ridicule by outsiders. This explanation, however, is unconvincing: Even if we concede that Aristotle wanted to take such care in manuscripts like the *Nicomachean Ethics* (which cannot have been widely available), it remains hard to see what he could have gained by suppressing his view that piety was a virtue. After all, whether it was called piety or not, his philosophical theology was revisionary enough to be resented or ridiculed.

51 Chrysippus: see Ch. 2. See also Ch. 7, on the sage's abilities to be a prophet, to be a priest, to be holy and to carry out religious rites. Aristotle: At *EN* 1122b19–21 the expenditure inevitably involved in the participation in religious cults is one of the objects of magnificence (*megaloprepeia*). Later Stoics: Seneca *Letters* 95.47–50, Epictetus *Ench.* 31.

52 See Ch. 12.

53 See *EN* 1120a1.

54 See Ch. 12 on Diogenes Laertius 7.107 and 109.

55 See *EN* 1156a3–5.

56 See *EN* 1155b32–4 and 1166b30–2.

57 See *EN* 1167a11.

58 On *oikeiōsis* see Ch. 8.

59 Annas (1993: 276).

60 See Ch. 12.

61 Erskine (1990: 115f.).

62 Not included in the Chrysippean virtue catalogue in Stobaeus and Pseudo-Andronicus, see Ch. 8.

63 An example: Aristotle's 'anonymous kind of friendliness which is close to friendship (φιλία)' ensures that the virtuous person is sociable, yet not overanxious to avoid dissent; he should acquiesce in the right things and likewise disapprove of the right things in the right manner (*EN* 1126b17–20).

Bibliography

Algra, K. (1988) The early Stoics on the immobility and coherence of the cosmos. *Phronesis* 33, 155–80.

—(1990) Chrysippus on virtuous abstention from ugly old women (Plutarch, *SR* 1038E–1039A). *Classical Quarterly* 40, 450–58.

—(2003a) The mechanism of social approbation and its role in Hellenistic ethics. *OSAP* 25, 265–96.

—(2003b) Stoic Theology. In Inwood (2003), 153–78.

—(2007) *Conceptions and Images: Hellenistic Philosophical Theology and Traditional Religion.* Amsterdam.

—, Barnes, J., Mansfeld, J. and Schofield, M. (eds) (1999) *The Cambridge History of Hellenistic Philosophy.* Cambridge.

Annas, J. (1989) Cicero on Stoic moral philosophy and private property. In Griffin and Barnes (1989), 151–73.

—(1993) *The Morality of Happiness.* Oxford.

—(1999) *Platonic Ethics, Old and New.* Ithaca, NY.

—(2002) My station and its duties: Ideals and the social embeddedness of virtue. *Proceedings of the Aristotelian Society* 102, 109–23.

Anscombe, E. (1958) Modern moral philosophy. *Philosophy* 33, 1–19.

Arnim, J. von (1890) Über einen stoischen Papyrus der Herculanensischen Bibliothek. *Hermes* 25, 473–95.

—(ed.) (1903–24) *Stoicorum Veterum Fragmenta.* Index by M. Adler. 4 vols. Leipzig.

Auvray-Assayas, C. (2005) Deux types d'exposé stoïcien sur la providence. In Romeyer Dherbey and Gourinat (2005), 233–46.

Ax, W. (ed.) (1938) *M. Tullius Cicero: De Divinatione. De Fato. Timaeus.* Leipzig.

Babbitt, F. C. (1927) *Plutarch: Moralia.* Vol. 1. Cambridge, MA.

Babut, D. (1974) *La religion des philosophes grecs.* Paris.

Banateanu, A. (2001) *La théorie stoïcienne de l'amitié: essai de reconstruction.* Fribourg.

Barnes, J. (1980) Proof destroyed. In Schofield, Burnyeat and Barnes (1980), 161–81.

Barney, R. (2003) A puzzle in Stoic ethics. *OSAP* 24, 303–40.

Bastianini, G. and Long, A. A. (eds) (1992) Hierocles. *Corpus dei Papiri Filosofici Greci e Latini* 1, vol 1**. Florence.

Bees, R. (2004) *Die Oikeiosislehre der Stoa. I. Rekonstruktion ihres Inhalts.* Würzburg.

Bénatouïl, T. (2006) *Faire usage: la pratique du stoïcisme.* Paris.

Betegh, G. (2003) Cosmological ethics in the *Timaeus* and early Stoicism. *OSAP* 24, 273–301.

Bindley, T. H. (ed.) (1889) *Quinti Septimii Florentis Tertulliani Apologeticus adversus Gentes pro Christiani.* Oxford.

Bobzien, S. (1986) *Die stoische Modallogik*. Würzburg.

—(1998) *Determinism and Freedom in Stoic Philosophy*. Oxford.

—(1999) Chrysippus theory of causes. In Ierodiakonou (1999), 196–242.

Borret, M. (ed. and trans.) (1967–76) *Origène: Contre Celse*. 5 vols. Paris.

Brandt, S. (ed.) (1890) Divinae Institutiones. In S. Brand and G. Laubmann (eds) *L. Caeli Firmiani Lactanti Opera Omnia*. Vol. 1. Vienna.

Bremmer, J. N. (1999) *Greek Religion* (*Greece & Rome, New Surveys in the Classics* No. 24). Oxford (repr. 2003).

—(2007) Atheism in antiquity. In M. Martin (ed.) *The Cambridge Companion to Atheism*. Cambridge, 11–26.

Brennan, T. (1998) The old Stoic theory of emotions. In Sihvola and Engberg-Pedersen (1998), 21–70.

—(2000) Reservation in Stoic ethics. *Archiv für Geschichte der Philosophie* 92, 149–77.

—(2003) Stoic moral psychology. In Inwood (2003), 257–93.

—(2005) *The Stoic Life: Emotions, Duties, and Fate*. Oxford.

Broadie, S. (2003) Aristotelian piety. *Phronesis* 48, 54–70.

Brouwer, R. (2002) Sagehood and the Stoics *OSAP* 23, 181–224.

Bruit Zaidman, L. and Schmitt, Pantel, P. (1992) *Religion in the Ancient City*. Trans. by P. Cartledge. Cambridge. (French original: *La religion grecque*. Paris 1989.)

Bruns, I. (ed.) (1887–92) *Alexandri Aphrodisiensis praeter Commentaria Scripta Minora*. 2 vols. Berlin.

Brunschwig, J. (1986) The cradle argument in Epicureanism and Stoicism. In Schofield and Striker (1986), 113–44.

—(1994) Did Diogenes of Babylon invent the ontological argument? In J. Brunschwig, *Papers in Hellenistic Philosophy*. Cambridge, 170–89.

—(2003) Stoic metaphysics. In Inwood (2003), 206–32.

—(2005) Sur deux notions de l'éthique stoïcienne: de la "réserve" au "renverse-ment." In Romeyer Dherbey and Gourinat (2005), 357–80.

—and M. C. Nussbaum (eds) (1993) *Passions & Perceptions: Studies in Hellenistic Philosophy of Mind*. Proceedings of the Fifth Symposium Hellenisticum. Cambridge.

Bryant, J. M. (1996) *Moral Codes and Social Structure in Ancient Greece: A Sociology of Greek Ethics from Homer to the Epicureans and Stoics*. Albany, NY.

Budé, G. de (ed.) (1916–19) *Dionis Chrysostomi Orationes*. 2 vols. Leipzig.

Burkert, W. (1985) *Greek Religion: Archaic and Classical*. Trans. by J. Raffan. Oxford. (German original: *Griechische Religion der archaischen und klassischen Epoche*. Stuttgart 1977.)

—(1987) *Ancient Mystery Cults*. Cambridge, MA.

Burnet, J. (ed.) (1900–07) *Platonis Opera*. 5 vols. Oxford.

Bury, R. G. (ed. and trans.) (1933–49) *Sextus Empiricus*. 4 vols. Cambridge, MA.

Bywater, I. (ed.) (1894) *Aristotelis Ethica Nicomachea*. Oxford.

Cherniss, H. (ed. and trans.) (1976) *Plutarch: Moralia*. Vol. 13, Part 2. Cambridge, MA.

Cohn, L., Wendland, P. and Reiter, S. (eds) (1896–1915) *Philonis Alexandrini Opera quae Supersunt*. Berlin.

Cooper, J. M. (ed.) (1997) *Plato: Complete Works*. Indianapolis.

—(1998a) The unity of virtue. In E. F. Paul et al. (eds) *Virtue and Vice*. Cambridge, 233–74.

Decleva Caizzi, F. (1993) The porch and the garden: Early Hellenistic images of the philosophical life. In A. Bulloch et al. (eds) *Images and Ideologies: Self-Definition in the Hellenistic World*. Berkeley and Los Angeles 1993, 303–29.

DeFilippo, J. G. and Mitsis, Ph. T. (1994) Socrates and Stoic natural law. In Vander Waerdt (1994b), 252–71.

De Lacy, P. H. (1977) The four Stoic personae. *Illinois Classical Studies* 2, 163–72.

—(ed. and trans.) (1978–84) *Galen: On the Doctrines of Hippocrates and Plato*. 3 vols. Berlin.

—and Einarson, B. (eds and trans.) (1959) *Plutarch's Moralia*. Vol. 7. Cambridge, MA.

Des Places, É. (1981) Platon et la langue des mystères. In É. Des Places, *Études platoniciennes*. Leiden 1981, 83–98 (repr. from *Annales d'Aix* 38 (1964)).

Diels, H. (ed.) (1879) *Doxographi Graeci*. Berlin.

—(ed.) (1882–95) *Simplicius: In Aristotelis Physica Commentaria*. 2 vols. Berlin.

Dorandi, T. (ed. and trans.) (1982) Filodemo, Gli Stoici (p. Herc. 155 e 339). *Cronache Ercolanesi* 12, 91–133.

Dover, K. J. (1988) The freedom of the intellectual in Greek society. In K. J. Dover, *The Greeks and their Legacy*. Oxford 1988, 135–58 (repr. from *Talanta* 7 (1975), with a postscript).

Dragona-Monachou, M. (1976) *The Stoic Arguments for the Existence and the Providence of the Gods*. Athens.

Duhot, J.-J. (1989) *La conception stoïcienne de la causalité*. Paris.

Dyck, A. R. (1996) *A Commentary on Cicero, De Officiis*. Ann Arbor.

—(2004) *A Commentary on Cicero, De Legibus*. Ann Arbor.

Edelstein, L. and Kidd, I. G. (eds, comm. and trans.) (1972–99) *Posidonius*. 3 vols. in 4. Cambridge.

Einarson, B. and De Lacy, P. H. (eds and trans.) (1967) *Plutarch's Moralia*. Vol. 14. Cambridge, MA.

Engberg-Pedersen, T. (1986) Discovering the good: oikeiōsis and kathēkonta. In Schofield and Striker (1986), 145–83.

—(1990a) *The Stoic Theory of Oikeiosis: Moral Development and Social Interaction in Early Stoic Philosophy*. Aarhus.

—(1990b) Stoic philosophy and the concept of the person. In Ch. Gill (ed.) *The Person and the Human Mind: Issues in Ancient and Modern Philosophy*. Oxford, 109–35.

—(2000) *Paul and the Stoics*. Edinburgh.

Erskine, A. (1990) *The Hellenistic Stoa: Political Thought and Action*. Ithaca, NY.

Forschner, M. (1993) *Über das Glück des Menschen: Aristoteles, Epikur, Stoa, Thomas von Aquin, Kant*. Darmstadt.

—(1995a) *Die stoische Ethik: Über den Zusammenhang von Natur-, Sprach- und Moralphilosophie im altstoischen System*. Second edition. Darmstadt.

—(1995b) Μόνον τὸ καλὸν ἀγαθόν—Oder von der Gleichgültigkeit des Wertvollen in der stoischen Ethik. *Perspektiven der Philosophie. Neues Jahrbuch* 21, 125–45.

—(1999) Theoria und stoische Tugend: Zenons Erbe in Cicero, Tusculanae disputationes V. *Zeitschrift für philosophische Forschung* 52, 163–87.

Fortenbaugh, W. W. (ed.) (1983) *On Stoic and Peripatetic Ethics: The Work of Arius Didymus*. New Brunswick, NJ.

Frede, D. (2002) Theodicy and providential care in Stoicism. In Frede and Laks (2002), 85–117.

—(2003) Stoic determinism. In Inwood (2003), 179–205.

—and Laks, A. (eds) (2002) *Traditions of Theology: Studies in Hellenistic theology, its Background and Aftermath.* Leiden.

Frede, M. (1974) *Die stoische Logik.* Göttingen.

—(1980) The original notion of cause. In Schofield, Burnyeat and Barnes (1980), 217–49.

—(2005) La théologie stoïcienne. In Romeyer Dherbey and Gourinat (2005), 213–32.

Fuhrmann, M. (1979) Persona, ein römischer Rollenbegriff. In O. Marquard and K. Stierle (eds) *Identität.* Munich, 83–106.

Gass, M. (2000) Eudaimonism and theology in Stoic accounts of virtue. *Journal of the History of Ideas* 61, 19–37.

Gelinas, L. (2006) The Stoic argument *ex gradibus entium. Phronesis* 51 (2006), 49–73.

Gerson, L. P. (1990) *God and Greek Philosophy: Studies in the Early History of Natural Theology.* London.

Gill, Ch. (1988) Personhood and personality: The four-personae theory in Cicero, *De officiis* I'. *OSAP* 6, 169–99.

—(1998) Platonic and Stoic thinking on emotions. In Sihvola and Engberg-Pedersen (1998), 113–48.

—(2005) Competing readings of Stoic emotions. In Salles (2005c), 445–70.

Glibert-Thirry, A. (1977) (ed.) Pseudo-Andronicus de Rhodes ΠΕΡΙ ΠΑΘΩΝ. Leiden.

Gomoll, H. (1933) *Der stoische Philosoph Hekaton: Seine Begriffswelt und Nachwirkung unter Beigabe seiner Fragmente.* Bonn.

Göransson, T. (1995) *Albinus, Alcinous, Arius Didymus.* Gothenburg.

Gould, J. B. (1970) *The Philosophy of Chrysippus.* Leiden.

Goulet, R. (2005) La méthode allégorique chez les stoïciens. In Romeyer Dherbey and Gourinat (2005), 93–119.

Gourinat, J.-B. (2005) Prédiction du futur et action humaine dans le traité de Chrysippe *Sur le destin.* In Romeyer Dherbey and Gourinat (2005), 246–73.

Graver, M. R. (2007) *Stoicism and Emotion.* Chicago.

Griffin, M. T and Atkins, E. M. (eds and trans.) (1991) *Cicero: On Duties.* Cambridge.

Griffin, M. and Barnes, J. (eds) (1989) *Philosophia Togata I: Essays on Philosophy and Roman Society.* Oxford.

Grube, G. M. A. (trans.) (1997) Crito. In Cooper (1997), 37–48.

Hadot, I. (1969) *Seneca und die griechisch-römische Tradition der Seelenleitung.* Berlin.

Hadot, P. (1995) *Qu'est-ce que la philosophie antique?* Paris.

—(2002) *Exercices spirituels et philosophie antique.* Second enlarged edition. Paris.

Hahm, D. E. (1977) *The Origins of Stoic Cosmology.* Columbus, OH.

—(1990) The ethical doxography of Arius Didymus. *ANRW* II.36.4, 2935–3055.

Halper, E. (1999) The unity of the virtues in Aristotle. *OSAP* 17, 115–43.

Hankinson, R. J. (ed.) (1998) *Galen on Antecedent Causes.* Cambridge.

—(1999) Determinism and indeterminism. In Algra et al. (1999), 513–41.

Helmbold, W. C. (ed. and trans.) (1957) *Plutarch's Moralia.* Vol. 6. Cambridge, MA.

Henrichs, A. (1974) Die Kritik der stoischen Theologie im PHerc. 1428. *Cronache Ercolanesi* 4, 5–32.

Hicks, R. D. (ed. and trans.) (1931) *Diogenes Laertius: Lives of Eminent Philosophers.* 2 vols. Cambridge, MA.

Hirzel, R. (1877–83) *Untersuchungen zu Ciceros philosophischen Schriften.* 3 vols. Leipzig (repr. Hildesheim 1964).

Hubbell, H. M. (ed. and trans.) (1949) *Cicero: De Inventione. De Optimo Genere Oratorum. Topica.* Cambridge, MA.

Hülser, K. (ed. and trans.) (1987–88) *Fragmente zur Dialektik der Stoiker: Neue Sammlung der Texte mit deutscher Übersetzung und Kommentaren.* Stuttgart-Bad Cannstatt.

Hunt, H. A. K. (1976) *A Physical Interpretation of the Universe: The Doctrines of Zeno the Stoic.* Melbourne.

Ierodiakonou, K. (ed.) (1999) *Topics in Stoic Philosophy.* Oxford.

Inwagen, P. van (1993) *Metaphysics.* Oxford.

Inwood, B. (1984) Hierocles: Theory and argument in the second century AD. *OSAP* 2, 151–83.

—(1985) *Ethics and Human Action in Early Stoicism.* Oxford (repr. 1999).

—(1986) Goal and target in Stoicism. *Journal of Philosophy* 83, 547–56.

—(1987) Commentary on Striker. *PBACAP* 2, 95–101.

—(1996) L'oikeiôsis sociale chez Epictète. In K. Algra, P. W. van der Horst and D. T. Runia (eds) *Polyhistor: Studies in the History and Historiography of Ancient Philosophy Presented to Jaap Mansfeld on his 60th Birthday.* Leiden 1996, 243–64.

—(1999) Rules and reasoning in Stoic ethics. In Ierodiakonou (1999), 95–127.

—(ed.) (2003) *The Cambridge Companion to the Stoics.* Cambridge.

—(2005) *Reading Seneca: Stoic Philosophy at Rome.* Oxford.

—and Donini, P. (1999) Stoic ethics. In Algra, et al. (1999), 675–738.

—and Gerson, L. P. (eds and trans.) (1997) *Hellenistic Philosophy: Introductory Readings.* Second edition, Indianapolis.

Ioppolo, A. M. (1980) *Aristone di Chio e lo Stoicismo Antico.* Naples.

Jaeger, W. (ed.) (1957) *Aristotelis Metaphysica.* Oxford.

Jedan, C. (2001) Zur Aktualität des stoischen Kompatibilismus. *Zeitschrift für philosophische Forschung* 55, 375–86.

—(2004) Chrysipp über Determinismus und moralische Verantwortlichkeit. In B. Guckes (ed.) *Zur Ethik der älteren Stoa.* Göttingen 2004, 141–64.

—and Strobach, N. (2002) *Modalities by Perspective: Aristotle, the Stoics and a Modern Reconstruction.* Sankt Augustin.

Kalbfleisch, K. (ed.) (1907) *In Aristotelis Categorias Commentarium.* Berlin.

Kerferd, G. B. (1972) The search for personal identity in Stoic thought. *Bulletin of the John Ryland University Library of Manchester* 55, 177–96.

—(1978a) The origin of evil in Stoic thought. *Bulletin of the John Ryland University Library of Manchester* 60, 482–94.

—(1978b) What does the wise man know? In Rist (1978), 125–36.

Kidd, I. G. (1971) Stoic intermediates and the end for man. In Long (1971), 150–72.

—(1978) Moral actions and rules in Stoic ethics. In Rist (1978), 247–58.

King, J. E. (ed. and trans.) (1927) *Cicero: Tusculan Disputations.* Cambridge, MA.

Kooten, H. G. van (2008) *Paul's Anthropology in Context*. Tübingen.

Kühn, C. G. (ed.) (1819–33) *Galeni Opera Omnia*. 20 vols. in 22. Leipzig (reprint Hildesheim 1965).

Lapidge, M. (1978) Stoic cosmology. In Rist (1978), 161–86.

—(1989) Stoic cosmology and Roman literature, first to third centuries A.D. *ANRW* II.36.3, 1379–429.

Laurand, V. (2005) *La politique stoïcienne*. Paris.

Lee, C.-U. (2002) *Oikeiosis: Stoische Ethik in naturphilosophischer Perspektive*. Freiburg.

Levett, M. J. (trans.) (1997) Theaetetus, rev. by M. Burnyeat. In Cooper (1997), 157–234.

Long, A. A. (1968) The Stoic concept of evil. *Philosophical Quarterly* 18, 329–43.

—(ed.) (1971) *Problems in Stoicism*. London.

—(1974) *Hellenistic Philosophy: Stoics, Epicureans, Sceptics*. London (second edition, London 1986).

—(1978) Dialectic and the Stoic sage. In Rist (1978), 101–24 (repr. in Long 1996, 85–106).

—(1983) Greek ethics after MacIntyre and the Stoic community of reason. *Ancient Philosophy* 3, 184–97 (repr. with a postscript in Long 1996, 156–78).

—(1985) The Stoics on world-conflagration and everlasting recurrence. In R. H. Epp (ed.) *Recovering the Stoics*. Spindel conference 1984. Supplement of *Southern Journal of Philosophy* 23 (1985), 39–56.

—(1988) Socrates in Hellenistic philosophy. *Classical Quarterly* 38, 150–71 (repr. with a postscript in Long 1996, 1–34).

—(1989) Stoic Eudaimonism. *PBACAP* 4, 77–110 (repr. in Long 1996, 179–201).

—(1991) The Harmonics of Stoic virtue. *OSAP, Suppl. vol.*, 97–116 (repr. in Long 1996, 202–23).

—(1992) Stoic readings of Homer. In R. Lamberton and J. J. Keaney (eds) *Homer's Ancient Readers: The Hermeneutics of Greek Epic's Earliest Exegetes*. Princeton 1992, 41–66 (repr. in Long 1996, 58–84).

—(1993) Hierocles on *oikeiōsis* and self-perception. In K. J. Boudouris (ed.) *Hellenistic Philosophy*. Vol. I. Athens, 93–104 (repr. in Long 1996: 250–63).

—(1996) *Stoic Studies*. Cambridge (repr. Berkeley and Los Angeles 2001).

—(1999) Stoic psychology. In Algra, et al. (1999), 560–84.

—(2002) *Epictetus: A Stoic and Socratic Guide to Life*. Oxford.

—(2003) Eudaimonism, divinity and rationality in Greek ethics. *PBACAP* 19, 123–43.

—and Sedley, D. N. (eds, comm. and trans.) (1987) *The Hellenistic Philosophers*. 2 vols. Cambridge.

Lukoschus, J. (1999) *Gesetz und Glück: Untersuchungen zum Naturalismus der stoischen Ethik*. Frankfurt am Main.

Mansfeld, J. (1979) Providence and the destruction of the universe in early Stoic thought. In M. J. Vermaseren (ed.), *Studies in Hellenistic Religions*. Leiden 1979, 129–88 (repr. in Mansfeld 1989).

—(1983) Resurrection added: The interpretatio christiana of a Stoic doctrine. *Vigiliae Christianae* 37, 218–33 (repr. in Mansfeld 1989).

—(1986) Diogenes Laertius on Stoic philosophy. *Elenchos* 7, 297–382.

—(1989) *Studies in Later Greek Philosophy and Gnosticism*. London.

—(1991) The idea of the will in Chrysippus, Posidonius, and Galen. *PBACAP* 7, 107–45.

—(1999) Theology. In Algra et al. (1999), 452–78.

Marcovich, M. (ed.) (1987) *Refutatio Omnium Haeresium*. Berlin.

—(ed.) (1999) *Diogenes Laertii Vitae Philosophorum*. 2 vols. Stuttgart.

Marshall, P. K. (1968) (ed.) *Aulus Gellius: Noctes Atticae*. Oxford.

Meijer, P. A. (1981) Philosophers, intellectuals and religion in Hellas. In H. S. Versnel (ed.) *Faith, Hope and Worship: Aspects of Religious Mentality in the Ancient World*. Leiden.

—(2007) *Stoic Theology: Proofs for the Existence of the Cosmic God and of the Traditional Gods*. Delft.

Menn, S. (1995) Physics as a virtue. *PBACAP* 11 (1995), 1–33.

—(1999) The Stoic theory of categories. *OSAP* 17, 215–47.

Merki, H. (1952) Ὁμοίωσις θεῷ: *Von der platonischen Angleichung an Gott zur Gottähnlichkeit bei Gregor von Nyssa*. Fribourg.

Minio-Paluello, L. (ed.) (1949) *Aristotelis Categoriae et Liber De Interpretatione*. Oxford.

Mitsis, Ph. T. (1986) Moral rules and the aims of Stoic ethics. *Journal of Philosophy* 83, 556–58.

—(1993) Seneca on reason, rules, and moral development. In Brunschwig and Nussbaum (1993), 285–312.

—(1994) Natural law and natural right in post-Aristotelian philosophy: The Stoics and their critics. *ANRW* II.36.7, 4812–50.

Mommsen, T. (ed.) (1895) Iustiniani Digesta. In P. Krueger and T. Mommsen (eds), *Institutiones. Digesta*. Berlin.

Monro, D. B. and Allen, T. W. (eds) (1920) *Homeri Opera*. Vol. 2. Third edition. Oxford.

Morani, M. (ed.) (1987) *Nemesius: De Natura Hominis*. Leipzig.

Mras, K. and Des Places, É. (eds) (1982–83) *Eusebius: Die Praeparatio Evangelica*. 2 vols. Second edition. Berlin.

Muir, J. V. (1985) Religion and the new education: The challenge of the sophists. In P. E. Easterling and J. V. Muir (eds) *Greek Religion and Society*. Cambridge 1985, 191–218.

Nehamas, A. and Woodruff, P. (trans.) (1997) Phaedrus. In Cooper (1997), 506–56.

Nussbaum, M. C. (1994) *The Therapy of Desire: Theory and Practice in Hellenistic Ethics*. Princeton.

—(1995) Commentary on Menn. *PBACAP* 11, 35–45.

Oldfather, W. A. (ed. and trans.) (1925–28) *Epictetus: The Discourses. Fragments. Encheiridion*. 2 vols. Cambridge, MA.

Pease, A. S. (ed. and trans.) (1958) *M. Tulli Ciceronis De Natura Deorum*. 2 vols. Cambridge, MA.

Peck, A. L. and Balme, D. M. (eds and trans.) (1965–91) *Aristotle: History of Animals*. 3 vols. Cambridge, MA.

Pembroke, S. (1971) Oikeiōsis. In Long (1971), 114–49.

Philippson, R. (1930) Das Sittlichschöne bei Panaitios. *Philologus* 85, 357–413.

Plasberg, O. (ed.) (1922) *M. Tullius Cicero: Academicorum Reliquiae cum Lucullo*. Leipzig.

—and Ax, W. (eds) (1933) *M. Tullius Cicero: De Natura Deorum*. Second edition. Leipzig.

Pohlenz, M. (1940) *Grundfragen der stoischen Philosophie*. Göttingen.

—(1959) *Die Stoa: Geschichte einer geistigen Bewegung*. Second edition. Göttingen (sev. repr.)

Pomeroy, A. J. (ed. and trans.) (1999) *Arius Didymus, Epitome of Stoic Ethics*. Atlanta.

Préchac, F. (ed. and trans.) (1961) *Sénèque: Des bienfaits*. Second edition. 2 vols. Paris.

—(ed. and trans.) (1963–64) *Sénèque: Lettres á Lucilius*. 2 vols. Fourth edition. Paris.

Price, A. W. (1995) *Mental Conflict*. London.

—(2005) Were Zeno and Chrysippus at odds in analysing emotion? In Salles (2005c), 471–88.

Price, S. (1999) *Religions of the Ancient Greeks*. Cambridge.

Rabbow, P. (1954) *Seelenführung: Methodik der Exerzitien in der Antike*. Munich.

Radice, R. (2000) *Oikeiosis': Ricerche sul Fondamento del Pensiero Stoico e sulla sua Genesi*. Milan.

Reydams-Schils, G. (2002) Human bonding and *oikeiōsis* in Roman Stoicism. *OSAP* 22, 221–51.

Reynolds, L. D. (ed.) (1998) *M. Tulli Ciceronis De Finibus Bonorum et Malorum*. Oxford.

Riedweg, Ch. (1987) *Mysterienterminologie bei Platon, Philon und Klemens von Alexandrien*. Berlin.

Rist, J. M. (1989) Seneca and Stoic orthodoxy. *ANRW* II.36.3, 1993–2012.

—(ed.) (1978) *The Stoics*. Berkeley and Los Angeles.

Roloff, D. (1970) *Gottähnlichkeit, Vergöttlichung und Erhöhung zu seligem Leben: Untersuchungen zur Herkunft der platonischen Angleichung an Gott*. Berlin.

Romeyer Dherbey, G. and Gourinat, J.-B. (dir. and ed.) (2005) *Les stoïciens*. Paris.

Roskam, G. (2005) *On the Path to Virtue: The Stoic Doctrine of Moral Progress and its Reception in (Middle-) Platonism*. Louvain.

Ross, W. D. (ed.) (1964) *Aristotelis Analytica Priora et Posteriora*. Oxford.

Rowe, C. and Schofield, M. (eds) (2000) *The Cambridge History of Greek and Roman Political Thought*. Cambridge.

Salles, R. (2001) Compatibilism: Stoic and Modern. *Archiv für Geschichte der Philosophie* 83, 1–23.

—(2003) Determinism and recurrence in early Stoic thought. *OSAP* 24, 253–72.

—(2005a) *The Stoics on Determinism and Compatibilism*. Aldershot.

—(2005b) Ἐκπύρωσις and the goodness of God in Cleanthes. *Phronesis* 50, 56–78.

—(ed.) (2005c) *Metaphysics, Soul, and Ethics in Ancient Thought*. Oxford.

Sambursky, S. (1959) *Physics of the Stoics*. London.

Sandbach, F. H. (1975) *The Stoics*. London.

Schofield, M. (1980) Preconception, argument and God. In Schofield, Burnyeat and Barnes (1980), 283–308.

—(1983) The syllogisms of Zeno of Citium. *Phronesis* 28, 31–58.

—(1984) Ariston of Chios and the unity of virtue. *Ancient Philosophy* 4, 83–96.

—(1995) Two Stoic approaches to justice. In A. Laks and M. Schofield (eds) *Justice and Generosity: Studies in Hellenistic Social and Political Philosophy*. Cambridge 1995.

—(1999) *The Stoic Idea of the City*. Second edition with an introduction by M. Nussbaum. Chicago.

—(2000) Epicurean and Stoic political thought. In Rowe and Schofield (2000), 435–56.

—(2003) Stoic ethics. In Inwood (2003), 233–56.

—and Striker, G. (eds) (1986) *The Norms of Nature: Studies in Hellenistic Ethics*. Cambridge.

—, Burnyeat, M. F. and Barnes, J. (eds) (1980) *Doubt and Dogmatism: Studies in Hellenistic Epistemology*. Oxford.

Sedley, D. N. (1989) Philosophical allegiance in the Greco-Roman world. In Griffin and Barnes (1989), 97–119.

—(1991) Commentary on Mansfeld. *PBACAP* 7, 146–52.

—(1993) Chrysippus on psychophysical causality. In Brunschwig and Nussbaum (1993), 313–31.

—(1999a) Hellenistic physics and metaphysics. In Algra et al. (1999), 355–411.

—(1999b) The Stoic-Platonist debate on *kathēkonta*. In Ierodiakonou (1999), 128–52.

—(2002) The origins of Stoic God. In Frede and Laks (2002), 41–83.

—(2003a) The ideal of godlikeness. In G. Fine (ed.) *Plato 2: Ethics, Politics, Religion, and the Soul*. Oxford, 309–28.

—(2003b) The school, from Zeno to Arius Didymus. In Inwood (2003), 7–32.

—(2007) *Creationism and its Critics in Antiquity*. Berkeley.

Sellars, J. (2003) *The Art of Living: The Stoics on the Nature and Function of Philosophy*. Aldershot.

—(2007) Téchnē perì tòn bíon. Zur stoischen Konzeption von Kunst und Leben. In W. Kersting and C. Langbehn (eds) *Kritik der Lebenskunst*. Frankfurt 2007, 91–117.

Sherman, N. (2005) *Stoic Warriors: The Ancient Philosophy behind the Military Mind*. Oxford.

Sihvola, J. and Engberg-Pedersen, T. (eds) (1998) *The Emotions in Hellenistic Philosophy*. Dordrecht.

Sorabji, R. (2000) *Emotion and Peace of Mind: From Stoic Agitation to Christian Temptation*. Oxford.

Stählin, O. (ed.) (1905–09) *Clemens Alexandrinus*. Berlin.

Steinmetz, P. (1994) Die Stoa. In H. Flashar (ed.) *Grundriß der Geschichte der Philosophie: Die Philosophie der Antike. Vol. 4: Die Hellenistische Philosophie*. Basle, 491–716.

Stephens, W. O. (1996) Epictetus on how the Stoic sage loves. *OSAP* 14, 193–210.

Striker, G. (1983) The role of *oikeiosis* in Stoic ethics. *OSAP* 1, 281–97.

—(1987) Origins of the concept of natural law. *PBACAP* 2, 79–94.

—(1991) Following nature: A study in Stoic ethics. *OSAP* 9, 1–73.

Thomson, J. A. K. (trans.) (1976) *Aristotle, The Nicomachean Ethics*. Rev. edition. Harmondsworth (1976).

Tieleman, T. (2003) *Chrysippus' On Affections: Reconstruction and Interpretation*. Leiden.

Todd, R. B. (1976) *Alexander of Aphrodisias on Stoic Physics: A Study of the* De Mixtione *with Preliminary Essays, Text, Translation and Commentary*. Leiden.

—(1978) Monism and Immanence: Foundations of Stoic physics. In Rist (1978), 137–60.

Usener, H. K. (1867) *M. Annaei Lucani Commenta Bernensia*. Leipzig.

Valente, M. (1956) *L'Éthique stoïcienne chez Cicéron.* Paris.

Vander Waerdt, P. A. (1994a) Zeno's republic and the origins of natural law. In Vander Waerdt (1994b), 272–308.

—(1994b) (ed.) *The Socratic Movement.* Cornell.

Vlastos, G. (1991) *Socrates: Ironist and Moral Philosopher.* Cambridge.

Voelke, A.-J. (1973) *L'idée de volonté dans le stoïcisme.* Paris.

—(1993) *La philosophie comme thérapie de l'âme.* Fribourg.

Vogt, K. (2005) Gibt es eine Lebenskunst? Politische Philosophie in der frühen Stoa und skeptische Kritik. *Zeitschrift für philosophische Forschung* 59, 1–21.

—(2008) *Law, Reason, and the Cosmic City.* Oxford.

Wachsmuth, C. and Hense, O. (eds) (1884–1923) *Ioannis Stobaei Anthologium.* Berlin.

Waszink, J. H. (ed.) (1947) *Quinti Septimi Florentis Tertulliani De Anima.* Amsterdam.

—(ed.) (1976) *Timaeus a Calcidio Translatus Commentarioque Instructus.* Revised edition. Leiden.

Watson, G. (1971) The natural law and Stoicism. In Long (1971), 216–38.

White, M. J. (2003) Stoic natural philosophy (physics and cosmology). In Inwood (2003), 124–52.

White, N. P. (1978) Two notes on Stoic terminology. *American Journal of Philology* 99, 111–19.

Wildberger, J. (2006) *Seneca und die Stoa: Der Platz des Menschen in der Welt.* 2 vol. Berlin.

Wilken, R. L. (2003) *The Spirit of Early Christian Thought: Seeking the Face of God.* New Haven.

Winterbottom, M. (ed.) (1970) *M. Fabii Quintiliani Institutiones Oratoriae.* Oxford.

—(ed.) (1994) *M. Tulli Ciceronis De Officiis.* Oxford.

Zagdoun, M.-A. (2005), Problèmes concernant l'*oikeiôsis* stoïcienne. In Romeyer Dherbey and Gourinat (2005), 319–34.

Zetzel, J. E. G. (trans.) (1999) *Cicero: On the Commonwealth and On the Laws.* Cambridge.

Ziegler, K. (ed.) (1979) *M. Tullius Cicero: De Legibus.* (Third rev. by W. Görler) Heidelberg.

Index of Cited Passages

General Index

Aetius 14, 84
akrasia 18–19
appropriate actions (καθῆκον) 5, 121, 125, 130–6, 138–9, 145, 147–9, 151, 168, 198 n. 12, 204 n. 26, 205 n. 32
appropriation (οἰκείωσις) 1, 100–1, 127, 143, 172, 195 n. 25, 200 n. 22, 203 n. 3
Alexander of Aphrodisias 15–16, 33, 43
Algra, Keimpe 25, 174 nn. 2, 11, 175 n. 5, 177 n. 40, 181 n. 43, 187 n. 42
Annas, Julia 160, 172, 184 n. 2, 190 n. 12, 197 n. 29, 205 n. 44, 206 n. 45
Aristo of Chios 53, 76–7, 90, 129, 189 n. 4, 202 n. 60
Aristotle 1, 59, 101, 130, 149–50, 160–73
Arius Didymus 5, 179 n. 69
Arnim, Johannes von 6, 54, 185 n. 8, 188 n. 45, 192 n. 17
assent (συγκατάθεσις) 18, 38–9, 42–4, 67–70, 73–4, 86
Auvray-Assayas, Clara 21

Babut, Daniel 2, 175 n. 1
belief (δόξα) 18–19, 189 n. 22
Bénatouïl, Thomas 187 nn. 39, 43, 188 n. 45, 192 n. 21, 204 nn. 22–4
blameless companionship (εὐσυναλλαξία) 82, 159, 164, 172–3
Bobzien, Susanne 32, 34, 36–7, 174 n. 13, 182 nn. 2, 9–11, 14, 16, 18–19, 21, 183 nn. 24, 27, 31–2
body 10–11, 15–17, 43–4, 57–8, 177 n. 42, 191 n. 10
breath *see pneuma*
Bremmer, Jan 107, 175 n. 5, 180 n. 17, 196 n. 14, 197 n. 24

Brennan, Tad 137–8, 141, 186 n. 23, 201 n. 34, 202 nn. 49–51, 53–6
Broadie, Sarah 207 n. 50

causation 15, 38–40, 42–4, 183 nn. 26, 28, 30
character (διάθεσις) 58–62
Cicero 21, 204 n. 26, 205 n. 27
Cleanthes 14, 34, 37, 62–3, 146–7, 189 nn. 18, 2
cognition (κατάληψις) 66–9, 188 n. 7
cognitive impression (καταληπτικὴ φαντασία) 68–9, 188 n. 7
commanding faculty (ἡγεμονικόν) 17, 20
confidence (θαρραλεότης) 158, 163
conflagration 14, 178 n. 53
constancy (ἀπαραλλαξία) 159, 192 n. 16
conviviality (συμποτική) 92–3, 159, 173, 193 n. 30
corporealism 4, 10, 17
cosmic city 46–8, 109, 111, 126, 184 n. 35
cosmos 10, 12, 14–15, 17, 25, 34
courage (ἀνδρεία) 52, 55–7, 68, 75, 81–2, 158, 169–70

death 17, 68, 108, 113, 165
decreta (philosophical doctrines) 127, 129, 199 n. 4
dialectic (διαλεκτική) 84–9, 91–2, 158
Dionysius of Heraclea 146
discretion (νουνέχεια) 82, 92, 159, 164, 167
divination 29–30
divine perspective 20, 99, 115–18, 136, 138, 197 n. 29, 199 n. 24
dog-and-cart simile 36–7, 182 n. 16
Dragona-Monachou, Myrto 21–3